Mussolini's National Project in Argentina

The Fairleigh Dickinson University Press Series in Italian Studies

**General Editor: Dr. Anthony Julian Tamburri, Dean
John D. Calandra Italian American Institute (Queens College-CUNY)**

The Fairleigh Dickinson University Press Series in Italian Studies is devoted to the publication of scholarly works on Italian literature, film, history, biography, art, and culture, as well as on intercultural connections, such as Italian-American Studies.

Recent Publications in Italian Studies

Aliano, David, *Mussolini's National Project in Argentina* (2012)
Parati, Graziella, *New Perspectives in Italian Cultural Studies—Volume 1: Definition, Theory, and Accented Practices* (2012)
Smith, Shirley Ann, *Imperial Designs: Italians in China, 1900–1947* (2012)
Rosengarten, Frank, *Giacomo Leopardi's Search for a Common Life through Poetry: A Different Nobility, a Different Love* (2012)
Baliani, Marco (au.), Nicoletta Marini-Maio, Ellen Nerenberg, Thomas Simpson (trans. and eds.), *Body of State: A Nation Divided* (2012)
Ducci, Lucia, *George P. Marsh Correspondence: Images of Italy, 1861-1881* (2012)
Verdicchio, Pasquale, *Looters, Photographers, and Thieves: Aspects of Italian Photographic Culture in the Nineteenth and Twentieth Centuries* (2011)
Parati, Graziella and Anthony Julian Tamburri (eds.), *The Cultures of Italian Migration: Diverse Trajectories and Discrete Perspectives* (2011)
Trubiano, Marisa S., *Ennio Flaiano and His Italy: Postcards from a Changing World* (2010)
Halliday, Iain, *Huck Finn in Italian, Pinocchio in English: Theory and Praxis of Literary Translation* (2009)
Serra, Ilaria, *The Imagined Immigrant: The Images of Italian Emigration to the United States between 1890 and 1924* (2009)
Lucamante, Stefania (ed.), *Italy and the Bourgeoisie: The Re-Thinking of a Class* (2009)
Van Order, Thomas, *Listening to Fellini: Music and Meaning in Black and White* (2008)
Billiani, Francesca, and Gigliola Sulis, *The Italian Gothic and Fantastic: Encounters and Rewritings of Narrative Traditions* (2008)
Parati, Graziella, and Marie Orton (eds.), *Multicultural Literature in Contemporary Italy, Volume 1* (2007)
Orton, Marie, and Graziella Parati (eds.), *Multicultural Literature in Contemporary Italy, Volume 2* (2007)
Scambray, Ken, *Queen Calafia's Paradise: California and the Italian-American Novel* (2007)
Polezzi, Loredana, and Charlotte Ross (eds.), *In Corpore: Bodies in Post-Unification Italy* (2007)
Francose, Joseph, *Socially Symbolic Acts: The Historicizing Fictions of Umberto Eco, Vincenzo Consolo, and Antonio Tabucchi* (2006)
Kozma, Jan (trans.), *Grazia Deledda, Marianna Sirca* (2006)

On the Web at http://www.fdu.edu/fdupress

Mussolini's National Project in Argentina

David Aliano

FAIRLEIGH DICKINSON UNIVERSITY PRESS
Madison • Teaneck

Published by Fairleigh Dickinson University Press
Co-published with The Rowman & Littlefield Publishing Group, Inc.
4501 Forbes Boulevard, Suite 200, Lanham, Maryland 20706
www.rowman.com

10 Thornbury Road, Plymouth PL6 7PP, United Kingdom

Copyright © 2012 by David Aliano

All rights reserved. No part of this book may be reproduced in any form or by any electronic or mechanical means, including information storage and retrieval systems, without written permission from the publisher, except by a reviewer who may quote passages in a review.

British Library Cataloguing in Publication Information Available

Library of Congress Cataloging-in-Publication Data

Aliano, David, 1977–
Mussolini's national project in Argentina / David Aliano.
p. cm.—(The Fairleigh Dickinson University Press series in Italian studies)
"Co-published with The Rowman & Littlefield Publishing Group"—T.p. verso.
Includes bibliographical references and index.
ISBN 978-1-61147-576-0 (cloth : alk. paper)—ISBN 978-1-61147-577-7 (electronic)
1. Italians—Argentina—History—20th century. 2. Immigrants—Argentina—History—20th century. 3. Italians—Argentina—Ethnic identity—History—20th century. 4. Nationalism—Argentina—History—20th century. 5. Argentina—Politics and government—1910-1943. 6. Mussolini, Benito, 1883-1945—Influence. 7. Fascism—Italy—History—20th century. 8. Italy—Relations—Argentina. 9. Argentina—Relations—Italy. I. Title.
F3021.I8A45 2012
982.06'1—dc23
2012022836

™ The paper used in this publication meets the minimum requirements of American National Standard for Information Sciences Permanence of Paper for Printed Library Materials, ANSI/NISO Z39.48-1992.

Printed in the United States of America

To the memory of Philip V. Cannistraro

Contents

Acknowledgments		ix
1	A National Project Outside of the Nation	1
2	Fascist Italy Looks Abroad	25
3	The "New Italy" in Argentina	53
4	An Italian National Identity in Argentina	85
5	The Nation Abroad Responds	115
6	Italian Identity and Argentina's National Debate	153
Conclusion		187
Bibliography		193
Index		203
About the Author		209

Acknowledgments

This study began in 2002 while I was a student under the direction of the late Philip V. Cannistraro, distinguished professor of Italian and Italian American history at Queens College, City University of New York. Without his help and encouragement, I would not have been able to conceive of and develop this project. A friend, a mentor, and a true scholar, he is missed by all.

The original version of this work was defended as a dissertation in February 2008. I would like to especially thank Marta Petrusewicz, who took over as my adviser and helped me develop and expand upon my initial argument, transforming it into the work that it has become. Marta has challenged me to produce the very best work that I am capable of and continues to inspire me intellectually. Mary Gibson also played in integral role in the development of this project by commenting on the original manuscript. I am also especially grateful to Emilio Gentile, whose advice and suggestions during my research trips to Rome helped enormously; Ruth Ben-Ghiat, who changed the way I approached the study of history as an undergraduate; and Silvana Patriarca, who introduced me to the theoretical questions of Italian identity that I explore here. Alfonso Quiroz and José Luis Renique both encouraged my interest in Latin American history and the development of this transnational topic. I would also additionally like to acknowledge Randolph Trumbach and Andrew Robertson, who read and commented on versions of my work.

The research required to complete this project involved an extensive use of the archival collections housed in Rome at the Archivio Centrale dello Stato, the Archivio Storico del Ministerio degli Affari Esteri, as well as the Archivio Storico della Camera dei Deputati, and in Buenos Aires at the Archivo Intermedio del Archivo General de la Nación, the Archivo del Congreso de la Nación, the Centro de Estudios Migratorios Latino Americanos, and the Biblioteca Nacional de la Republica Argentina. I would therefore like to thank the archives and the Italian and Argentine governments for granting me access to their collections as well as the archivists who helped me navigate through the inventories and folders related to my topic.

Since completing the initial manuscript in 2008, this work underwent four years of further revision as I worked hard to sharpen my argument and relate my work to new developments in the field. Portions of this work were presented at a number of conferences at which I received invaluable feedback from my co-panelists and fellow participants. I would therefore like to thank the participants in the Annual Conference of the American Italian Historical Association in 2005; the Concordia University History in the Making Conference in 2007; the Italians in the Americas Conference at the John D. Calandra Italian American Institute in 2008; the American Historical Association Annual Conference in January 2011; and New Directions in Italian and Italian American History: A Conference in Honor of Philip V. Cannistraro in November 2011. I am especially grateful to my friends in the Columbia University Seminar in Modern Italian Studies, who provided important comments and suggestions when I presented my work there in February 2010. I would also like to thank my friends, especially Alejandro Quintana, who helped me navigate my final revisions, as well as David H. Golland, Joseph Sramek, Kris Burrell, Peter Vellon, Marcella Bencivenni, Sarah Covington, and Alex Stavropoulos, each of whom gave freely of their precious time to read and comment on drafts of chapters as well as offer their own insight and advice on the writing process. I would like to also thank my colleagues at the College of Mount Saint Vincent, who gave me support and guidance throughout the revising process.

Finally, this work would not have been possible were it not for the love and support of my family. I would therefore like to thank my parents, David and Gloria; my late grandmother, Viola; my sister Claudia; Alan, my brother-in-law; and Santos and Bella Herrera, my father- and mother-in-law. Most importantly, I am eternally grateful to my wife, Bella, whose love and companionship sustained me throughout the many years in which I have labored on this project.

NOTE ON THE TEXT

Portions of this book originally appeared as part of an article for *Ethnic Studies Review* in 2010 (vol. 33, no. 1). They are reprinted with permission from the publisher.

Chapter One

A National Project Outside of the Nation

A few years ago, while attending a banquet held in New York City in honor of Ecuador's Independence Day, it struck me how different a national project appears when outside of its nation of origin. As an outsider listening to patriotic speeches, Ecuadorian anthems, and traditional folkloric dances, I realized that what seems natural in one environment can be quite jarring and unusual in another. The truth is that few of us really make a conscious effort at critically examining our own nationalism. Nation-states ensure that their citizens from an early age are immersed in a patriotic culture so that its national project seems natural and almost innate. For example, as an American, nothing could seem more innocuous than the Pledge of Allegiance, Thanksgiving, and the Fourth of July. The peculiarities of a national project are in fact all the more apparent when viewed from outside the community or, better yet, when outside of their national setting. But what happens when a national project leaves the nation-state of origin? How are the ideas and ideologies within the boundaries of a nation-state transformed when they are transplanted into a new environment and divorced from the sociopolitical and cultural context from which they were born? How are national identities conceived of and negotiated across borders and political divides? What does it mean to belong to one nation while living in another?

To answer the questions posed here, this book examines the historical experience of one nation's attempt to spread its national project outside its borders through its emigrant community in Argentina. It details how Bonito Mussolini's Italian fascist regime conceived of and disseminated its version of an Italian national identity abroad, how that national project looked fundamentally different within Argentina, as well as how the Italian community in Argentina and the Argentine public countered with their own original conceptions of the nation. Through its examination of Italian national identity in Argentina, this work illustrates both the possibilities as well as the limitations of a national project outside of the nation-state, demonstrating how an emigrant community, informed by the values of its new nation, can actively contest and reshape the project from abroad and, in so doing, challenge us to rethink the ways in which we interpret the construction and negotiation of national projects.

Far from being a unique historical experience, the case of the Italian regime's project in Argentina treated in this book is an exemplary model of what happens to national projects when they operate within another nation-state. The questions this book examines are therefore especially relevant to today's world as the ability of people to travel and communicate with one another across national boundaries is challenging the ways we identify ourselves and define our place in the world. The traditional model of a territorially defined national identity seems to be losing its relevance in a new globally integrated world. The European Union, NAFTA, Mercosur, multinational corporate affiliations, and virtual communities on the Internet are all fast creating new collective forms of identity, filling a role traditionally associated with the nation-state. Many nation-states have responded to these new transnational realities by granting extraterritorial rights as well as dual citizenship to its emigrants living abroad, changing our understanding of how national identities work. Modern nations with significant emigrant populations, especially those in Latin American and Asia, are in fact actively promoting their national projects among their citizens abroad, establishing special government agencies at home and overseas to strengthen emigrant loyalty and identification with their nation of origin.

The question of an extraterritorial national project is, however, not a new one. For over a century the Italian government has played an active role in cultivating transnational relationships with its emigrants. Between 1875 and 1975 over twenty-five million Italians emigrated out of Italy. Emigrating primarily out of socioeconomic necessity, many Italians traveled back and forth between Italy and their new adopted homes, influencing in the process both their new nation as well as Italy. Through their investments and remittances, consumption and cultural assimilations they created their own unique transnational identity. As Donna R. Gabaccia in her groundbreaking study *Italy's Many Diasporas* explains, "Migration made transnationalism a normal dimension of life for many, perhaps even most, working class families in Italy in the nineteenth and twentieth centuries. Family discipline, economic security, reproduction, inheritance, romance, and dreams transcended national boundaries and bridged continents."[1] With its citizens already leading transnational lives by the late nineteenth century, the Italian government responded early to the new realities posed by migration.

More active than most governments of the time, the liberal regime in Italy (1870–1922) attempted to maintain formal connections with its emigrant communities abroad by investing state resources in services for its emigrants. According to the historian Mark I. Choate in his *Emigrant Nation: The Making of Italy Abroad*, the liberal regime's active involvement with its emigrant population represented a conscious effort to "nationalize its emigration by intervening transnationally, levering diplomatic resources to influence international travel, the dissemination of media, transnational religious activity, and ethnic economic activity abroad to achieve specific national benefits."[2] Seen from this perspective, liberal Italy's overtures toward its citizens abroad were as much a reflection of a traditional national agenda as it was an innovative response to a transnational reality.

After taking power, Mussolini was especially interested in taking advantage of Italy's emigrant population. During the 1920s and 1930s the fascist regime in Italy attempted to create and propagate a fascist Italian national identity tailored to Italian communities abroad in an effort to reclaim these emigrants for Italy's national project. As Piero Parini, the director of Italians abroad during the 1930s, declared, "If there is a sector in which fascism has radically renovated a mentality and consciousness, it is undoubtedly that of Italian identity outside of its borders . . . across the world there are eight million Italians; *a nation outside of the Nation.*"[3] Even more important than the initiative itself are its implications: what it really means to belong to one nation while living in another, and how national discourses change when a public overseas participates in the debate.

While fascist Italy's national project abroad operated in many countries throughout the world, this book uses Argentina as a case study both because it was seen by the regime as offering the greatest potential and because it ended up becoming one of its most spectacular failures. At the time of the fascist seizure of power in Italy, the Italian Foreign Ministry counted 1,797,000 Italian citizens in the Republic of Argentina. For Il Duce, this number alone demonstrated the importance of reaching out to this Italian emigrant community. Although it is perhaps too much to claim that Argentina was one of the fascist regime's first priorities, Italian fascist interest in the South American republic is undeniable. Some of the regime's most talented propagandists, along with high-ranking cultural and political figures, traveled to and wrote about Argentina and its potential value to the regime. Encouraged by the large number of Italians living in Argentina, Mussolini invested a significant amount of resources in bombarding the republic with propaganda. Although the Italian regime failed abjectly in promoting its political program overseas, this propaganda did succeed in changing the debate at home and abroad over the question of an Italian national identity outside of the nation-state. Once within Argentina's public sphere, Italians in Argentina rejected the regime's national project while affirming in its place their own equally valid versions of Italy's national identity. By propagating an Italian national identity within another sovereign state, Mussolini's initiative also had the unintended consequence of inspiring heated debate among native Argentines over their own national project. The presence of this foreign project on their soil forced Argentines to define how they understood their own national project in sharp contrast to the Italian one they confronted.

Using the content and experiences of Il Duce's national project in Argentina, this book demonstrates how national projects take on different meanings once they enter a contested public space. The Argentine context in which the Italian nation was debated fundamentally changed the very nature of that national discourse. Outside of the coercive mechanism of state control, the regime's national project entered into a relatively free public space in which the official state discourse was but one voice among many. The very fact that the regime had to openly compete with and engage other alternative Italian national narratives in and of itself changes the way in which we understand that nationalization project. Rather than imposed from above, it interacted on an equal plain with its opponents. This study further demonstrates that Mussolini's national project did more than simply compete with Argentina's own national project but instead became entangled with and informed by the New World context in which it operated. A national narrative is in fact understood differently by different people when they are living in another nation. Rather than simply choosing one national project over another, members of the Italian community instead created their own alternative vision of Italy's national project, a vision that reflected a New World conceptualization of national belonging. Both members of the Italian immigrant community as well as native Argentines engaged in reimagining and reshaping the Italian national discourse, in the end transforming it into an ideational national project framed within the parameters of New World notions of national identity informed by democratic principles.

A QUESTION OF NATIONAL IDENTITY

There is a growing literature that has begun to analyze Mussolini's fascist propaganda efforts directed toward Italian emigrants abroad. This new interest in the regime's activities abroad began especially in the 1990s and has continued to the present. Emilio Gentile, for example, in a 1995 issue of *Storia Contemporanea* details the activities of the Fasci Italiani all'Estero, the Italian fascist party abroad.[4] This article was followed soon after by a number of other articles and books that have analyzed this formerly neglected aspect of the Italian fascist regime. Luca de Caprariis examines the organization and goals broadly, focusing on the regime's policies, while a number of other historians examine its experiences in specific countries. Philip V. Cannistraro, for example, focuses on its activities among Italian immigrants in the United States, while Claudia Baldoli examines the impact of these fascist activities on Italian immigrants in Great Britain in her work.[5]

An excellent collection of essays edited by Emilio Franzina and Matteo Sanfilippo, *Il Fascismo e gli emigrati: La parabola dei Fasci italiani all'estero (1920–1943)*, comparatively analyzes the various experiences of the Italian fascist party abroad in a number of countries throughout the world, including Argentina and Brazil in Latin America, evaluating its presence and relative successes or failures.[6] In terms of specifically analyzing South America and especially Argentina, Eugenia Scarzanella's edited volume titled *Fascisti in Sud America* filled an important void in the field. Her work analyzes a variety of issues, including creating community consensus for the fascist regime, fascism's influence on Latin American societies, as well as the question of Italian patriotism and the construction of immigrant identities. Its contributors focus especially on Italian fascism in Argentina as expressed through the Italian language daily *Il Mattino d'Italia*. Scarzanella asserts that fascism created for the Italian communities in South America a new ideological form of Italian patriotism that was universal in scope, which enabled Italians to integrate themselves into the political landscapes of their new countries.[7] She suggestively concludes that many of the ideas contained in the Italian fascist propaganda influenced Italian immigrant identities both before as well as after the war, asserting that after the war, "The fascists did not disappear nor lose their prestige . . . nor their corporatist ideology, anti-Americanism, distrust in democracy, and cult of the leader."[8] Federica Bertagna, in *La patria di riserva: L'emigrazione fascista in Argentina*, extends this discussion of fascism's influence on political identities into the postwar years by exploring the relationship between Italian fascist exiles, member of the Italian community, and their later relationship to Perón's rule in Argentina.[9] Most recently, Matteo Pretelli's *Il fascismo e gli italiani all'estero* offers a comprehensive overview of the fascist regime's overall agenda toward Italian emigrants abroad. He traces the evolution of the regime's policy and ties together earlier scholarship that focused on individual countries or individual fascist initiatives, providing key insights into the regime's strategy abroad and the content of the fascist program tailored toward its emigrants. Most significantly, his work broadens the narrative of fascist activities to cover all of the regime's organizational structure abroad, including the work of Piero Parini and the Direzione degli Italiani all'Estero, the Società Nazionale Dante Alighieri, the Dopolavoro, and especially the Scuole Italiani all'Estero.[10]

In contrast to many of the above works, my study argues that the regime's Italian national agenda was actually at odds with and would ultimately undermine its universal fascist one. By reading similar material evidence in the context of a contested national project operating within a foreign state, this work interprets the Italian regime's effort as one which worked against immigrant integration and failed abjectly as a national project abroad in Argentina when it was confronted with alternative national discourses provided by the immigrants themselves that were shaped by the democratic New World context of the national debate. My work also draws different conclusions from Scarzanella's volume in particular, in that it argues that a belief in liberty and democracy underlay both pro- and antifascist notions of an Italian national identity in Argentina.

Furthermore, these recent works have not incorporated into their analyses the active role of antifascists in challenging the regime's national and political projects abroad. Rather than treating this as a separate topic, this work will argue that analyzing the antifascist movement abroad in fact fundamentally alters our understanding of the regime's national project. Ever since Charles Delzell's classic study of the antifascist movement, *Mussolini's Enemies: The Italian Anti-Fascist Resistance*, many others have in fact written specifically on the antifascist experience in Latin America.[11] Studies on Argentina and Uruguay, especially those by Pietro Rinaldo Fanesi; Ronald C. Newton, who analyzed both the fascist and antifascist movements in Argentina; and Clara Aldrighi, have all highlighted the ways in which antifascists outmaneuvered fascist supporters and undermined many of the regime's efforts. María Victoria Grillo's work in particular provides an important contribution to the field by demonstrating how the antifascists in Argentina countered the regime's propaganda by offering the community their own alternative antifascist Italian identity.[12] Federica Bertagna's recent analysis of the antifascist periodical *Italia del Popolo* among other Italian community newspapers in her recent work *La stampa italiana in Argentina* is also an important counterbalance to works that have focused exclusively on fascist activities in Argentina. Her overall work is also a key addition to the literature in that it highlights the centrality of the Italian-language press within the political debates the community had with the Italian regime, an argument that is also supported by Pantaleone Sergi's article on the final days of the storied community newspaper *La Patria degli Italiani*.[13]

Taken together these works on fascism and antifascism in Argentina and elsewhere have sketched a clear narrative portrait of fascist Italy's political activities and their influence in the various countries they targeted. They have outlined fascist Italy's major policy initiatives toward its emigrant communities as well as identified the key individuals and organizations responsible for advancing the fascist agenda. In so doing, these authors have demonstrated the centrality of Mussolini's emigrant propaganda to the regime's overall international agenda. They have also validated the importance of studying the community press as a way of understanding the propaganda and its reception.

Building upon this scholarship, my work uses similar sources to answer a different set of questions, moving the field in a new direction by asking what theoretical implications these activities have on Italian national discourses. Almost all of the recent works do in fact recognize that Italian patriotism and spreading Italian national identity abroad were key components of the fascist agenda, adding that both fascists and antifascists conflated "Italian-ness" with their own political ideologies, and yet few have explored in depth the theoretical implications that these activities have had on the creation of contested national narratives. Those works that do address the issue of Italian national identity approach this theme from the perspective of fascism (or antifascism) and its ideological influence on the community. This work instead separates fascism's ideological political agenda from its nationalization project abroad, arguing that these two agendas worked at cross-purposes from one another. Furthermore, by examining the changing discourses on national identity the Italian propaganda provoked rather than its politics, this study does more than trace the experiences of fascist Italy's program in Argentina but rather uses these experiences to understand more generally how national projects work outside of the nation-state and how national narratives change when contested and reimagined from abroad. In other words, the goal of this work is not to recount fascist and antifascist activities in Argentina or their ideological influence on politics and identity, a task that has been done quite effectively by others, but instead to analyze the discursive debate over the Italian national project abroad that emerged from those activities, activities that themselves look different when framed as a national project rather than a fascist one. This alternative focus is significant in that it leads me to draw different conclusions from many of the works discussed above.

As the title suggests, this work interprets the activities of Il Duce's regime from the context of a state-sponsored national project not unlike other national projects abroad created by other nation-states both before and after the years of fascism. By approaching the topic from this perspective, the study identifies the peculiar dynamics of a national identity outside of the national context. Unlike much of the current scholarship, this work asserts that the significance of Mussolini's efforts abroad lies not in the propaganda effort itself and whether it was rejected or accepted but rather in the dynamic national conversation it provoked, in which both supporters and opponents of the regime's national project articulated their own original understandings of the Italian nation. The focus of this study is therefore on the theoretical implications that the Italian fascist agenda and reactions to it had on changing the nature of a national discourse, rather than on the agenda itself.

IMAGINING THE ITALIAN NATION

This work centers on public discourse, examining the issue of national identity from a cultural perspective through a close analysis of textual material and analyzing the ways in which its subjects conceived of and articulated their notions of identity. It uses the material evidence of the fascist propaganda effort and the published responses the effort provoked in Argentina to explore how different members of the Italian and Argentine communities defined and debated their national identities. The discourses on national identity that the book examines are, however, firmly grounded in the social and political context in which they were written, providing both a narrative of events and personalities as well as a textual analysis of the debates themselves. This approach highlights the interrelatedness of imagined communities and the realities that they reflect and are informed by.

Il Duce's national project in Argentina is used here as an optic for understanding the broader question of Italy's national identity and the changing ways in which it was conceptualized. In examining the various ways in which members of the Italian community envisioned the nation and conceptualized their identity, it becomes clear that fascist officials and antifascist exiles were not the only ones creating the national discourses. Members of the Italian community also articulated their own original conception of the nation, replete with their own set of national myths, images, and historical narratives.

Benedict Anderson's definition of national identity provides a useful starting point for understanding Italy's national project both at home and abroad. Anderson moved away from sui generis and static definitions of the nation and instead defined national identities as cultural constructs, which are imagined, contested, and reelaborated over the course of a nation's history. According to Anderson, the nation is "a cultural artefact," "an imagined political community imagined as both limited and sovereign." Central to Anderson's view is the question of how the nation is conceived and delimited, creating a sense of commonality among a people living within the boundaries of a nation-state.[14] Thinking of a nation as an "imagined community" enables us to understand the dynamics of its creation on a discursive level, which makes the ways in which the nation is envisioned and defined central to understanding Italy's national project in Argentina.

Anderson's characterization of national identity as an imagined cultural construct has in particular led to a number of studies on Italian identity that analyze the origins of discourses on the nation and the particular national characteristics and ideological ingredients that coalesce during crucial historical junctures into the creation of a national identity.[15] Silvana Patriarca, for example, in *Numbers and Nationhood: Writing Statistics in Nineteenth-Cen-*

tury Italy illustrates how statistical information was used for the development of an Italian national identity in the nineteenth century by arguing that statisticians not only interpreted the nation but also helped create it. In her more recent work, *Italian Vices: Nation and Character from the Risorgimento to the Republic*, Patriarca approaches the question of Italian identity by examining discourses on Italian national character, and in so doing demonstrates the importance of cultural tropes and narratives in the formation of national identity.[16]

Making and Remaking Italy: The Cultivation of National Identity around the Risorgimento, edited by Albert Russell Ascoli and Krystyna von Henneberg, and *Immagini della nazione nell'Italia del Risorgimento*, edited by Alberto Mario Banti and Roberto Bizzocchi, similarly approach the question of Italian national identity through the optic of the myths and images that came to be associated with the Risorgimento.[17] Relying primarily on cultural sources, including literature, the visual arts, music, and later film, the contributors to these collections examine much of the iconography employed by intellectuals and politicians in their construction of an Italian national identity designed to unify the country culturally and politically.[18] Lucy Riall's study of the Risorgimento leader Giuseppe Garibaldi, *Garibaldi: The Invention of a Hero*, also traced the way in which the myth of Garibaldi was consciously cultivated by Italian political leaders during as well as after his death in order to promote their own visions of Italian identity.[19] More than mere representations of the nation, these conceptualizations provided a powerful intellectual framework from which Risorgimento leaders and liberal politicians set out to establish a unified nation.

Taken together, these recent works demonstrate the tremendous impact intellectual conceptions of the nation played in the creation of a particular national identity. They have also established the importance of ideas and the power of discourse in shaping national realities. Though dealing with a later time and place, this book sees the same creative power of discourse at work among the Italians in Argentina as they put forth a vision of the Italian nation at odds with the one emanating from Rome.

STATE FORMATION THROUGH NATIONAL DISCOURSE

Il Duce's propagandists in Argentina tried to monopolize the conversation on Italy's national identity abroad. As is true of most modern nations, once unified the Italian state strove to exert a hegemonic control over the national discourse. Anderson made note of this relationship between state building and nationalism, describing the process as "a systematic, even Machiavellian, instilling of nationalist ideology through the mass media, the educational system, administrative regulations and so forth." [20] For Anthony Smith, "national agencies of mass socialization" were also central to what he defines as the civic, or Western, model of national identity, "whose members were united, if not made, homogenous by common historical memories, myths, symbols, and traditions."[21] Eugen Weber's *Peasants into Frenchmen: The Modernization of Rural France, 1870–1914* illustrates in great detail how this process of nation building worked on a local level by demonstrating how socioeconomic change and government involvement integrated peasants into France's national project during the Third Republic. In particular, Weber highlights the role of military service as well as a state school system in promoting a national culture and identity.[22]

Mussolini's national project in Argentina included almost all of the same fascist symbols and myths that the regime employed in its nationalization project at home. Theorists of nationalism highlight in particular this promulgation of national symbols, myths, historical memories, and images to create a sense of unity among a people and devotion to the state.[23] George L. Mosse was among the first to examine how a nation-state employed such devices to promote a national project. According to Mosse, monuments, aesthetics, symbols, and ceremony were used in Germany to inspire unity and a national German identity. This national spirit was expressed through a combination of classical Greek ideals with German *volk* traditions. National monuments, linked to public festivals, which promulgated national mythology, developed into a new secular religion, attracting mass appeal and designed to transcend class lines and political divisions.[24]

Emilio Gentile illustrates in detail how the Italian state, especially while under the fascist regime, imposed its vision of the Italian nation on the Italian people. He argues that fascism in particular established itself as a political religion whose goal was to complete Italy's nationalization project. According to Gentile, through solemn rituals fascists honored patriotic symbols, such as the flag and war monuments, and associated themselves with the Italian nation, and mixed their own rituals and symbols with those of the state. As the regime became more powerful, fascist holidays honoring Mussolini's March on Rome and the founding of the party were added to the litany of national holidays and celebrations. Religious symbols, such as the use of bells and holy relics, were also co-opted by the fascists, and locations such as fascist headquarters and memorials became sacred sanctuaries. Carefully orchestrated processions, bonfires, ceremonies, and celebrations were all designed to instill a collective sense of identity and communion with the fascist regime.[25]

The Italian government, especially during the fascist period, similarly attempted to nationalize its Italians living in Argentina by offering an Italian education through a state-sponsored network of Italian schools abroad, by calling on Italian emigrants to return to serve in the Italian military, and through the use of mass media. Of course, if the methodology was similar, the context was quite different. Lacking the coercive mechanisms of the state, the Italian fascists had no way of requiring Italian emigrants in Argentina to attend their schools or join their military. This speaks to the fundamental difference between fascist Italy's national project at home and its project abroad, making us question the nature of nationalism outside of the territory of the nation-state.

Members of the Italian community in Argentina as well as native Argentines complicated fascist Italy's nationalization project by challenging and redefining it from below, creating an identity replete with its own alternative set of national symbols and images. Michael E. Geisler in his introduction to *National Symbols, Fractured Identities* highlights this "coexistence of competing and contested national narrative systems," explaining that "the role played by national symbols in the formation and maintenance of collective identity is an ongoing, dynamic process in which historical symbolic meanings are constantly recycled, actualized, challenged, renegotiated, and reconfirmed, or re-written."[26] In the case of Argentina, many members of the Italian community did not receive the fascist message in the way in which the regime intended; instead, they attached their own meanings and symbolism to the fascist national liturgy, providing it with their own assumptions and conceptualizations of the nation.

In analyzing fascism's national project in Argentina, one must question whether the fascists truly succeeded in identifying their regime with the Italian nation. Geisler further explains that the power of symbolic national imagery in defining a nation depends "on changes in public consensus or the ability or inability of a particular hegemonic societal group to maintain its hold on the collective imaginary."[27] Central to the issue at hand, therefore, is whether or not fascism held hegemonic sway over Italy's national discourse.

In reflecting on the national discourse after the war in his *Finis Italiae: Declino e morte dell'ideologia risorgimentale*, the journalist Sergio Romano among others seemed to think that they did, writing that "if Mussolini had brought to the king 'the Italy of Vittorio Veneto' as he declared at the Quirinale on October 30, 1922, it was by then [after the war] impossible to speak of Vittorio Veneto with patriotic accents. National pride was hijacked by the fascist-inspired radical right and became anomalous, illegitimate."[28] The shadow of fascism did seem to loom over postwar national discourses. Fascism's apparent appropriation of Italy's national identity as well as its use of patriotic imagery complicated how Italians after the Second World War redefined the nation. The new postwar republic had to avoid much of the tainted nationalist themes associated with fascism, marshaling alternative myths surrounding the role of the antifascist resistance and the Italian people during the war years and highlighting the universal values of justice and liberty.[29]

Some scholars, Ernesto Galli della Loggia first among them, have viewed this new postwar identity as antinationalist, creating a crisis in Italy's identity as a nation.[30]

This book's evaluation of the Italian regime's experiences in Argentina, however, calls into question whether the fascists ever truly succeeded in co-opting the national discourse, at least when viewed from abroad. Along the same lines, for some time there has been much debate among historians over the extent to which Mussolini's regime sought after and achieved public consensus in Italy.[31] Whatever degree of consensus was or was not achieved at home, this study will show that the regime exerted little control over its national project once it crossed the Atlantic.

The Italian fascist nationalization project entered a contested public space when it arrived on Argentina's shores. Without the tools of coercion and armed only with the power of persuasion, the fascists had to compete openly with alternative visions of the Italian nation. Following the Italian fascist propaganda and the public reactions it provoked in Argentina, therefore, provides the unique opportunity to examine how an authoritarian dictatorial regime operates within a relatively free democratic society. This situation makes it possible to examine how fascism's vision of the Italian nation was publicly debated, challenged, contested, and redefined. Although the degree to which Italians in Argentina supported the regime is difficult to measure quantifiably, in terms of controlling national discourse, this study conclusively demonstrates that fascism's "hold over the collective imaginary" was far from hegemonic.

It is useful to consider the experiences of the Italian national debate in Argentina in terms of Jürgen Habermas's concept of the public sphere. Italian citizens abroad were afforded access to a free public space in Argentina not readily available within Italy while under Mussolini's authoritarian regime. This enabled the Italian public in Argentina to resemble what Habermas defines as a public sphere in which "citizens act as a public when they deal with matters of general interest without being subject to coercion; thus with the guarantee that they may assemble and unite, and express their opinions freely."[32] Once established, Habermas explains, this public sphere can "mediate between state and society, [and be] a sphere in which the public, as the vehicle of public opinion, is formed."[33] In a shift from the past, the public therefore had the ability to actively engage in a nation's public discourse, participate fully, and interpret for themselves topics of national relevance, including discourses on the nation itself.[34] Interestingly, Habermas has in mind the role of the public sphere as an outgrowth of bourgeois society that operated within the specific context of a democratic constitutional model. However, as historian Geoff Eley explains in a critique of Habermas's concept, "the public sphere makes more sense as the structured setting where cultural and ideological contest or negotiation among a variety of publics takes place."[35] The experiences within Argentina substantiate this understanding of the public sphere. By creating "a nation outside of the nation," the regime itself created an Italian public sphere within Argentina. Furthermore, and quite ironically, the regime validated that public sphere by asserting that its Italian emigrants abroad were just as integral to the Italian nation as Italians living at home. What they could not have realized was that by expanding their national project to incorporate citizens outside of the nation-state, they also opened the door to a national public space in which the national project itself could be debated and reimagined outside of the state's control.

REIMAGINING THE NATION FROM ABROAD

Fascist Italy recast its national project to encompass its emigrant population abroad, and emigrants in Argentina and throughout the world in turn challenged this conceptualization by reimagining the Italian nation to encompass their own collective identities. By actively engaging in a debate with the fascist regime's propagandists over Italian identity, the Italian emigrants in Argentina involved themselves in the construction of Italy's national discourse. The heart of this analysis is therefore the question of how Italian emigrants imagined their own identity and interacted with their nation of origin.

As Smith explains, a national identity is "fundamentally multi-dimensional": "it can never be reduced to a single element, even by particular factions of nationalists, nor can it easily or swiftly be induced in a population by artificial means."[36] Mussolini did in fact try to artificially impose on Italian communities abroad his own politicized fascist identity. That he failed in this endeavor sustains Smith's point, as does the fact that members of the community abroad created their own sense of a nation abroad that transcended the simple ideological dichotomy between fascist and antifascist definitions of the nation.

This work is informed especially by new transnational approaches to the study of Italian emigration and Italy's national project. In his classic work *A History of Italy, 1871–1915*, Benedetto Croce wrote, "The persistency of national character among emigrants is primarily determined by the prestige of their home country and the vitality of its culture."[37] Historians are now examining in depth the relationship Croce suggestively posed between emigrant communities and the national identity of their homeland. While there are a number of works detailing the various Italian immigrant experiences in their adopted countries, emigration has in the past received all too little attention in a transnational perspective. Historical works on Italian emigration have generally focused on contributions made by Italians to their adopted country as well as on their socioeconomic conditions within their new countries. Donna R. Gabaccia and Fraser M. Ottanelli are among the first to place Italian emigration in a transnational context, relating as much as possible the emigrant experience to developments in Italian history as well as the history of emigrants' new nations.[38] In her highly suggestive work, Gabaccia wrote that "national histories obscure the most outstanding characteristics of migrations from Italy—their worldwide dimensions and their circulatory character—and ignore connections between Italy's villages, towns, and government and the Other Italies around the world."[39] Pasquale Verdicchio in *Bound by Distance: Rethinking Nationalism through the Italian Diaspora* similarly adopts this transnational approach to the study of Italian nationalism. Through his textual analysis of a variety of literary works, Verdicchio connects emigration to the turn-of-the-century Italian national debate, illustrating how a critique of the mass emigration out of Italy was used as a device to promote a new society at home and an imperialist agenda abroad.[40]

Mark I. Choate's *Emigrant Nation: The Making of Italy Abroad* further links emigration directly to debates over Italy's national project by examining the different ways in which liberal and nationalist figures debated the role of emigration in terms of Italian national expansion, linking it to the debates over colonization in Africa.[41] His approach to the changing contours of the Italian debate over emigration during the liberal period parallels this book's treatment of the debate during the fascist period and also highlights the interconnectedness between Italian emigration and national discourse in shaping the way in which the Italian nation was defined. While exploring a related theme, this study, however, decenters the debate over emigration and identity by not only focusing on the Italian perspective but also examining how it was debated across the Atlantic among members of the Italian community in Argentina as well as by the wider Argentine population.

Adopting a truly transnational perspective on the national debate makes an understanding of the social and political realities faced by the Italian immigrant community in Argentina integral to my interpretation of its cultural discourse on Italy's national project abroad. According to Eric Hobsbawm, "The progress of national consciousness is neither linear nor necessarily at the expense of other elements of social consciousness," and "the acquisition of national consciousness cannot be separated from the acquisition of other forms of social and political consciousness during this period. They all go together."[42] For Hobsbawm, these social and political factors influence a subject's social consciousness, and a people's priorities and loyalties shift over time depending on the context.

Over the past thirty years there has been a significant number of historical studies examining the sociopolitical aspects Italian immigration to Latin America, especially to Brazil and Argentina. Fernando Devoto, Angelo Trento, Gianfausto Rosoli, and, in English, Samuel Baily have provided a tremendous amount of analysis of Italian immigration to these nations, especially during the period of mass immigration during the late nineteenth and early twentieth centuries. Recently, historians have moved beyond works of social history and begun to examine Italian immigrant cultural and political identities in a transnational perspective. This renewed interest is no doubt also in part the result of Italy's recent transition from a nation of emigration to a nation of immigration. More and more historians are in fact adopting transnational and comparative approaches to the Argentine experience. Well-established historians, such as Emilio Franzina, Trento, and Scarzanella have led the way, writing, editing, and introducing many new volumes that address these themes. These pioneering authors have highlighted the transnational bonds many Italians in Latin America maintained with Italy throughout the nineteenth and twentieth centuries. In so doing, they have demonstrated the relevance of emigration to the study of modern Italian history.[43] Many of these scholars also highlight the importance of the 1920s through 1930s as a key moment in the Italian community's social and political integration into Argentine society. It is in fact impossible to understand the Italian emigrant national discourses examined in this book without taking into account the social and political experience of Italian immigration to Argentina that informed and shaped those discourses.

Over the past few years these new transnational approaches to understanding nationalism from the Italian diaspora have fundamentally changed the way we understand the formation of national identities by validating the active role of emigrants in reshaping those discourses from abroad. By applying this framework to the specific case of fascist Italy's project in Argentina, this work analyzes not only the content and impact of Italy's national program in Argentina, but also the ways in which Italian emigrants actively participated in shaping that national discourse. Viewing national discourse through this transnational lens enables this book to argue that the emigrants' different conceptualizations of the nation within Argentina were no less valid than that of the fascist regime and equally important to our understanding of how national identities are constructed and negotiated over time and across space.

REFRAMING THE NATION: A NEW WORLD PERSPECTIVE

The debate this book analyzes over how to envision the nation among Italians at home and abroad did not take place in a vacuum. The Argentine context in which the Italian discourse played out is also of fundamental importance, raising the question of how the dynamics of identity formation change across the Atlantic. The various articulations of Italian national identity from within the Italian community were each informed and shaped by Argentina's New World nationalism. The resulting national project was in effect a European national identity framed within an American national discursive model.

In a very important recent collection of essays on New World nationalisms, Don H. Doyle and Marco Antonio Pamplona explain how the contours of the debate on national identity differ significantly from European models. According to Doyle and Pamplona, "The pluralism as well as the newness of American nations undermined any attempt to envision the nation along the lines of the European paradigm as a people bound and distinguished by common descent, a deep collective past, or homogeneous cultural traditions."[44] Although this New World context changes the contours of the debate over identity, it does not lesson the importance of creating a national conscious. As Doyle and Pamplona explain, "The need to construct a common national identity was every bit as pressing in the multiethnic immigrant societies of the Americas as in other countries, but immigrant nations had to work with different materials."[45] Nations of immigrants therefore tended to stress a shared set of values and beliefs rather than ethnicity or a shared cultural heritage.

Though the context was quite different, Argentina's national project was no less complex and no less valid than that of Italy. At the very same moment that the Italian Risorgimento intellectuals attempted to construct a unified Italian cultural identity, Argentine elites were also struggling to forge their own national culture. Just as was the case in Italy, several national factors in Argentina complicated this project: its vast territorial expanses and sparse population, Spain's ambiguous cultural legacy, and the divide culturally between the city and countryside and politically between the provinces and Buenos Aires. Furthermore, unlike in other parts of Latin America, Argentina lacked a rich indigenous cultural heritage that Creole elites could use to construct a distinctive national narrative. Without much of a mythical past to fall back on, Argentina was by necessity defined as a nation of the future. In light of these obstacles to a cultural construction of identity, Argentine elites relied on ideational definitions of the nation.

Civic virtue and democratic ideals figured prominently in the formation of the Argentine nation in the early nineteenth century. According to the historian Jorge Myers in his recent work on Argentine identity, "a persistent theme in Argentine life from independence onward has been the emergence of a powerful republican discourse." As Myers goes on to explain, "the tendency was toward the establishment of a national identity defined primarily in terms of political principles and objectives rather than the cultural attributes of the country's inhabitants."[46] Along these lines, Argentine leaders like Domingo Faustino Sarmiento and Juan Bautista Alberdi in the nineteenth century encouraged immigration as well as a public education system based on the North American model in the hopes of creating an inclusive national identity based on the principle of an informed and democratic civil society.

All this began to change in the early twentieth century. The new and emerging Argentine nationalist movement formulated its own ethnic-cultural version of Argentine national identity that would soon dominate the national debate. Ricardo Rojas, one of the leading intellectuals of this movement, defined the Argentine race by exalting its Creole national character, which was symbolized by idyllic representations of the gaucho and the pampas. According to Rojas, new immigrants would be transformed by the Creole environment in which they lived and become ethnically Argentine by assimilating Argentine customs and receiving a state education that exalted Argentina's history, literature, and geography. Other nationalists like Manuel Gálvez defined Argentine identity more narrowly, highlighting its Spanish and Catholic roots.[47]

Historians of Argentine nationalism agree that the 1920s and 1930s were a key moment in the elaboration of this ethno-cultural nationalism that would later lay the groundwork for Argentina's future authoritarian regimes. By then Argentine nationalism had become more of a right-wing political movement, and nationalist visions were increasingly nativist and xenophobic in character. These nationalists resented Britain's historical dominance over the economy but were far more troubled by the menacing anarchist and radical tendencies of the immigrant working classes and wrote on the corrupting influences of immigration to Argentina that tarnished the purity of Argentina's Spanish-Creole cultural heritage. Unlike earlier nationalists, they openly criticized Argentina's civil traditions and democratic paradigms.[48] As a counterbalance to these histories of the rise of right-wing nationalism in Argentina, Andrés Bisso's *El antifascismo Argentino* reminds readers that not all Argentines were nationalist-fascist sympathizers by highlighting the importance of the Argentine antifascist movement and the diverse intellectuals and activists who struggled for democracy and social justice against the threats posed by both foreign and local fascisms.[49]

It is at this critical juncture in Argentina's national and political struggle that Italian fascist propaganda arrived on Argentina's shores. Federico Finchelstein in his recent *Transatlantic Fascism: Ideology, Violence, and the Sacred in Argentina and Italy, 1919–1945* specifically analyzes the transnational relationship between Italian fascism and Argentine nationalism. He highlights the influence that Italian fascist propaganda played in the development of Argentina's own original right-wing political ideology.[50] Finchelstein also identifies in the Italian regime's efforts the uneasy, at times contradictory, coexistence in the propaganda of fascist Italy's national appeal to its immigrants as well as its universal ideological appeal to Argentine nationalists. As he explains, "fascist propaganda was aimed at two imagined audiences: Argentine society and Italian immigrants. To be sure the audiences were often the same imagined communities, but fascism never addressed this situation."[51] While Finchelstein goes on to explore fascism's ideological influence on Argentine nationalism, my work goes in the other direction by exploring instead its nationalization project directed toward its emigrants, a project that I argue undermined the ideological message. My work is also a good complement to Finchelstein in that it conversely analyzes the role played by Argentine national discourses in shaping the debate over Italian national identity that took place on Argentine soil.

CONCLUSION

This work begins by focusing on what members of the fascist regime in Italy said and wrote about the notion of an Italian identity outside of Italy and analyzes how they attempted to transmit that identity through the print propaganda they sent to Argentina. Subsequent chapters analyze Argentina's Italian-language press to determine how prominent members of the Italian community created their own discourses on Italian national identity and explore the wider Argentine public debate on national identity and fascist propaganda through an analysis of Argentine newspapers as well as the proceedings of Argentina's congressional debate.

Using the articles, speeches, and reports of key cultural and political figures, chapter 2 analyzes the overall Italian fascist mission to promote its national identity throughout the world and the inherent contradictions it entailed. Analyzing the telegrams and dispatches sent by Italian consuls and fascist envoys to the Ministry of Foreign Affairs in Rome, it details the evolution of the regime's national agenda abroad, focusing especially on the regime's creation and co-optation of Italian organizations abroad to advance its national project at the expense of its own more radical fascist ideology.

Chapter 3 focuses exclusively on the activities of the Italian fascist regime in Argentina. After providing an overview of Italian immigration to Argentina, this chapter examines why the South American republic attracted so much of the regime's attention, making it one of the focal points of its worldwide agenda. The chapter then goes on to detail the regime's various activities within Argentina, highlighting the increasing importance placed on promoting the national agenda through Italian cultural organizations.

Chapter 4 is a close textual analysis of the Italian propaganda materials sent to Argentina in the context of its promotion of an Italian national identity abroad. It examines a wide array of materials sent by the Ministry of Popular Culture and other fascist ministries to Argentina. The main focus of this chapter is on the school textbooks produced by the Italian fascist regime and disseminated to the Italian schools in Argentina. It analyzes how the regime articulated its conceptualization of Italian identity and communicated it to the children of Italian emigrants in Argentina. Most importantly, it uses the textual materials sent to Argentina to demonstrate how the content of national projects is fundamentally different when articulated to a public living within another sovereign state.

Chapter 5 explains the various ways in which members of the Italian community responded to fascist Italy's national project at their doorstep. Focusing on the public debate in the Italian-language press over the fascist regime's claims on Italian identity, it examines both profascist and antifascist perspectives. These members of the community actively engaged in a lively discussion of Italian national identity within Argentina. Whether they supported or opposed Mussolini's regime, this chapter contends that these community members expressed an Italian identity fundamentally different from the version emanating from the regime in Rome. Anxious to assimilate into Argentine society and influenced by Argentine notions of identity, these Italians developed their own original understanding of an Italian national identity abroad, an identity informed by Argentina's democratic traditions.

Chapter 6 studies the reception of the Italian project by the wider Argentine population and places the question of an Italian national identity abroad into the context of Argentine debates over its own identity as a nation. From the congressional halls where politicians delivered impassioned speeches defending Argentina's democratic character against the totalitarian menace, to the pages of the nationalist press that used the fascist identity to create their own concept of the nation, Argentines of all persuasions used the propaganda to advance their own politically charged definitions of national identity. From this debate, this chapter demonstrates the continued importance of democratic values in the formation of an ideational Argentine national identity, a departure from much of the current Argentine historiography on the period. This chapter also contrasts New and Old World national identities through a comparative analysis of Italian and Argentine identity formation. And it concludes by recounting the centrality of Italy's national project in the Argentine government's investigation of Italian fascist activities during the war and the congressional debates over Argentine identity that it inspired.

The question of national identity is a complex one, informed by many different elements of collective identity. In exploring the way in which nations are imagined, constructed, and recast, both from above as well as from below, this work provides a transatlantic example of the dynamic interplay between the Italian state and its emigrant communities in the conceptualization of the nation, shedding new light on the intricate ways national identities are imagined and negotiated. Using the case of Mussolini's promotion of an

Italian national identity in Argentina, it illustrates the intersections between culture and politics, ethnicity and ideology, and the state and the collective in the construction of a national discourse.

The concept of an extraterritorial national identity is especially relevant in today's increasingly transnational world. Studying a national project and the way in which it was reshaped and debated outside of the national territory offers us a different paradigm for understanding the dynamics of identity formation. It is, in short, a transnational perspective on what it means to belong to a nation.

NOTES

All translations from the original Italian and Spanish are my own unless otherwise noted.

1. Donna R. Gabaccia, *Italy's Many Diasporas* (Seattle: University of Washington Press, 2000), 9, 11.
2. Mark I. Choate, *Emigrant Nation: The Making of Italy Abroad* (Cambridge, MA: Harvard University Press, 2008), 18.
3. Piero Parini, *Gli Italiani nel mondo* (Rome: Fasci all'Estero, 1935), 9.
4. Emilio Gentile, "La politica estera del partito Fascista: Ideologia e organizzazione dei Fasci italiani all'estero (1920–1930)," *Storia Contemporanea* 26, no. 6 (1995): 897–956.
5. Luca de Caprariis, "'Fascism for Export?' The Rise and Eclipse of the Fasci Italiani all' Estero," *Journal of Contemporary History* 35, no. 2 (April 2000): 151–83; Philip V. Cannistraro, *Blackshirts in Little Italy: Italian Americans and Fascism, 1921–1929* (West Lafayette, IN: Bordighera,1999); Claudia Baldoli, *Exporting Fascism: Italian Fascists and Britain's Italians in the 1930s* (Oxford: Berg, 2003).
6. Emilio Franzina and Matteo Sanfilippo, eds., *Il Fascismo e gli emigrati: La parabola dei Fasci italiani all'estero (1920–1943)* (Rome: Laterza, 2003). See also Renzo Santinon, *Fasci all'estero* (Rome: Edizioni Settimo Sigillo, 1995); Domenico Fabiano, "I fasci italiani all'estero," in *Gli Italiani fuori d'Italia: Gli emigranti italiani nei movimienti operai dei paesi d'adozione, 1880–1940*, ed. Bruno Bezza, 221–36 (Milan: Franco Angelli Editori, 1983); Juan Oddone, "Serafino Mazzolini: Un misionario del Fascismo en Uruguay, 1933–1937," *Estudios Migratorios Latinoamericanos* 12, no. 37 (1997): 375–87; João Fábio Bertonha, "Emigrazione e politica estera: La diplomazia sovversiva di Mussolini e la questione degli italiani all'estero, 1922–1945," *Altreitalie* 23 (2001): 39–61; João Fábio Bertonha, "Fascism and the Italian Communities in Brazil and America," *Italian Americana* 19, no. 2 (2001): 146–57; João Fábio Bertonha, *O fascismo e os imigrantes italianos no Brasil* (Porto Alegre: EDIPUCRS, 2001). Most historians have focused only on Brazil and Argentina, which had the largest Italian collectivities; articles by Orazio A. Ciccarelli and Franco Savarino, however, stress the importance of studying Peru and Mexico as well, countries that had relatively small yet very influential middle-class Italian collectivities greatly influenced by fascism. Orazio A. Ciccarelli, "Fascism and Politics in Peru during the Benavides Regime, 1933–39: The Italian Perspective," *Hispanic American Historical Review* 70, no. 3 (August 1990): 405–32; Orazio A. Ciccarelli, "Fascist Propaganda and the Italian Community in Peru during the Benavides Regime, 1933–39," *Journal of Latin American Studies* 20, no. 2 (November 1988): 361–88; Franco Savarino, "Bajo el signo del *Littorio*: La communidad italiana en México y el fascismo 1924–1941," *Revista Mexicana de Sociología* 64, no. 2 (January–March 2002): 113–39.
7. Eugenia Scarzanella, ed., *Fascisti in Sud America* (Florence: Le Lettere, 2005), xi. Eugenia Scarzanella, Vanni Blengino, and Camilla Catarułla focus on Italian fascism in Argentina as expressed through *Il Mattino d'Italia*. Scarzanella examines Vittorio Valdani's life and the role of *Il Mattino d'Italia* in promoting fascism. Cattarulla examines a survey published by the paper in 1934 that asked the question, "What would you say to the Duce if you had the

opportunity to speak to him?" She argues that respondents' use of language as well as their thoughts and ideas reflect a mix of pride and nostalgia for their homeland and their own anxieties and desires within their new nation. Blengino examines how Argentine nationalists contributed to *Il Mattino* in an attempt to appeal to the wider public.

8. Scarzanella, *Fascisti in Sud America*, xiii.

9. Federica Bertagna, *La patria di riserva: L'emigrazione fascista in Argentina* (Rome: Donzelli, 2006).

10. Matteo Pretelli, *Il fascismo e gli italiani all'estero* (Bologna: Clueb, 2010).

11. See, for example, Ronald C. Newton, "Ducini, Prominenti, Antifascisti: Italian Fascism and the Italo-Argentine Collectivity, 1922–1945," *Americas* 51, no. 1 (1994): 41–66; M. L. Leiva, "Il movimiento antifascista italiano in Argentina (1922–1945)," in Bezza, *Gli Italiani fuori d'Italia*, 553–82; Pietro Rinaldo Fanesi, "El anti-fascismo italiano en Argentina (1922–1945)," *Estudios Migratorios Latinoamericanos* 4, no. 12 (1989): 319–352; and Clara Aldrighi's work on Luigi Fabbri's activities in Uruguay: *Antifascismo italiano en Montevideo: El dialogo politico entre Luigi Fabbri y Carlo Rosselli* (Montevideo: Universidad de la Republica, 1996), and "Luigi Fabbri en Uruguay, 1929–1935," *Estudios Migratorios Latinoamericanos* 12, no. 37 (1997): 389–422.

12. Judith Casali de Babot and María Victoria Grillo, *Fascismo y antifascismo en Europa y Argentina en el siglo XX* (San Miguel de Tucumán: Instituto de Investigaciones Historicas, Universidad Nacional de Tucumán, 2002).

13. Federica Bertagna, *La stampa italiana in Argentina* (Rome: Donzelli Editore, 2009); Pantaleone Sergi, "Fascismo e antifascismo nella stampa italiana in Argentina: Cosí fu spenta 'la Patria degli Italiani,'" *Altreitalie* 42 (2007): 4–44.

14. Benedict Anderson, *Imagined Communities: Reflections on the Origin and Spread of Nationalism* (London: Verso, 1983), 1–11.

15. Linda Colley's *Britons: Forging the Nation* (New Haven, CT: Yale University Press, 1993) is illustrative of this approach. Colley argues that over the course of the sixteenth century British elites cultivated a national self-image unified by a set of values premised on Protestantism, commercial enterprise, imperial expansion, and patriotic images of the monarchy, in opposition to all things French. Alberto Mario Banti, in *La nazione del risorgimento* (Turin: Einaudi, 2000), adapts this approach by focusing on the literary "canon" of the Risorgimento: the writings of the young intellectual patriots who developed their own particular vision of a unified national community during the first half of the nineteenth century. Beginning especially with the Jacobin period of French occupation, Banti argues that intellectuals in their writings began to envision Italy as an indivisible and sovereign national community.

16. Silvana Patriarca, *Numbers and Nationhood: Writing Statistics in Nineteenth-Century Italy* (Cambridge: Cambridge University Press, 1996); *Italian Vices: Nation and Character from the Risorgimento to the Republic* (Cambridge: Cambridge University Press, 2010). See also Silvana Patriarca, "Indolence and Regeneration: Tropes and Tensions of Risorgimento Patriotism," *American Historical Review* 110, no. 2 (2005): 1–26.

17. Albert Russell Ascoli and Krystyna Von Henneberg, *Making and Remaking Italy: The Cultivation of National Identity around the Risorgimento* (Oxford: Berg, 2001); Alberto Mario Banti, and Roberto Bizzocchi eds, *Immagini della nazione nell'Italia del Risorgimento* (Rome: Carocci, 2002).

18. Ascoli and Von Hennenberg, *Making and Remaking Italy*, 7.

19. Lucy Riall, *Garibaldi: The Invention of a Hero* (New Haven, CT: Yale University Press, 2007).

20. Anderson, *Imagined Communities*, 113–14.

21. Anthony Smith, *National Identity* (Reno: University of Nevada Press, 1991), 11.

22. Eugen Weber, *Peasants into Frenchmen: The Modernization of Rural France, 1870–1914* (Stanford, CA: Stanford University Press, 1976), 336.

23. Anderson, *Imagined Communities*; Smith, *National Identity*, 11.

24. George L. Mosse, *The Nationalization of the Masses: Political Symbolism and Mass Movements in Germany from the Napoleonic Wars through the Third Reich* (New York: Howard Fertig, 1975), 27–34.

25. Emilio Gentile, *The Sacralization of Politics in Fascist Italy* (Cambridge, MA: Harvard University Press, 1996), 32–53, 80–102. Also see more recently Emilio Gentile, *La grande Italia* (Rome: Laterza, 2006). Two other works of note that explore national identity through symbolic imagery and ritual are Bruno Tobia, *L'altare della patria* (Bologna: Il Mulino, 1998), and David Atkinson and Denis Cosgrove, "Urban Rhetoric and Embodied Identities: City, Nation, and Empire at the Vittoriano Emanuele II Monument in Rome, 1870–1945," *Annals of the Association of American Geographers* 88, no. 1 (1998): 28–49. Both works explore the changing symbolic role in national discourses of the Victor Emmanuel Monument in Rome.

26. Michael E. Geisler, ed., *National Symbols, Fractured Identities* (Middlebury, VT: Middlebury College Press, 2005), xviii.

27. Ibid.

28. Sergio Romano, *Finis Italiae: Declino e morte dell'ideologia risorgimentale* (Milan: All'Insegna del Pesce d'Oro, 1995), 54.

29. Over time, however, these images were in turn challenged by a number of scholars. Renzo De Felice argued that there was in fact a large measure of popular consensus for the fascist regime during the 1930s, and from a different ideological perspective Claudio Pavone defined the period from 1943 to 1945 as a "civil war" between fascists and antifascists. See Renzo De Felice, *Fascism: An Informal Introduction to Its Theory and Practice* (New Brunswick, NJ: Transaction, 1976); Claudio Pavone, *Una guerra civile: Saggio storico sulla moralità nella resistenza* (Turin: Bollati Boringhieri, 1991) .

30. Ernesto Galli della Loggia and Gian Enrico Rusconi are particularly harsh in their assessment of Italy's postwar identity, characterizing the war years as a period of crisis and defeat for the concept of the Italian nation. See Ernesto Galli della Loggia, "La morte della patria," in *Nazione e nazionalità in Italia: Dall'alba de secolo ai nostri giornii*, ed. Giovanni Spadolini, 125–61 (Bari: Laterza, 1994); Gian Enrico Rusconi, *Se cessiamo di essere una nazione* (Bologna: Il Mulino, 1993), 45–101.

31. The question of consensus in Italy for the Italian fascist regime has been much debated ever since De Felice's second volume of his biography, *Mussolini Il Duce: Gli anni del consenso, 1929–1936* (Turin: Giulio Einaudi Editore, 1974). De Felice asserts that after Mussolini consolidated fascist control over the mechanisms of the state, his regime worked toward and largely achieved popular Italian consensus for fascism, a consensus that culminated in the Italian invasion of Ethiopia. Philip V. Cannistraro also examines the fascist regime's search for consensus in *La fabbrica del consenso: Fascismo e mass media* (Bari: Laterza, 1975). He argues that the regime's cultural policies and use of the mass media were indeed intended to achieve a broad base of popular support. For Cannistraro this "cultural revolution" was limited, however, and not as complete as De Felice suggests. Victoria De Grazia directly challenged De Felice's thesis in *The Culture of Consent: Mass Organization of Leisure in Fascist Italy* (New York: Cambridge University Press, 1981) by arguing that consumerism and religion, as well as other social factors, exerted far more influence over the Italian populace than the fascist regime's cultural attempts at remaking the Italian people. Paul Corner recasts the debate over consensus by questioning whether consensus can in fact truly be determined under a dictatorship. He argues that historians from De Felice on who have drawn definitive conclusions on the issue have failed to take into account not only the repressive nature of the fascist dictatorship but also what he calls "aspects that are not directly repressive but that nonetheless constitute instruments of a fairly rigid social control." Given the coercive mechanisms at the disposal of the fascist state, Corner effectively challenges historians' ability to truly measure fascism's influence over the Italian people. See Cannistraro, *La fabbrica del consenso*; Philip V. Cannistraro, "Mussolini's Cultural Revolution: Fascist or Nationalist?" *Journal of Contemporary History* 7, no. 3 (1972): 115–39; De Grazia, *Culture of Consent*; Paul Corner, "Italian Fascism: Whatever Happened to Dictatorship?" *Journal of Modern History* 74 (2002): 325–51.

32. Jürgen Habermas, *On Society and Politics: A Reader*, ed. Steven Seidman (Boston: Beacon Press, 1989), 231–32.

33. Ibid.

34. Craig Calhoun, ed., *Habermas and the Public Sphere* (Cambridge, MA: MIT Press, 1992), 21–39.

35. Geoff Eley, "Nations, Publics, and Political Cultures: Placing Habermas in the Nineteenth Century," in Calhoun, *Habermas and the Public Sphere*, 306.
36. Smith, *National Identity*, 14.
37. Benedetto Croce, *A History of Italy, 1871–1915*, trans. Cecelia M. Ady (Oxford: Clarendon Press, 1929), 229.
38. See, for example, Donna R. Gabaccia and Fraser Ottanelli, eds., *Italian Workers of the World: Labor Migration and the Formation of Multiethnic States* (Urbana: University of Illinois Press, 2001), and most recently, Loretta Baldassar and Gabaccia's fascinating collection on gender and Italian identity: *Intimacy and Italian Migration: Gender and Domestic Lives in a Mobile World* (New York: Fordham University Press, 2011).
39. Donna Gabaccia, *Italy's Many Diasporas* (Seattle: University of Washington Press, 2000), 9.
40. Pasquale Verdicchio, *Bound by Distance: Rethinking Nationalism through the Italian Diaspora* (Madison, NJ: Fairleigh Dickinson University Press, 1997), 42.
41. Mark I. Choate, *Emigrant Nation: The Making of Italy Abroad* (Cambridge, MA: Harvard University Press, 2008).
42. Eric Hobsbawm, *Nations and Nationalism since 1780: Programme, Myth, and Reality* (Cambridge: Cambridge University Press, 1990), 130.
43. In addition to the works mentioned above, also see, for example, Emilio Franzina, *L'America gringa: Storie italiane d'immigrazione tra Agentina e Brasile* (Reggio Emilia: Diabasis, 2008), and Eugenia Scarzanella, *Sin fronteras encuentros de mujeres y hombres entre América Latina y Europa, siglos XIX–XX* (Madrid: Iberoamericana, Vervuert, 2008).
44. Don H. Doyle and Marco Antonio Pamplona, eds., *Nationalism in the New World* (Athens: University of Georgia Press, 2006), 5.
45. Ibid., 6.
46. Jorge Myers, "Language, History, and Politics in Argentine Identity, 1840–1880," in Doyle and Pamplona, *Nationalism in the New World*, 121.
47. See Jean H. Delaney, "Imagining *El Ser Argentino*: Cultural Nationalism and Romantic Concepts of Nationhood in Early Twentieth Century Argentina," *Journal of Latin American Studies* 34 (2002): 625–58.
48. David Rock, *Authoritarian Argentina: The Nationalist Movement, Its History and Its Impact* (Berkeley: University of California Press, 1993). For discussions on Argentine cultural nationalism, see Eduardo J. Cárdenas, *El primer nacionalismo argentino en Manuel Gálvez y Ricardo Rojas* (Buenos Aires: A. Peña Lillo, 1978); Sandra McGee Deutsch and Ronald H. Dolkart, eds., *The Argentine Right: Its History and Intellectuals Origins, 1910 to the Present* (Wilmington, DE: SR Books, 1993); Marisa González de Oleaga, *El doble juego de la Hispanidad: España y la Argentina durante la Segunda Guerra Mundial* (Madrid: Universidad Nacional de Educación a Distancia, 2001).
49. Andrés Bisso, *El antifascismo Argentino* (Buenos Aires: Editorial Buenos Libros, 2007).
50. Federico Finchelstein, *Transatlantic Fascism: Ideology, Violence, and the Sacred in Argentina and Italy, 1919–1945* (Durham, NC: Duke University Press, 2010).
51. Ibid., 39.

Chapter Two

Fascist Italy Looks Abroad

On March 30, 1923, just six months after the March on Rome, Benito Mussolini gave his first speech on emigration, famously declaring that, "For better or for worse, emigration is a physiological necessity of the Italian people. We are forty million people enclosed in our narrow peninsula that has too many mountains, a land that cannot feed everyone."[1] Mussolini did not come into power with a coherent strategy for Italian emigrants abroad. Over the course of the 1920s, however, the presence of Italians throughout the world soon inspired the regime to develop one of its most expansive policies abroad.

At first, the new agenda was all talk but little action. The first battle abroad was a rhetorical one at home. Mussolini, followed by a cadre of fascist writers, strove to convince the public that this "physiological necessity" was actually a great Italian victory. Emigrants were supposedly the pioneers of the "New Italy," spreading Italian fascism throughout the world. Beyond the founding of the fascist party abroad, Mussolini did little in his first years in power to advance his ambitious national agenda. The regime's actions abroad were disorganized and counterproductive. In these early years, the expectation was that Italian emigrants would naturally gravitate toward the Italian regime. By the midtwenties this expectation began to change.

In order for the regime to succeed abroad, Mussolini realized, he would have to systematically target Italian emigrant communities by infiltrating them through Italian organizations and convincing them to become a part of the New Italy. As Mussolini consolidated his power at home, the regime developed much more organized programs abroad. By 1930 all of the regime's efforts abroad were centralized and well coordinated from Rome. Yet as the organizational structure was coming together, inherent tensions within the regime's project became more and more apparent. On the one hand, the regime was promoting a radical international political agenda that strove to spread the fascist movement throughout the world through its emigrants; on the other hand, many of its initiatives instead promoted a more traditional national project that strove to instill within Italians emigrants a renewed sense of belonging to the Italian nation. While not necessarily mutually exclusive endeavors, this chapter will highlight the many instances in which the two strategies worked at cross-purposes with one another. Ultimately, its more narrowly defined national project abroad, not substantially unlike the regime's liberal predecessor, would overshadow its fascist ideological agenda. The result was a program whose primary focus was to nationalize Italian emigrants and their children and in so doing to create a nation without borders.

In analyzing the development of fascism's policy toward its emigrants, historians have in general striven to integrate that policy into the regime's broader ideological program. For example, by tracing the evolution of fascist policies toward emigration from its nationalist precursors through 1920s, Emilio Gentile links fascist views on emigration to nationalist stances on the issue during the immediate postwar years. According to Gentile, the fascists actively promoted an ambitious and expansionist agenda in Argentina until 1927, when they reformulated their stance on emigration, adopting a decidedly negative view on the issue. This evaluation is also supported by Alessandra Ruberti in her article on Argentina in the fascist press.[2] Other historians, however, most recently Matteo Pretelli, have pushed the narrative further into the 1930s by highlighting the importance of the regime's more coordinated efforts toward its emigrants, identifying it as an ambitious, well-organized attempt to garner support for the fascist agenda.[3] Together these works underscore the importance of the regime's activities abroad and shed light on a previously neglected aspect of the fascist period. While the narrative recounted here substantiates much of this current scholarship, this chapter also represents a departure in that rather than viewing the regime's emigration policy in the service of a fascist political agenda abroad, it instead argues that the national project actually operated at the expense of the political one. By focusing on the regime's policies more narrowly in terms of a state-sponsored national project, we also see even more similarities not only between the liberal and fascist regimes but also between Italy and other countries' national projects. In the end, as the policy developed, the national agenda abroad, an outgrowth of liberal Italy, actually won out over the other, more radical fascist political initiatives directed toward emigrants.

By tracing the development of Mussolini's policy abroad in a national rather than a fascist context, this chapter provides an answer to the questions of how a nation promotes its national project outside its territory and what challenges and limitations such an agenda encounters along the way. Mussolini would soon realize that the realities of emigration, international law, and domestic policies of the host countries were daunting obstacles to his national project abroad. These challenges pushed the regime to develop innovative strategies and mechanisms to attain their ambitious goals.

Whether or not fascist Italy's fully developed initiatives toward its emigrants were as coordinated or as effective as those of Italy's liberal regime has been debated by historians.[4] In highlighting the continuities between the two projects, the focus of this chapter is instead on what these strategies toward emigrants tell us about how one national regime conceived of its national project abroad, and how both the strategies employed as well as the content of that agenda differ from its project at home. What follows is the story of how that agenda came about as well as the contradictions inherent in it.

FASCISM CONFRONTS EMIGRATION

In the late nineteenth and early twentieth centuries millions of Italians left their homeland in search of a better life, prompting lively debates among many prominent public figures of the liberal era. Volumes of speeches, essays, and monographs on the emigration problem flooded the presses of liberal Italy. During this period three distinct ways of viewing Italian emigration emerged. Sidney Sonnino, along with a number of other politicians of the time, viewed emigration as a social safety valve and, by the turn of the century, a possible solution the "Southern Question," while Luigi Einaudi, in *Un principe mercante*, argued that emigration presented the possibility of expanding Italy's cultural and commercial influence and power overseas, creating an informal mercantile empire. These positive representations of emigration were followed by the more negative image of emigration as a national disgrace and a drain on Italy's pool of creative manpower.[5] The poet Giovanni Pascoli and later the nationalist Enrico Corradini used emigration to emphasize the need for new formal colonies as an outlet for Italian emigration. By the end of the liberal era, the nationalists and their negative view of emigration came to dominate the debate.[6]

Fascism had supposedly ushered in a new age, creating a bold and regenerated Italy from the ashes of the disgraced and prostrate liberal regime. Yet in Mussolini's first years in power, emigration, the nationalists' symbol of Italy's weakness as a nation, was still prevalent. Its continued presence made it an unavoidable issue. Mussolini's initial strategy was to redefine the emigration problem by turning a supposed weakness into a strength by declaring:

> Italian expansion in the world is a problem of life or death for the Italian race. I say expansion, expansion in every sense: moral, political, economic, demographic. I declare here that the government intends to protect Italian emigration: it cannot be indifferent to those who travel beyond the ocean, it cannot be indifferent because they are men, workers, and above all Italians. And wherever there is an Italian, there is the tricolor, there is the *patria*, there is the government's defense of these Italians.[7]

By turning emigration into expansion, Mussolini attempted to put a positive spin on the debate. According to Mussolini, rather than losing vital manpower, emigrants, by retaining their Italian identity, expanded and strengthened the *patria*, creating an "empire without borders."[8] In a 1923 message to Italians living in North and South America, Mussolini went on to claim that Italians, even after emigrating, kept the *patria* close to their hearts. He declared, "The government does not make its appeal to its citizen emigrants abroad in vain because it knows that distance makes love for the *patria* more alive and cogent. . . . Italy to the Americas is like a gigantic extended arm, the *patria* extends out to its distant sons, to attract them to itself, enabling them to participate ever more in its pain, its joy, its work, its greatness, and its glory."[9]

Mussolini's pronouncements changed the way emigration was viewed in fascist Italy. As one writer explained, "Emigration is no longer considered from the point of view of the need for assistance and the protection of individuals, but is now a collective manifestation of the national life . . . no longer a thing of shame but a vibrant expression of vigor and energy."[10] No longer an anonymous mass of manual laborers, Italian emigrants thanks to the fascist regime were now ambassadors of the New Italy abroad: "the pioneers of Italian civilization."[11]

Throughout the 1920s fascist writers and journalists, in books and newspapers, followed Mussolini's lead and worked to incorporate emigration into the larger constellation of fascist myths, one such myth being the failure of the liberal regime. They argued that if emigrants did in the past lack a sense of pride in their Italian identity, this was entirely due to the incompetence of liberal government, which could not stir the hearts and minds of Italians, neither at home nor abroad. It was, therefore, the liberal government's neglect in its obligation to the *patria* and its lack of imagination in policymaking that emigration was long thought of as a weakness in Italy's national character. According to one fascist writer, liberal parliamentarians mistook emigration as "a sign of pauperism" and depicted the emigrants themselves as poor humble masses "abandoned and derelict on top of a bundle of bags."[12] Ignoring the many positive and expansive contributions to the emigration debate of the liberal period, fascist writers made the liberals easy scapegoats and provided yet another justification for the fascist revolution. Liberals were of course to blame for all that went wrong. Leaving the emigrants to their own devices without the proper government support had made them vulnerable to assimilation in their new societies and a loss for Italy. To these writers, because of liberal Italy's abandonment, Italian emigrants were nothing more than a pool of anonymous manual laborers open to exploitation, "the Chinese of Europe."[13] Fascist Italy, however, would succeed where liberal Italy had failed.

This fascist narrative has had an enduring influence. In reality, liberal Italy had played an exceptionally active role in supporting its emigrants and cultivating relationships with them. As the historian Mark I. Choate aptly demonstrates in *Emigrant Nation: The Making of Italy Abroad*, liberal Italy provided a variety of services to its emigrant communities and, just like the fascists, strove to preserve Italian identity abroad to the benefit of the homeland.[14] Historians have also cited the return of thousands of Italian emigrants to Italy to serve in the First World War as a measure of liberal Italy's success among its emigrant communities.[15] To fascist ideologues, however, it was the war itself that had inspired emigrant patriotism, in spite of liberal Italy's abandonment.

Fascist journalists went on to speak of Italy's victory in the First World War as the "great spiritual redemption" of Italy's emigrants, making use of another well-known fascist trope. To these writers, the crucible of war reawakened emigrants who had been abandoned by liberal Italy and were losing their Italian identity. In a 1922 message to Italians living in America, Mussolini himself declared, "A greater, more august Italy emerged from Vittorio Veneto, and this renewed consciousness must give you pride to feel Italian and to carry tall everywhere the name of Italy."[16] Others described the cheering crowds of Italians throughout the Americas who greeted General Diaz, the victorious Italian World War I commander, demonstrating "these Italian communities' impassioned attachment to Italy." Likewise, the contributions Italian emigrants made to the war effort, in both money and manpower, was "the most beautiful proof of the devotion Italians beyond the ocean feel for the mother country, a source of great pride and hope for the future."[17] Italy's victory and the fascist "revolution," so the story went, reawakened long dormant national pride among emigrants and created renewed interest in the *patria*. It was up to the fascist regime to cultivate these sentiments of Italian-ness abroad and to put them to the service of the New Italy.

"In the name of Italy you move in compact legions, always advancing ever further, like the legions of Ancient Rome, to the Empire's frontiers, creating works of peace with your new empire of labor."[18] The fascist articulations of an expansive Italian emigration led to bold, if imprecise, rhetoric that was militaristic in tone. For "emigration is a battle, those who are the most tenacious and relentless in their work will win . . . conquering the world with their tireless energy."[19] It was to be a "battle" like so many in the past, "the greatness of Italy in the world lies in the memory of its fifteen battles from Isonzo to the Piave, in Vittorio Veneto, and in the valorization of our emigrants."[20]

Other than their somewhat hollow fascist rhetorical devices, these writers were the first to articulate the goals of what would become the regime's national project abroad. According to these writers, it was up to the regime to instill a sense of national consciousness in the emigrants: "making such a consciousness, creating such a personality, means not only elevating the tone of a worker's life but creating a dignified spirit that would not allow themselves to be exploited and humiliated; it means raising their moral level and the prestige of the *patria* in the eyes of the civilized world."[21] With this consciousness and pride in their Italian identity reestablished, "Then through the force of expansion, emigrant social groups abroad will not only maintain the esteem of their native civilization but will gradually impose it on their new country, to the moral and political advantage of the mother country, raising its prestige and dignity."[22] While still ill defined, it is unmistakably evident that it was up to the state to provide emigrants with a new sense of belonging to the Italian nation.

The "valorization" of emigrant communities was in fact the cornerstone of the regime's developing concept of an Italian national identity abroad. Valorization meant reclaiming the emigrant for the *patria* by providing the Italian abroad an important role to play in the New Italy. This implied validating the emigrant's natural inclinations toward their homeland and channeling this primordial sense of Italian-ness into collective action abroad, enhancing Italian prestige and spreading Italian culture. As one writer explained, national valorization abroad meant "converting our demographic strength into an instrument to expand the *patria* abroad." Since the advent of fascism, emigration was "no longer a question of demographic congestion, but rather a question of moral and economic valorization." Italy was no longer supplying laborers for the nations of the world, but instead sending forth its sons to spread the "proud genius of its race."[23] Validating emigration also meant validating the emigrants themselves as legitimate members of the Italian nation: "Italians far from the country are not inferior to those living on Italian soil; in fact distance and the painful separation from the homeland can inspire the most beautiful idealism and render an Italian abroad a better and more pure Italian than those living in Italy." Citizenship was, therefore, "not so much the result of residing in the territory of the state as love and attachment to a national sentiment."[24]

Fascist writers optimistically predicted that by maintaining their Italian national identity and validating their mission, emigrants could spread Italian influence throughout the world: "With a population in need of expanding, for Italy today imperialism means the rush of its masses onto the roadways of the world to conquer the labor market with the sweat of their brows and their hardworking hands, enabling us to better compete with the other peoples of the world."[25] In practical terms, this expansion meant the increase in Italian prestige and influence through the establishment and maintenance of communities abroad, which remained loyal to the *patria* and true to their Italian identity.

Through the veneer of fascist imagery, what these writers are actually advocating for is a program that is essentially a national project abroad. There is in fact nothing uniquely fascist in the content of their emigrant policies. Instead, with an expressed goal to reclaim emigrants for the Italian nation, fascist Italy's project abroad is best understood as a state-sponsored national program. To realize this national mission abroad, writers called on much more aggressive action on the part of the regime and its diplomatic corps, lest these emigrants be lost to the *patria*. What was needed were new schools abroad to educate the children of immigrants, as well as the establishment of new fascist organizations to serves as beacons of Italian identity in distant lands. Since Mussolini and members of the regime continually conflated fascism with Italian national identity, they no doubt assumed that by promoting a national identity abroad they would in turn garner support for fascism. Not only are these two goals not one in the same, they did not always work well together, not even within the regime's own organizational efforts.

FASCIST ITALIAN ACTIVITIES ABROAD

In terms of actual policy, little in fact changed during Mussolini's first five years in power. He chose to rely primarily on preexisting liberal institutions, which operated relatively unaltered though placed under fascist supervision. At the top, Mussolini left the Commissariato Generale dell'Emigrazione relatively unchanged. The Commissariato Generale dell'Emigrazione was founded in 1901 for the task of providing services to Italian emigrants abroad. Oft criticized for its overly technocratic approach to the problems emigration entailed, the Commissariato compiled vital statistics about the various countries of emigration. It also published numerous manuals and handbooks for emigrants. These works provided travel information, compared the labor markets of various countries, provided data on salaries and job opportunities abroad, as well as collected foreign legal codes relevant to emigrant laborers. The main organ of the Commissariato was the monthly *Bollettino dell'Emigrazione*, which provided readers with reports and telegrams from the various Italian embassies, legal codes, travel advisories, parliamentary debate, and statistical information on Italian emigration as well as feature-length articles on important international political developments.[26]

During the early 1920s, Mussolini allowed the head of the Commissariato, Giuseppe De Michelis, to continue unhindered, and the Commissariato's activities under the fascist regime differed little from those of the previous liberal governments.[27] In 1923 Mussolini placed the Commissariato Generale dell'Emigrazione under the direct authority of the Ministry of Foreign Affairs. Such a move demonstrated the potential political and diplomatic importance of emigration at the time. With emigrants viewed as potential political capital for the regime, close and more direct coordination with the government through its embassies and consular services was essential.[28] Thereafter, the Commissariato's manuals for emigrants gave high praise to Mussolini's new call for the spread of Italian identity abroad, although much of its work continued to focus narrowly on the more mundane issues of providing emigrants with technical training, economic assistance, and assurances of employment.[29]

Other than the preexisting Commissariato and Italian Consulates throughout the world, the fascist regime also created the Fasci Italiani all'Estero, the fascist party abroad, and restructured the Scuole Italiane all'Estero, the Italian elementary school program targeting foreign-born children of Italian descent. The regime hoped that these efforts would expand fascist Italy's influence over its emigrant communities abroad.[30]

In 1923, soon after the March on Rome, Mussolini inaugurated the Fasci Italiani all'Estero and appointed Giuseppe Bastianini to head the new branch of the party. Bastianini, a former Socialist, was a devoted follower of Mussolini and a fascist from the movement's inception, active in the *squadristi* violence of the early 1920s.[31] In July of 1923 the Fascist Grand Council gave the new Fasci Italiani all'Estero its marching orders: to unite Italian emigrants, to keep alive their love of the *patria*, and to spread fascism's ideology abroad. The Fasci were given a relatively free hand, with the only restrictions that they "avoid any action that could damage relations between Italy and the foreign states that host them" and that they "respect the laws of the host countries and abstain from local politics."[32] Bastianini was only answerable to the Duce. For each of the major countries or regions abroad, he appointed a fascist delegate, below whom were presidents of the local Fascist Party sections, each of whom were ordered to organize (1) an office of inspection and organization, to form the party's male, female, and youth groups; (2) an administrative office; and (3) a press and propaganda office, charged with founding the party's local paper and disseminating information about fascism abroad. Members of the Fasci had to be of Italian blood and could not be Italian army deserters. Each member swore to "obey the Duce's orders without question and to serve with all my strength and if necessary with my blood the great Fascist Italy."[33] The now officially sanctioned organization was unleashed on Italian communities throughout the world, becoming the first truly Italian fascist initiative abroad.

The Grand Council's directive left much to interpretation, inspiring lively debate among members of the various local Fasci during the first years of the organization's existence. Many understood their mission as internationalist in scope: to spread fascism's political ideology abroad, targeting foreign as well as Italian communities. Others saw their mission in national terms: to unite Italian emigrants by instilling patriotism and loyalty to the New Italy of the fascist regime. How to go about accomplishing their mission and what relationship, if any, they were supposed to have with the Italian government's embassies abroad remained unclear. Articles in *Il Legionario*, the official organ of the Fasci all'Estero, illustrate a confused and often contradictory sense of mission throughout the 1920s. Under the young and ambitious Bastianini, *Il Legionario* articles stress fascism's universal mission. One contributor to the magazine wrote that having "saved the *patria*," fascism's new mission through the Fasci abroad was to serve as "a North Star guiding other *patrie* to their salvation."[34] Although acknowledging that the Grand Council had prohibited the Fasci from interfering in other nation's politics, Bastianini pushed the internationalist agenda, suggesting that communication and in some cases alliances could be made between the Fasci all'Estero and foreign fascist parties. In an article in *Il Legionario*, Bastianini insisted that fascism was indeed an international movement to save the world from the "degeneration of society caused by parliamentarian democracy and international bolshevism."[35]

From 1923 to 1925 the Fasci Italiani all'Estero did not enjoy much success, doing far more harm than good to the regime's image abroad. Historians of the Fasci all agree that during this early radical period of their existence they were a failure.[36] They were for the most part only able to recruit an extremist and marginal following, which was often outnumbered or outmaneuvered by antifascist members of the community. Their parades and ceremonies sparked violent street disturbances and succeeded only in alarming the host nations and, in so doing, endangering Italy's diplomatic relations with these countries. This in turn created tension within the Italian regime between the diplomatic corps and the Fascist Party. Bastianini openly criticized Italy's diplomats for their questionable commitment to fascism's revolutionary mission, while diplomats responded that the Fasci were fast undermining the regime's credibility abroad.

In 1923, after sending his Fasci out, Mussolini turned his attention to the Italian school system abroad. Its headquarters located in Rome, with instructional material and curricula provided directly through the Italian consulates, the Scuole Italiane all'Estero was a shadow school system often operating outside of its host nations' supervision. These schools were designed as alternatives to the primary schools of the host nations. While the Fasci all'Estero attracted more attention both at the time as well as among historians today, the Scuole Italiane all'Estero would have a more lasting impact on Italian communities around the world.[37]

The Scuole Italiane all'Estero were founded by Francesco Crispi in 1889 with the mission to "promote the diffusion abroad of the Italian language and the education and instruction of Italian emigrant communities by maintaining government schools abroad and subsidizing other academic institutes not directly dependent on the government."[38] Under the authority of the Ministry of Foreign Affairs, and run by a central committee appointed by parliament, the schools followed the pedagogical guidelines of Italian public schools within the kingdom with a focus on basic literacy.[39] In 1923 Mussolini identified the Scuole Italiane all'Estero as a subject of "special importance." In a circular sent to the Italian embassies, he declared, "We must with all of our energy ensure the existence and efficiency of our Italian schools abroad, because as shining lights of Italian-ness, they defend and conserve the national character among our emigrants."[40] Beginning in 1923, new fascist government decrees reorganized the schools. Teachers were now required to swear an oath "to instill in their students love for our country, and deep devotion to the king and to the *patria*'s institutions."[41] Historian Giorgio Floriani, who analyzed at length all of the laws and decrees related to the schools abroad, asserts that the reference to "the *patria*'s institutions" in the new oath was quite significant. Requiring loyalty to the state's institutions, then in the process of being infiltrated by the fascists, implied by extension loyalty to the emerging fascist regime.[42] Mussolini also placed all of the system's authority in the hands of a Rome-based director general who was answerable only to the Foreign Minister.[43] In a *Gerarchia* article, Ciro Trabalza, the director general of schools from 1923 to 1929, made clear the new turn the schools had taken, defining as its new mission "to preserve and defend the national character of our emigrants across the ocean. And expand our nation's culture."[44] As was happening in many other facets of government during the 1920s, fascist politicians found it convenient to blame lack of will and commitment on the part of the liberal regime for the schools' perceived failures. For rather than a pedagogical or technical problem, it was "essentially and above all else a problem of conscience, will, and national pride within the government, the country, and the colonies."[45] In other words, with a dose of fascist patriotic fervor and force of will, the new Italian regime would supposedly succeed where the old had failed.

Rhetoric notwithstanding, under Trabalza's tenure the schools remained disorganized, had inconsistent enrollment, relied on outdated curricula, and failed to coordinate its activities with the regime's other initiatives abroad.[46] Thus, while not as controversial as the Fasci all'Estero, they were similarly ineffective in promoting the regime's agenda during the 1920s.

FASCIST ILLUSIONS CONFRONT EMIGRANT REALITIES

The realities of Italian emigration fast exposed the illusionary nature of Mussolini's bold rhetoric. Far from expanding Italian power and influence through its emigrants, as fascist writers were proclaiming, Italy was on the defensive throughout the 1920s. It was scrambling to protect its emigrant masses from legal abuses and attempting to turn back the severe restrictions being placed on immigration in many countries, most notably the 1924 United States immigration quota act, which limited Italian immigration to 3,800 people per year. The regime also struggled to maintain existing Italian institutions abroad designed to help Italian emigrants, such as savings banks and credit institutions. The defensive tone of fascist writers in the face of a United States campaign to nationalize foreign savings banks reveals the difficulties the regime was encountering. In an article in *Gerarchia*, Gino Arias wrote, "We must resist these nationalistic North American policies by opposing propaganda with propaganda, organization with organization. . . . We must come to the defense of the Italian nationality wherever it is threatened in the world. . . . We must preserve the right of our emigrants to remain Italian and operate in an Italian manner."[47] At the very same moment that fascist theorists were proclaiming Italian expansion abroad through emigration, the actual Italian emigrants themselves were facing legal restrictions and prejudicial legislation in their adopted nations.

Mussolini responded to the pressures placed on Italian emigration by convening the first International Conference on Emigration and Immigration in Rome on May 15–31, 1924. Inaugurated with much publicity by Mussolini himself, the expressed purpose of the conference was nothing less than to establish an international accord regulating the flow of immigration and standardizing legal protections and services for immigrants, although the underlying idea, without a doubt, was to enhance Mussolini's international prestige.[48]

The Italian delegation at the conference pushed an ambitious emigration agenda: defining citizenship on the principle of jus sanguinis, based on blood, the delegation insisted that emigrants and their children, wherever they may be, legally remained subjects of their nation of origin. To that end, the Italian delegation introduced resolutions that would ensure that emigrants were placed under the legal protection of their original nation's government and, since priority was given to their nation of origin, that emigrants should be exempt from their host nation's military service and instead be obligated to return home to serve in their nation of origin's military. Needless to say, these assertions provoked heated debate at the conference. The delegations from all of the nations in the Americas rejected the Italian *jus sanguinis* definition of citizenship. They argued on the principle of *jus soli* that once emigrants chose to live and have children in a new nation, they became citizens of that nation. No longer obligated to serve their former nation, nor under its protection, these immigrants had the same rights and duties of all other citizens living in their adopted nation.[49] With two fundamentally different and irreconcilable definitions of citizenship on the table, any agreement between Italy and the nations that received its emigrants was unlikely.

In the end, few resolutions of substance were passed at the conference. Only those resolutions that affirmed immigrant laborers' human rights were approved, while those that attempted to promote Mussolini's expansive agenda were not.[50] In the final acts of the conference, most of the foreign delegations approved resolutions that provided for the passage of emigrants, their reception in the host country, the assurance of sanitary conditions and medical attention, and the protection of women and children traveling alone. Also approved were measures providing for the cooperation between immigration and emigration services.[51] The regime's more ambitious proposals did not, however, succeed. The Italian delegation tried to pass proposals that would have given its consular officials the authority to intervene in the judicial proceedings of other nations, would have required emigrants to serve in their birth country's military, and would have allowed government-sponsored "patriotic organizations" to operate unrestricted within the host nations. Seen as a violation of their national sovereignty, most nations rejected these proposals.[52]

Mussolini's proposals at the conference are in fact important in that unlike the regime's vague rhetorical flourishes, they provide us with a specific concrete articulation of what the regime was hoping to accomplish. The undeniable implication of these proposals is that emigrants should not simply remain emotionally bound to their homeland but legally bound as well. Taken together, these proposals did nothing less than attempt to redefine traditional notions of citizenship by giving priority to the emigrants' nation of origin over their nation of residence and in so doing to de-territorialize the nation-state. With such a radical underlying agenda, it is no wonder the conference produced little results.

While Italian commentators claimed that this conference demonstrated the leading role played by Mussolini and the fascist regime in promoting an expansive policy of emigration and validating the work of Italians abroad, the conference did little to ebb the tide of international restrictions.[53] Fascist organizations abroad were also ineffective and failed to accomplish their ambitious goal of exporting Italian fascism. The Fasci all'Estero's activities provoked outbreaks of violence that terrified the local governments where they were operating and seriously undermined the Italian diplomatic missions in these countries, while the schools abroad remained throughout the 1920s in a state of disarray and did little to promote or teach the fascist agenda. Emigration, even dressed up by the fascists as "expansion," was fast becoming an issue that could only serve to tarnish the image of the regime and was clearly not a policy that Mussolini was willing to favor much longer.

FROM EMIGRANTS TO ITALIANS ABROAD

Beginning in 1925, Mussolini tightened his grip over the state by making himself dictator and outlawing the opposition. The interests of state were now taking precedence over those of the Fascist Party, and the party's extremist tendencies were curtailed. Mussolini's appointment of Dino Grandi, a moderate fascist, as undersecretary of foreign affairs signaled this new direction.[54] Grandi had been the leader of the fascist movement in Bologna in 1920–1921 during the height of Blackshirt violence in the countryside. He led the provincial faction of the Fascist Party, which challenged Mussolini's hold over the National Fascist Party (PNF), but after reconciling with Mussolini in 1921 he became one of the Duce's most trusted men and a key member of the Fascist Grand Council. A lawyer by profession, Grandi was particularly adept at diplomacy and was a voice of moderation in the regime. Under Grandi's direction, the Ministry of Foreign Affairs began to reevaluate fascist Italy's strategy toward its emigrants.

In line with the creation of a more professional and well-organized Foreign Ministry, Mussolini also attempted to reign in the activities the Fasci all'Estero. An article in *Il Legionario* on the eve of the first congress of the Fasci all'Estero in October 1925 made the regime's new position clear: "Fascism is action and doctrine, as action it must remain strictly within the territorial confines of the peninsula, and its doctrine abroad must be restricted to the cultural and economic valorization of our emigrants."[55] While many ideas were debated at the congress, Mussolini of course had the final say, closing discussions by issuing his "Seven Commandments" to the Fasci all'Estero:

1. Obey the laws of the host countries and show this obedience to the law in your daily activities, setting an example for those nations' citizens.
2. Do not participate in the internal politics of the host countries.
3. Do not create discord within the Italian communities but heal division under the sign of the Lictor.
4. Be an example of public and private integrity.
5. Respect the representatives of the Italian government abroad.
6. Defend Italian identity past and present.
7. Offer assistance to Italians in need.[56]

Mussolini further exhorted them to "consider yourselves in all of your works and in every moment of your life like pioneers, like missionaries, like the bearers of Latin, Roman, Italian civilization."[57] Stressing the need to obey the law and respect diplomatic officials, along with the more limited goals of assisting Italians in need and promoting Italian identity, ultimately signaled the end of the Fasci all'Estero's intransigent-internationalist stage. Articles in *Il Legionario* from 1925 onward stressed instead the national mission to promote and defend Italian national identity abroad. As one contributor put it, "The defense of the nationality of Italians living abroad is a duty that fascism has understood perfectly and fascist propaganda developed by fascists abroad is the valorization of Italy. If the Blackshirts speak of fascism, it is because fascism has allowed them to speak with pride of Italy."[58] While claiming that fascism and Italy's national project are one and the same, left unsaid was how exactly this new national turn would advance fascism's ideological mission abroad.

This new mission to promote an Italian national identity among emigrants was not limited to the Fasci all'Estero. These directives were in fact an indication of a new policy direction Mussolini and Grandi were developing. In addition to reforming the Fasci all'Estero, the regime created new social and cultural organizations to support their efforts: the Opera Nazionale Dopolavoro, and the Opera Nazionale Balilla. Founded in 1925 the Dopolavoro was a government-run after-work program whose mission statement was to "improve the daily domestic and family life of the Italian laborer" through recreational activities, physical fitness and sports, and evening adult education programs, which included lectures, readings, and film screenings.[59] Mussolini envisioned a more nationalistic propaganda role for the Dopolavoro abroad:

> I think that this work of education and uplifting would also be valuable to our masses of emigrant laborers. In addition to the physical, moral, and intellectual improvement of our emigrants, which serve our national program of valorizing the emigrant, the Dopolavoro can also prevent our communities in foreign nations from falling into political subversion.[60]

It was in short an activity that would promote the "moral and patriotic" well-being of the emigrant living in different countries throughout the world.[61] The Dopolavoro all'Estero's founding charter also emphasized the central importance of instilling love for the *patria*. In addition to providing recreational and cultural events, it added the task of spreading "patriotic propaganda to keep alive the emigrants' affection for the mother *patria*: to remember its history and be aware of its future."[62]

Mussolini's first national effort targeting youth was the Opera Nazionale Balilla (ONB); as he himself declared, "I hear the thundering shout of our young fascists as a challenge to the future. That shout contains a certainty: in that shout vibrates the soul of the great Italian people."[63] Founded in 1926, it was the youth section of the PNF. The ONB recruited young children and was designed to inculcate fascist ideas in the next generation of Italians through physical fitness and pre-military training. After school and while attending Balilla summer camps, children learned to obey orders, march in step, and prepare for military life. This youth organization was later reorganized into the Gioventú Italiana del Littorio, which comprised three groups: the Balilla for boys ages six to twelve, the Avanguardisti for adolescent boys aged thirteen to seventeen, and the Piccole Italiane for girls. The ten rules or commandments of the Gioventú Italiana del Littorio included "to give your body and soul to the country and to serve Mussolini without questioning," as well as "to thank God every day that he has made you an Italian and a fascist."[64] Over time, the regime's youth organizations were incorporated into the Italian national school system and exported abroad.

On March 31, 1927, in front of the Chamber of Deputies, Grandi formally acknowledged the regime's new and still developing national agenda abroad. Fascist deputy Carlo Del Croix set the stage. Del Croix, a war veteran who had lost his sight and both arms in the war, was the national hero of choice employed by Mussolini and the Fascist Party to stir patriotic emotion. On this occasion, he declared before the Italian Chamber of Deputies that the Commissariato Generale dell'Emigrazione, "the Sultanate of Via Boncampagni," was an anachronistic institution filled with liberal technocrats who had little appreciation for fascism's expansive vision and had failed miserably in their mission to preserve and promote Italian identity abroad. It was "one of many of the inheritances that fascism must liquidate," for, according to Del Croix, "in Via Boncompagni there are still the same men with the same mentality of that bygone era when we were a poor people who had the shame of having too many children who had to leave in search of bread, and of men of power who used to do nothing but cry over this misery."[65] Placing the blame squarely on the Commissariato rather than the regime, Del Croix declared that "we must have the courage to confess that until yesterday our great collectivities for the most part lost their Italian identity after the first generation." Del Croix concluded with rousing praise for the regime's efforts through the Foreign Ministry and the Fascist Party abroad: "the New regime has given pride back to those of our people, even those farthest away. . . . Fascism has made our human abundance a source of pride and joy."[66]

Grandi followed up Del Croix by announcing the dissolution of the Commissariato Generale dell'Emigrazione. In a less harsh critique of the Commissariato, Grandi argued that in its "technical" functioning the Commissariato had served the Italian nation well; however, the changes brought about by emigration restrictions abroad and the fascist revolution in politics at home had rendered not only its work but also the very notion of emigration as outmoded.[67] No longer the "pioneers of Italian civilization," emigration was now seen as a loss to the nation, and as "denationalization," which was defined by Grandi as the "total and violent assimilation of men, groups, and classes of people who live within the orbit of other civilizations and races." *Denationalization*, rather than *valorization*, became the key word used to describe the fate of the Italian emigrant. While Grandi maintained that the government through the Ministry of Foreign Affairs would continue to promote Italian identity among Italians living abroad, emigration as a policy was now a dead issue. "From now on there will no longer be emigrants, only Italians abroad."[68]

The 1927 reorientation of fascist policies on emigration was in many ways a logical response to the political situation both at home and abroad. The age of mass migration was ending, and by 1927 it was no longer necessary for the regime to advocate it. Never enamored with emigration from the start, Mussolini took advantage of the opportunity created by the international situation, highlighted by the new restrictions on immigration being imposed abroad, to put a halt to what was from its inception a very problematic policy and to put forth instead a more realistic solution.

Many historians have cited Grandi's speech as evidence of the regime's abandonment of it ambitious emigration agenda, while others have seen Grandi's suggestive reference to "Italians abroad" as providing a new impetus to the regime's efforts among existing emigrant communities.[69] Rather than a dramatic shift in policy, I would argue that it was instead the logical culmination of policies that had been developing since the regime's inception. Nevertheless, with the issue of Italian national identity abroad no longer chained to the debate over emigration, the regime's nationalization project was broadened rather than diminished. With the mass emigration of Italians now over, the possibility remained of establishing a new relationship between Italian emigrant collectivities and Italy. The two goals of preserving Italian national identity abroad and winning the support of Italian collectivities for fascism's international policies characterized the fascist regime's new interest in its emigrants. With its more narrow focus on the promotion of an Italian national identity outside of the national territory throughout the many Italian communities abroad, the Ministry of Foreign Affairs would implement a strategy that was more national rather than fascist in scope but no less ambitious.

Not long after Grandi's speech, Mussolini set his sights on completely revamping the Fasci all'Estero. In 1927 Mussolini dismissed Bastianini, who had continued to promote his own internationalist agenda and clash with consular officials despite the regime's new directives. He was replaced by Cornelio di Marzio. A professor of literature and a nationalist before joining the PNF in 1920, Di Marzio had previously served the regime as a commercial attaché and press secretary to the Italian embassy in Istanbul.[70] During his tenure, Di Marzio reorganized the Fasci, emphasizing its public image and cultural initiatives. He supervised the founding of Fasci publications, worked to improve relations with Italian societies abroad, and urged local Fasci to coordinate their activities with the Italian consulates.[71] Di Marzio wanted his Fasci to take the leading role in directing the regime's efforts abroad but was frustrated at every turn by Dino Grandi's Foreign Ministry. Grandi, who had at the same time been working to consolidate all of the regime's efforts under his own authority, had grown tired of what he saw as the Fasci all'Estero's amateurish meddling in affairs of state. Grandi was also disturbed by Di Marzio's ambitious agenda, which undercut the role of the Italian embassies abroad. Di Marzio complained privately to the Duce about Grandi's interference, but to no avail.[72] It was a confrontation that Di Marzio could not win; Mussolini had already decided to favor Grandi and the state over Di Marzio and the party.

On January 7, 1928, Mussolini replaced Di Marzio with Piero Parini as head the Fasci all'Estero, which he then placed under the direct authority of the Foreign Ministry.[73] There was no longer any ambiguity in the relationship between the Foreign Ministry and the Fasci all'Estero. Parini was a subordinate of Grandi and reported directly to him. With the dismissal of Di Marzio, the Fasci Italiani all'Estero, much like the Fascist Party at home after the 1926 dismissal of Roberto Farinacci, lost what was left of its autonomy and political activism. This changing of the guard demonstrated Mussolini's new direction in policy. Promoting the new Italian national identity abroad was the order of the day.

PROMOTING THE ITALIAN NATION ABROAD

Piero Parini was a young fascist zealot who had joined the movement early in 1920 and participated in the Blackshirt violence of 1920–1922. A savvy self-promoter, Parini understood perfectly that he was Grandi's subordinate and part of the regime's bureaucratic structure. He thrived in his role as the new secretary general of the Fasci Italiani all'Estero, earning the trust of the Duce and gaining greater authority over the regime's efforts abroad. In 1929 he was promoted to the rank of minister plenipotentiary and appointed to head the Direzione Generale degli Italiani all'Estero; this office soon merged with the Direzione delle Scuole all'Estero, concentrating all of the regime's efforts abroad, outside of its diplomatic and consular missions, into the hands of one man. Having a keen sense of survival, Parini would remain in office until 1937, an unusually long duration for an official in Mussolini's Italy. He would go on to form a volunteer "legion" of Italians abroad to fight in Ethiopia and during the Second World War governed part of Italian-occupied Greece, earning him the dubious distinction of becoming one of the few Italians convicted of war crimes.

When Parini assumed control of the Direzione Generale degli Italiani all'Estero e Scuole (DIES), the Fasci all'Estero became but one of many components to Parini's larger apparatus promoting the Italian national project abroad. The newly formed DIES was a bureaucratic leviathan: it had inherited the intricate social and labor offices of the Commissariato Generale dell'Emigrazione, had swallowed up the Direzione delle Scuole Italiane all'Estero, and now absorbed the Fasci all'Estero. A failure as an extremist political party abroad in its first expression from 1923–1928, the Fasci all'Estero became a vehicle for promoting the regime's Italian national project abroad. It was now an official part of the Italian government's program and was no longer an autonomous political party answerable only to Mussolini.

According to Parini, this new consolidated structure of the DIES "solved all of the disputes over competence that had poisoned the atmosphere in many of the communities that are difficult to manage."[74] There were many in the diplomatic corps, however, who were far from thrilled with Parini's quick rise through the bureaucracy. In a confidential letter to the Duce, one Italian consul called Parini's appointment "a legal absurdity," insisting that no one other than the Duce himself should be allowed to occupy at the same time both high-ranking state and party positions.[75]

In January 1928, Parini issued his first marching orders to the Fasci Italiani all'Estero. *Discipline*, *obedience*, and *seriousness* were the catchwords of his message. Gone were the days when Fasci felt free to clash with consular officials and act on their own initiative, as they had done under Bastianini's tenure. Defining fascism as a "regime of authority," Parini lashed out at Fascist Party members abroad who challenged the authority of Italian consulates and created discord among fascists in the community, declaring, "We have other things to do than to waste time with this childish nonsense!"[76] Parini also berated those who "overvalued the *fuorusciti*," commanding his Fasci not only to fight against them but more importantly to show that "fascism is not afraid of them." At the same time, Parini reiterated that the Fasci must abstain from local politics and obey the laws of host countries. In line with Mussolini's new directives, Parini emphasized the central importance of spreading Italian national identity abroad: "While living abroad among foreign races with other traditions, you must be living representations of the new Italian."[77] To accomplish this task, Parini instructed his Fasci to educate and assist Italian emigrants in need, to teach them about the New Italy and rekindle their love of the *patria*, "to win over their hearts so they may become among the best Italians."[78]

In 1929 Piero Parini assumed control of the Direzione Generale delle Scuole Italiane all'Estero, which merged into the DIES. Parini quickly moved to reorganize the schools, tighten supervision, and emphasize the new Italian national program abroad.[79] In a memorandum to Mussolini, using imagery the Duce no doubt appreciated, Parini characterized the schools under his direction as engaged in a "battle" over national identity, declaring, "We are in fact involved in an international struggle over language and culture. . . . And in this struggle we must be present: wherever there is a nucleus of Italian-ness to defend, there is also the possibility of attracting new people into the orbit of our millenarian culture."[80] Critical of what he perceived as the missed opportunities and lost ground of the previous administration, Parini wrote with a sense of urgency: "Never has the spiritual climate been more favorable for our cultural expansion. We must seize the moment—a missed opportunity, a pause, or a moment of uncertainty represents a lost battle in this international struggle for culture."[81] Rather than a political struggle, Parini focused squarely on the regime's new nationalization agenda abroad.

Parini increased funding, opened new schools (preferably run by the Fasci), and reorganized the existing system to allow for tighter supervision. He also appointed better trained and ideologically more qualified teachers from Italy and required frequent reports from the schools to ensure their compliance with the new directives from Rome. Parini also hoped to expand the scope of the schools' mission to attract foreign students to Italian universities and institutes of higher education through a scholarship program so that they may become upon their return home "the best propagandists of our culture."[82]

In 1930 Parini commissioned a standardized series of textbooks specifically geared toward the fascist schools abroad. In justifying the need for an entirely new series of texts, the DIES textbook commission explained, "As a result of the advent of fascism, which has moved Italy and the world in a new direction, a complete revision of values and judgments in the moral sciences is necessary."[83] The texts to be commissioned for adaptation must, therefore, "fully adhere to the spirit and actions of the regime."[84] These texts were widely disseminated: they were sent not only to schools directly run by the government but to schools throughout the world teaching in Italian.[85] For Parini, more than new schoolbooks were needed, however: someone had to ensure that these texts were being used to promote the fascist agenda. To that end, in 1932 Parini established national competitions for teacher-agents to serve three-year appointments in the schools abroad. In addition to teaching, their task was to supervise the schools within their assigned area. Applicants were required to be Italian citizens between the ages of twenty-one and thirty-five. This requirement was in order to avoid two of the major problems with the current teachers, who were either well advanced in age or foreign nationals, making their knowledge of and commitment to the regime suspect in both cases.[86] Applicants were further required to pass an oral exam that would test their knowledge of "the history of Italy, the organization, ideas, and achievements of the fascist state, as well as the geographic and political characteristics of the target nations."[87] By the late 1930s teachers were also forced to sign an affidavit certifying that they were "not of the Hebrew race" or "a member of an Israelite community" or a "practitioner of the Israelite religion," a disturbing indication that the schools abroad were not immune to the regime's increasing anti-Semitism.[88]

Once selected, teachers were given the task of "founding in your assigned destination an Italian school, if one is not yet established, and promoting and developing an intensive program of activity in the heart of the Italian community of the area until the school itself becomes an active center in the diffusion of Italian language and culture."[89] The teachers' contracts additionally required them "to promote the diffusion of Italian culture in the students' families, and in all Italian compatriots in residence, through conferences, projections, theatrical performances, libraries, and etc."[90] Given the ever-present need of money to run the schools, teacher-agents were additionally assigned the task of fundraising.[91] These new positions took over the work of consular officials and community leaders, who had been seen as questionably committed to the regime's ideology. Parini hoped that the appointment of new handpicked teachers, given the added tasks of supervision, organization, and fundraising would better advance the regime's national project through the schools. The new texts and teachers together ensured Rome's tighter control over the schools and the material being taught.

In a 1932 letter to Mussolini, Parini boasted that "the Scuole Italiane all'Estero are without a doubt the most powerful and effective instrument for the defense of Italian-ness abroad and the diffusion of our language in foreign countries."[92] After assuming directorship of the schools, Parini had turned the schools into the centerpiece of the regime's national program abroad. He coordinated all of the other initiatives with school system. Many of these schools were organized and run by members of the local Fascist Party sections, others were operated by the "Dante Alighieri," all of the school children were enrolled in the ONB, and Dopolavoro events made use of the classrooms after school. In the end, the regime's national project abroad would succeed or fail in the classrooms of these schools.

In 1933 Mussolini added the final piece to his national project abroad by co-opting the Società Nazionale Dante Alighieri. Founded in 1889, the society's goals were to preserve Italian culture and language abroad and support irredentism. By the time Mussolini came to power, the Dante Alighieri was already the largest Italian initiative abroad. Thousands of students attended its cultural and language courses, and countless more made use of their extensive Italian-language library collections. By 1933 the Dante Alighieri counted 174 committees abroad, with over 126,000 members and 304,050 participants in their programs.[93] With the promotion of Italian identity central to its mission statement, the usefulness of the society to the fascist regime was readily apparent. In 1933 the regime stripped away its autonomy, turning it into yet another vehicle to promote the regime's programs.[94] New clauses were added to the society's statutes explicitly linking their promoting of Italian national identity to the fascist cause. Article 1 of its new statute declared, "The Società Nazionale Dante Alighieri's mission is to promote and defend the Italian language and culture outside of the kingdom and to hold high feelings of Italian identity in accordance with the spirit of the fascist revolution."[95] Article 8 placed members of the fascist regime on the society's governing body, including the director of the DIES and representatives of the PNF, Balilla, and Dopolavoro.

Mussolini chose Felice Felicioni to head the revamped Dante Alighieri. Felicioni, a longtime associate of Il Duce and a lawyer by profession, had joined the Fascist Party in 1920 and was the head of the Fascio in Perugia during the party's violent rise to power. Before his appointment, he had served on the PNF National Committee and was a fascist delegate to the Chamber of Deputies. While president of the Dante Alighieri, Felicioni worked closely with the Ministry of Popular Culture to, in his words, "spread the culture and ideals of the fascist revolution throughout the world."[96] He also collaborated with the Ministry of Press and Propaganda and Italian diplomatic authorities abroad, and provided Mussolini with annual reports of his society's activities.[97]

Parini, always looking after his own self-advancement, saw the Dante Alighieri as a rival rather than an ally. Before its incorporation into the fascist regime, Parini had attempted to block many of its efforts, claiming that all activities abroad were the sole responsibility of the DIES. When the regime took over the Dante Alighieri, Parini had hoped he would be named the new president and that it would be incorporated into his DIES. No doubt disappointed by the appointment of Felicioni, Parini tried to undermine and discredit him. In a letter to Galeazzo Ciano, by then the foreign minister, Parini called the work of the society a "bluff," its directives "inconsistent," and its committee members the "most anticultural people imaginable." [98] Felicioni responded in kind, insisting in a letter to Mussolini that Parini had been given a dangerous amount of authority over fascist activities abroad and recommended that he be removed from at least one of his positions.[99] Throughout the 1930s both vied for the favor of the Duce, taking credit for each other's accomplishments. Their power struggle, reminiscent of the earlier internecine fights between the Ministry of Foreign Affairs and the Fasci all'Estero, is a telling example of the competing ambitions and personal agendas that characterized the fascist power structure.

More important than the personal rivalries it provoked, the incorporation of the Dante Alighieri illustrates the turn the regime had made in the 1930s toward focusing on Italy's national project abroad. The change in the society's statutes is also a telling example of how the regime attempted to identify that national project with the fascist regime. The new statute made explicit what had been implied all along in the other national initiatives the regime developed, namely that in addition to an ethnic-cultural national project, the regime also attempted to add a belief in fascism to Italy's identity abroad. To be an Italian abroad you had to be ethnically and culturally Italian and identify with the fascist regime's values and beliefs.

It was thought that advancing Italy's cultural mission of promoting its national identity would inevitably lead to fascist recruits. Evidence of this comes from confidential reports sent to Rome from consular officials around the world. For example, in response to an inquiry on the possible creation of an Italian scholastic and cultural center in Bahia Blanca, Argentina, the Italian Consul of La Plata candidly explained, "An institution with the appearance of Italian and Argentine membership and under the pretext of a cultural exchange would enable us to attract the children of our emigrants. It would then be possible to accomplish an educational mission beyond mere didactics by forming a 'breeding ground' for youths to later place in Fascist Sections."[100] This association would only work, however, if the children of emigrants identified their Italian-ness with fascism, something that the regime took for granted would be the case.

As it will be shown in subsequent chapters, this conflation of the two would prove fatal to the regime's agenda in Argentina. The nationalization project would undercut the regime's more universal fascist ideological agenda, and the fascist component of the new Italian identity would lead many within the community to challenge and ultimately reject its national project. This association had in fact the consequence of opening up a discursive space in which Italian emigrants in Argentina could contest the national narrative.

CONCLUSION

While not among its chief priorities or even a policy by design, the mass emigration of Italians, which was still prevalent in the early 1920s, imposed on the regime the challenge of formulating a response to an issue long associated with the defunct policies of liberal Italy. Mussolini first responded by spinning a perceived weakness into a strength by conflating emigration with expansion. Emigrants were not abandoning the *patria* but instead spreading its influence throughout the world. This treatment of emigration could not stand the test of time. The reality of Italian emigrant experiences simply did not match Il Duce's bold vision of a nation expanding through emigration. In practice, the fascists were unable to turn their triumphal prose into a cohesive program of action, relying instead on the preexisting liberal-era bureaucratic structure to pursue much of the same policies as the Italian governments of the past.

The failure of Mussolini's International Migration Conference in 1924 had exposed the legal limitations to promoting a national agenda outside of the nation-state. National projects abroad can succeed only to the point that they do not come into direct confrontation with the national projects of the host nations since domestic laws within those host nations are designed to ensure their immigrant citizens remain loyal to their new nation. The regime soon learned that in order to accomplish its national agenda abroad, it would have to adopt more indirect and subtle—though still subversive—tactics.

Beginning with Grandi's directorship of the Foreign Ministry, the ambitious goal of spreading fascism's political doctrine abroad gave way to the more pragmatic though no less significant goal of spreading the Italian national program abroad. Under the less threatening guise of sociocultural programs, the regime was better equipped to deflect criticism, while still propagandizing an Italian national identity abroad. The regime would no longer talk of conquering the world through its emigration but would instead operate more quietly through cultural organizations abroad. From 1927 onward Italy's propaganda strategy would consist of instilling Italian national identity abroad in the Italian community. Within the emigrant community, the regime would attempt to push back the tide of assimilation and preserve Italian identity, while at the same time engaging in the project of spreading its national project beyond the community.

Charged with implementing the new agenda, Parini reorganized all of the Italian regime's efforts abroad. By the 1930s these efforts were undeniably more coordinated and effective than they had been in the previous decade. Their focus had also shifted to promoting Italian national identity rather than the more expansive project of spreading the fascist revolution. In the end, although they would be loath to acknowledge it, fascist Italy's newly developed agenda was not much different from liberal Italy's earlier efforts at promoting the nation, as illustrated by the fact that most of the institutions abroad had been established prior to the fascist seizure of power. Ultimately, Mussolini's new agenda toward Italy's emigrants was fascist only to the extent that fascism succeeded in identifying itself with Italy's national project. It is upon this rather tenuous connection that the regime's agenda came to rely and explains why it would ultimately fail. Most Italians within fascist Italy probably would not have questioned that association, at least not openly. However, this would not be the case abroad, as the regime's experiences in Argentina would demonstrate.

A 1933 propaganda booklet written by Parini captures best the regime's fully developed national agenda. According to Parini, "The great migratory movement that culminated towards the late nineteenth century has ceased. The fascist regime is hostile to emigration. Proving capable of creating work in the country, multiplying industries and reclaiming lands, fascism intends to keep Italians for Italy."[101] Separating Italian identity abroad from the emigration debate, however, Parini went on to declare that "there remain nine or ten million Italians of the old emigration who live beyond Italy's borders. . . . The fascist government feels united with them by the spiritual solidarity of a common origin and culture."[102] Thus, while rejecting emigration as a policy, the regime was more committed than ever to spreading an Italian national identity abroad. By the time this pamphlet was published, fascist Italy's national agenda abroad had developed into a focused strategy armed with the necessary institutional apparatus to implement it. By the end of the 1920s, Rome had a blueprint for promoting the Italian nation abroad. The question remains what happened once that national project arrived on foreign soil and how the experiences on the ground shaped and reshaped those strategies.

As the regime searched the horizon for potential testing grounds for its new agenda, no nation seemed better suited for the task than Argentina. To many within the fascist regime, Argentina was the nation that seemed to offer the best potential for the realization of its expansive emigration designs. Italian observers enthusiastically noted that Italians composed the largest single ethnic group within Argentina, a land in which the Italian language and culture was widespread. Argentina in the fascist imagination at once offered great possibilities along with troubling obstacles. It was a land that seemed to have swallowed up and assimilated the millions of Italians who arrived on its shores, but that also for the same reason showed the greatest potential for realizing Il Duce's national project abroad.

NOTES

1. Benito Mussolini, "Il problema dell'emigrazione," *Il Popolo d'Italia*, April 1, 1923, included in Benito Mussolini, *Opera omnia di Benito Mussolini*, ed. E. Sumsel and D. Susmel (Florence: La Fenice, 1957), 19:191.

2. Emilio Gentile, "L'emigrazione italiana in Argentina nella politica di espansione del nazionalismo e del Fascismo," *Storia Contemporanea* 17, no. 3 (1986): 355–96. Alessandra Ruberti ("Il fascismo e l'emigrazione italiana in Argentina nella stampa di Regime (1922–1930)," *Affari Sociali Internazionali* 20, no. 3 [1992]: 107–16), makes a similar argument, suggesting that international and specifically Argentine resistance to fascism's expansive overtures toward its emigrants was the main reasons for the Italian regime's abandonment of its emigration agenda. See also Ludovico Incisa Di Camerana, *L'Argentina, gli Italiani, e l'Italia: Un'altro destino* (Milan: Servizi Promozioni Attività Internazionali, 1998).

3. Matteo Pretelli *Il fascismo e gli italiani all'estero* (Bologna: Clueb, 2010). This chapter makes use of some of the same sources as Pretelli. Like Pretelli, my own reading of this archival evidence confirms his assertion that the regime's institutions abroad did develop into a well-organized apparatus. Pretelli's work should be consulted by those interested in an comprehensive overview of the regime's activities throughout the world. The focus of my work is instead the national discourses themselves and how they were contested within Argentina, to be discussed in subsequent chapters. See also Aldo Albonico, "Immagine e destino delle communità italiane in America Latina attraverso la stampa Fascista degli anni '30," in *Studi Emigrazione* 65 (March 1982): 41–51; Incisa Di Camerana, *L'Argentina, gli Italiani, e l'Italia*; Mario Mugnaini, "L'Italia e l'America Latina (1930–1936): Alcuni aspetti della politica estera fascista," *Storia delle Relazioni Internazionali* 2 , no. 2 (1986): 199–244.

4. For example, Mark I. Choate highlights liberal Italy's ambitious project toward its emigrants, asserting that this project was not as important or effective during the fascist regime (*Emigrant Nation: The Making of Italy Abroad* [Cambridge, MA: Harvard University Press, 2008], 217). In contrast, Pretelli argues that while many of the initiatives during the fascist regime had begun during the liberal period, fascism's efforts abroad were actually more aggressive and better coordinated (*Fascismo e gli italiani*, 23–24).

5. Angelo Trento, "Argentina e Brasile come paesi d'immigrazione nella pubblicistica italiana 1860–1920," in *L'Italia nella società Argentina*, ed. Fernando J. Devoto and Gianfausto Rosoli, 211–40 (Rome: Centro Studi Emigrazione, 1988), 213. For a more detailed discussion of liberal Italy's viewpoints on emigration, see Choate, *Emigrant Nation*.

6. Gentile, "L'emigrazione italiana."

7. Mussolini, "Il problema dell'emigrazione," 192.

8. Ibid.

9. Benito Mussolini, "Agli italiani del nord e sud America," *Popolo d'Italia*, April 19, 1923, included in Mussolini, *Opera omnia*, 19:408.

10. Celestino Arena, *Italiani per il mondo: Politica nazionale dell'emigrazione* (Milan: Alpes, 1927), 6.

11. Giovanni Borsella, *L'emigrante italiano e l'Argentina* (Milan: Fratelli Treves, 1925), 1.

12. Ibid., 3.

13. Alighiero Micci, *L'emigrazione* (Rome: A. Mondadori, 1925), 16.

14. Choate, *Emigrant Nation*.

15. Ibid., 189–217; Eugenia Scarzanella, "Cuando la patria llama: Italia en guerra y los inmigrantes italianos en Argentina," *Nuevo Mundo Mundos Nuevos*, March 12, 2007, http://nuevomundo.revues.org/3735.

16. Benito Mussolini, "Agli Italiani dell'America del Nord," *Il Popolo d'Italia*, November 5, 1922, included in Mussolini, *Opera omnia*, 19:407.

17. Antonino Cordova, *Gli aspetti presenti e futuri dell'emigrazione* (Turin: Lattes, 1923), 59.

18. Borsella, *L'emigrante italiano*, 11.

19. Ibid., 14.

20. Ibid., 182–83.

21. Micci, *L'emigrazione*, x–xi.

22. Ibid., 15.

23. Arena, *Italiani per il mondo*, 9.

24. Cordova, *Gli aspetti presenti e futuri*, 63.

25. Arena, *Italiani per il mondo*, 4–5.

26. *Il Bollettino dell'Emigrazione*, 1922–1927.

27. Benito Mussolini, "Per il consiglio superiore dell'emigrazione," *Il Popolo d'Italia*, January 23, 1925, included in Mussolini, *Opera omnia*, 21:245–46.

28. Mussolini, "Per il consiglio superiore, *Opera omnia*, 21:245.

29. Commissariato Generale dell'Emigrazione, *Manuale di geografia economica di legislazione sociale e di notizie utile per gli Italiani all'estero* (Rome: Commissariato Generale dell'Emigrazione, 1926).

30. There is a recent and quite extensive literature on Italian fascist activities abroad. A number of articles, though still very few books, have analyzed the various Italian operations. The historiography on the Fasci Italiani all'Estero is the most well developed within this area of study. These historical treatments, however, judge the success or failure of the Fasci Italiani all'Estero by its political influence and ability to spread fascism politically, and only discuss tangentially the role the party played in promoting their version of Italian identity abroad. See, for example, Emilio Gentile, "La politica estera del partito Fascista: Ideologia e organizzazione dei Fasci italiani all'estero (1920–1930)," *Storia Contemporanea* 26, no. 6 (1995): 897–956; Claudia Baldoli, *Exporting Fascism: Italian Fascists and Britain's Italians in the 1930s* (Oxford: Berg, 2003); and Emilio Franzina and Matteo Sanfilippo, ed., *Il Fascismo e gli emigrati: La parabola dei Fasci italiani all'estero (1920–1943)* (Rome: Laterza, 2003) and Matteo Pretelli, *Il Fascismo e gli italiani all'estero*. While a number of works have studied fascist culture in the context of the regime's search for consensus within Italy, few have examined its efforts in Latin America. A notable exception is Marco Pluviano and Irene Guerrini, "L'Opera Nazionale Dopolavoro in Sud America," *Studi Emigrazione* 32, no. 119 (1995): 518–37.

31. *Dizionario biografico degli Italiani* (Rome: Istituto della Enciclopedia Italiana, 1960–).

32. *Il Legionario: Organo dei Fasci italiani all'estero edito dalla segreteria generale*, October 3, 1925.

33. Fasci italiani all'estero, "Statuto," undated, Carte Cornelio di Marzio, file 47, Archivio Centrale dello Stato (hereafter cited in notes as ACS).

34. Orazio Laorca, "Il Fascismo in Italia e all'Estero," *Il Legionario*, January 3, 1925.

35. Giuseppe Bastianini, "Fasci italiani e Fasci stranieri: L'ultilità di una intesa," *Il Legionario*, July 4, 1925.

36. See, for example, Gentile, "La politica estera del partito Fascista"; Philip V. Cannistraro, *Blackshirts in Little Italy : Italian Americans and Fascism, 1921–1929* (West Lafayette, IN: Bordighera, 1999); and Franzina and Sanfilippo, *Il Fascismo e gli emigrati*.

37. Among the histories of fascist activities abroad, Baldoli, *Exporting Fascism*; Pretelli, *Fascismo e gli italiani*; and João Fabio Bertonha, *O fascismo e os imigrantes italianos no Brasil* (Porto Alegre: EDIPUCRS, 2001) are among the few works other than my own to emphasize the important role of the schools to the regime's agenda.

38. Legge Crispi, "Regio Decreto 8 dicembre 1889," no. 6566, *Raccolta ufficiale delle leggi e dei decreti del regno d'Italia* (Rome: Regia Tipografia, 1889), 4941–91 (hereafter cited in notes as RD).

39. "Regolamento," RD no. 6566.

40. Mussolini to ambassadors and agents abroad, "Circolare n. 94," Rome, December 9, 1923, Archivio Scuole (1923–1928), file 634, Achivio Storico del Ministero degli Affari Esteri (hereafter cited in notes as ASMAE).

41. RD no. 932, April 19, 1923.

42. Giorgio Floriani, *Scuole italiane all'estero: Cento anni di storia* (Rome: A. Armando Editore, 1974).

43. RD no. 933, April 19, 1923; RD no. 1481, June 17, 1923.

44. Ciro Trabalza, *Gerarchia*, November 11, 1923.

45. Ibid.

46. Italian consular reports from Argentina in the 1920s to be discussed in detail in the next chapter bear this out.

47. Gino Arias, "La nuova politica dell'emigrazione," *Gerarchia*, 1924, 33.

48. Conference Internationale de l'Emigration et de l'Immigration, Rome, May 15–31, 1924, "Travaux de la Conference" (Rome: Commissariat General Italien de L'Emigration, 1924), 255.

49. Ibid.

50. Ministero das Relações Exteriores, *Mensagem apresentado pelo Senhor Presidente da Republica ao Congresso Nacional em 3 de maio de 1925*, 54.

51. Conference Internationale de l'Emigration et de l'Immigration, Rome, May 15–31, 1924, "Acte Finale" (Rome: Commissariat General Italien de L'Emigration, 1924).

52. Ibid.

53. Arena, *Italiani per il mondo*, 162–65.

54. Cannistraro, *Blackshirts in Little Italy*, and Gentile, "La politica estera del partito Fascista," both highlight in particular Grandi's important role in reorganizing the regime's efforts abroad.
55. "Il Fascismo all'Estero," *Il Legionario*, October 3, 1925.
56. Mussolini, "I compiti dei fasci all'estero" *Il Popolo d'Italia*, October 31, 1925, included in Mussolini, *Opera omnia*, 21:430; a copy is also filed in Carte Cornelio di Marzio, file 47, ACS.
57. Mussolini, "I compiti dei fasci all'estero," 431.
58. E. Ceresole, "L'Italia e il Fascismo all'estero," *Il Legionario*, October 30, 1926.
59. Opera Nazionale Dopolavoro, *Scopi ed Organizzazione, Bollettino Ufficiale*, January 1, 1927.
60. Mussolini to foreign embassies, November 30, 1926, Archivio Scuole (1923–1928), file 634, ASMAE.
61. Ibid.
62. "Le providenze del regime per gli Italiani emigrati: Il dopolavoro all'Estero," *Il Legionario*, March 22, 1930.
63. Benito Mussolini "Tempo di giovinezza," in Scilla de Glauco, ed., *La Nuova Italia* (New York: Nikolas Press, 1939) 101–109.
64. "Il decalogo dei giovani Fascisti" in *La Nuova Italia*, 101.
65. Carlo Del Croix, speech to the Chamber of Deputies, March 31, 1927, *Atti del Parlamento italiano: Discussioni* 7:7415.
66. Ibid., 7:7414.
67. Dino Grandi, "Discorso alla Camera dei Deputati," March 31, 1927, in *La politica estera dell'Italia dal 1929 al 1932*, ed. Paolo Nello (Rome: Bonacci Editore, 1985), 132.
68. Ibid.
69. See, for example, Gentile, "L'emigrazione italiana in Argentina"; Ruberti, "Il fascismo e l'emigrazione italiana"; Pretelli, *Fascismo e gli italiani*.
70. "Cornelio di Marzio," *Il Legionario*, January 15, 1927.
71. Cornelio di Marzio, "Relazione al Duce per la seduta del gran consiglio Fascista del 7 novembre 1927," Carte Cornelio di Marzio, file 47, ACS.
72. Carteggio riservato, Segretaria Particolare del Duce, file 74, ACS.
73. Ibid.
74. Parini to Grandi, October 7, 1930, Le Carte del Gabinetto del Ministro e della Segretaria Generale dal 1923 al 1943, file 821-4, ASMAE.
75. Consul of Cologne to Mussolini, November 5, 1932, Le Carte del Gabinetto del Ministro e della Segretaria Generale dal 1923 al 1943, file 819, ASMAE.
76. Piero Parini, "Ai Camerati d'Oltralpe e d'Oltremare," *Il Legionario*, January 14, 1928.
77. Ibid.
78. Ibid.
79. Floriani, *Scuole italiane all'estero*, 76.
80. Parini, "Pro-memoria per S.E. Il Capo del Governo," August 5, 1932, Le Carte del Gabinetto del Ministero e della Segretaria Generale dal 1923 al 1943, file 819-2, ASMAE.
81. Ibid.
82. Ibid.
83. DIES Undersecretary of Schools to Parini, June 6, 1930, Le Carte del Gabinetto del Ministero e della Segretaria generale dal 1923 al 1943, file 821-4, ASMAE.
84. Ibid.
85. "Le nostre scuole d'oltre confine," *Diritti della Scuola*, Rome, July 15, 1933. The content of these new textbooks is the focus of chapter 4.
86. Secretary of State to Ministry of Foreign Affairs, "Decree," Rome, May 16, 1932, Archivio Scuole (1929–1935), file 776, ASMAE.
87. Ibid.
88. The affidavit that I found was undated but was included with other materials all dating prior to 1935. This dating is significant since it predates institutionalized anti-Semitism, which began in Italy with the passage of the racial laws of 1938. Given that Parini himself was an outspoken anti-Semite, it is possible that he instituted this policy prior to the racial laws and

Italy's alliance with Nazi Germany. It is, however, a claim I am reluctant to make based on an undated piece of evidence. Ministry of Foreign Affairs, Direzione Generale degli Italiani all'Estero, "Scheda personale riservatissima," Archivio Scuole (1929–1935), file 778, AS-MAE.

89. Secretary of State to Ministry of Foreign Affairs, "Decree," Rome, May 16, 1932, Archivio Scuole (1929–1935), file 776, ASMAE.

90. Direzione Generale degli Italiani all'Estero, "Schema di contratto per maestri e per maestri agenti in Argentina," 1932, Archivio Scuole (1929–1935), file 776, ASMAE.

91. Ibid.

92. Parini, "Pro-memoria per S.E. Il Capo del Governo," August 5, 1932, Le Carte del Gabinetto del Ministero e della Segretaria Generale dal 1923 al 1943, file 819-2, ASMAE.

93. Felicioni to Mussolini, "Relazione del Presidente della Società Nazionale 'Dante Alighieri,'" January 1934, Ministero della Cultura Popolare (hereafter cited in notes as Minculpop), Gabinetto, file 91, ACS.

94. Beatrice Pisa, *Nazione and politica nella Società "Dante Alighieri"* (Rome: Bonacci Editore, 1995), 435.

95. "Il Nuovo Statuto della Società Nazionale 'Dante Alighieri,'" *Le Pagine della Dante*, November–December, 1933.

96. Felicioni to Pavolini, Minculpop, Gabinetto, file 91, ACS.

97. There are a number of letters by Felicioni that indicate this collaboration in Minculpop, Gabinetto, file 91, ACS.

98. Parini to Undersecretary of State, September 28, 1933, Le Carte del Gabinetto del Ministero e della Segretaria Generale dal 1923 al 1943, file 820, ASMAE; Parini to the Consul in Rosario di Santa Fe, December 14, 1934, Archivio Scuole (1929–1935), file 780, ASMAE.

99. Felicioni to Mussolini, Segretaria Particolare del Duce, Carteggio Riservata, ACS.

100. Romolo Bertuccioli, Consul in La Plata, February 12, 1930, Archivio Scuole (1929–1935), file 780, ASMAE.

101. Piero Parini, "Italians in the World," in *Italy* (Chicago: Chicago Tribune, 1933), 26.

102. Ibid.

Chapter Three

The "New Italy" in Argentina

Argentina appeared to be the ideal land to advance the new Italian national project abroad. But if it offered great potential, it also carried with it great risk. Much was at stake precisely because of the strong Italian presence in the South American republic. Without the coercive apparatus of the state at their disposal, these fascist propagandists had to compete publicly with Italian antifascists for control of the national discourse. Were the fascist regime's efforts in Argentina to fail, its claims over Italian national identity abroad would be called into question. The fascists therefore went to great lengths to penetrate the Italian community in Argentina and realize their goal of creating the Italian nation abroad. It is for this reason that the Italian regime's experience in Argentina is an invaluable case study, providing insight into the question of what happens to national projects outside of the national territory.

This chapter follows the Italian regime's activities in Argentina, with a focus on the organizations that the Benito Mussolini regime sent to infiltrate the community and propagandize its national project. From an abrasive, disorganized, political movement abroad, this chapter shows how fascist activities in Argentina evolved and adapted to the situation in Argentina. In the end, reorganization at the top in Rome, along with the work of the regime's operatives on the ground in Argentina, created a much more organized propaganda operation that over time shifted its focus away from exporting the fascist political ideology toward promoting instead an Italian national identity abroad.

There is now extensive literature that narrates the political activities of Italian fascists abroad. While this chapter also provides an overview of those activities in Argentina, the focus is instead on the regime's attempt to promote its national project rather than on the spread of their political ideology; although, without a doubt, the two goals were informed by one another, they often worked at cross-purposes. In this discussion of all of the organizations abroad, particular emphasis is placed on the Fasci Italiani all'Estero, which failed as an activist political organization in Argentina but later served the regime as an important vehicle for promoting its national identity, and on the Scuole Italiane all'Estero, which had been neglected and disorganized during the 1920s but emerged as the regime's most central nationalization initiative in Argentina by the 1930s.[1]

THE ITALIAN COMMUNITY IN ARGENTINA

Italian immigrants and their children are interwoven into the history of Argentina from the nation's inception. Manuel Belgrano, one of Argentina's founding fathers, was in fact the son of an Italian merchant, while the famed Italian Risorgimento leader Giuseppe Garibaldi honed his skills as a revolutionary on the Argentine Pampas. Mass immigration to Argentina began during and in the years immediately following Italian unification, a full generation before the period of Italian mass immigration to the United States. The number of Italians entering Argentina jumped from approximately 3,000 annually in 1857 to 23,000 annually by 1870.[2] Between 1871 and 1930, approximately 1.4 million Italians entered Argentina, constituting 43 percent of all immigrants entering Argentina and roughly 16 percent of Argentina's total population of nine million in 1930, a percentage that does not include the children and descendants of Italian immigrants.[3] In all it is commonly accepted that over 40 percent of all Argentines are Italian or at least partially of Italian descent, making Italians the largest single ethnic group in Argentina. The majority of the Italian immigrants came from northern Italy, mainly from Liguria, Piedmont, Friuli, and the Veneto. Between 1876 and 1895, roughly 75 percent of Italians arriving in Argentina were from northern and central Italy. After the turn of the century, more southern Italians began to arrive, and by 1914 only 55 percent of arriving Italians were from the north, which still differs from Italian immigration to the United States, in which the majority came from southern Italy.[4]

During the nineteenth century, Argentine presidents encouraged and in some cases even subsidized Italian immigration in an effort to whiten or Europeanize their population, as well as to populate their vast, sparsely inhabited territorial expanses; as the Argentine statesman Juan Bautista Alberdi famously declared, "To govern is to populate."[5] The first Italian immigrants were contracted as rural tenant farmers cultivating wheat, and they played a key role in the commercialization of agriculture on the Argentine Pampas.[6]

Italian immigrants migrated to the city of Buenos Aires and other urban centers right when Argentina began to industrialize and represented an especially high proportion of the nation's industrial proprietors as well as laborers. In 1887 56 percent of all industrial proprietors and 51 percent of industrial laborers were Italian born, and as late as 1935, even after the period of mass immigration, 21 percent of all Argentine industry was in Italian immigrant hands.[7] The vast majority of these businesses were small or midrange manufacturing establishments, mainly in textiles, shoes, metallurgy, furniture, ceramics, and other crafts, although a few immigrant families would emerge as leading Argentine capitalists, such as the De Marchi's in pharmaceuticals, the Devoto's in commerce and banking, and the Di Tella's in heavy industry. Already established Italian entrepreneurs also set up shop in Argentina around the turn of the century, such as Enrico Dell'Acqua, Gaetano Dellachà, and Ernesto Piaggio. They were soon followed by major Italian companies such as Pirelli, Fiat, and Cinziano, which each set up regional factories and offices in Argentina by 1923.[8] In spite of these individual Italian investors, Great Britain continued to dominate all foreign investors in Argentina's economy. In 1900 Britain was the source of 81 percent of all foreign investments, and in 1927 British capital continued to account for 58 percent of all foreign investments, followed by the United States at a distant second with 14 percent. Great Britain also remained Argentina's main trading partner, in 1927 accounting for 28 percent of all Argentine exports and 20 percent of all imports.[9]

Between 1887 and 1914, 35 percent of all real estate owners were Italian, just behind native Argentines, who made up 42 percent, and well ahead of the next foreign group, the Spanish, who made up 11 percent. The vast majority of Italian-held properties were small in size, however, while the native Argentine elite continued to control most of the nation's land and resources.[10]

Italians were also at the forefront of Argentina's labor movement. According to the historian Samuel L. Baily, in 1914 approximately 40 percent of all organized workers in Argentina were Italian, many occupying leadership positions in unions.[11] In 1878 three of the nine organizers of Argentina's first strike were Italian born, and in 1889 the majority of leaders in a strike led by Freemasons were of Italian origin. By 1890 Italian workers ran seventy-nine mutual-aid societies, comprising 42 percent of the total such organizations in Argentina. In 1901 Italians were again prominent in the founding of Argentina's first major labor confederation, the Federación Obrera Regional Argentina, making up 52 percent of the participants at its founding congress.[12]

In short, by the time the fascists came to power in Italy in 1922, Italian immigrants had firmly established themselves within Argentina's socioeconomic landscape. Although only a very few had managed to enter into Argentina's closed circle of elite landowners, Italian immigrants swelled the ranks of its growing middle- and working-class populations, becoming an integral component of Argentine society.

During the First World War many members of the Italian community responded to their homeland's call, donating millions of pesos to the Italian war effort and volunteering to serve in the Italian army. All told, 32,430 Italians living in Argentina returned to serve in the war, including many elite members of the community, like Antonio De Marchi and Torcuato Di Tella.[13] This expression of Italian patriotism, along with the community's numerical and economic significance, would not be ignored for long by the new fascist regime in Italy. Argentina would in fact figure prominently in the debates over Italian emigration during the 1920s.

THE ALLURE OF ARGENTINA

Italian writers believed that their emigrants to Argentina, thanks to their Latin culture, European roots, and proportionally higher numbers, would be able to assume positions of high prominence in the Argentine nation without being forced to assimilate into a foreign culture.[14] These writers contrasted Argentina with the United States, where it was thought that Italian emigrants were forced to either assimilate or remain a marginalized ethnic minority in an Anglo-Saxon cultural milieu. Giovanni Borsella, one of the first writers to produce a monograph on Argentina's potential value to the fascist regime, explained that "the United States views emigration as a form of servitude. . . . Our countrymen find themselves in the powerful republic of the 'dollar' always between the devil and the deep blue sea, in unstable positions and risky situations, victims of political and social change and of 'trusts.'"[15] The increasing restrictions placed on Italian immigration by the United States government led Borsella to conclude that "the United States has now closed its door on us. After all of their labor and all the wealth we have created we have been labeled 'undesirables.'"[16] In contrast, "One could say that Argentina is the great nation best suited for our emigration . . . especially if one wanted to establish a position for themselves. . . . One could have great luck in countries like Argentina, especially in the field of commerce and industry."[17] To demonstrate how Argentina was a favorable destination for Italian emigration, Borsella filled his account with evidence of the prosperity of Italian immigrants and their cultural penetration of Argentine society.

In 1924 Mussolini dispatched one of his trusted *gerarchi*, Giovanni Giuriati, to serve as the regime's special emissary in Latin America, accompanying Prince Umberto's goodwill tour to the region on board the *Italia*. Giuriati, an irredentist and nationalist, had served with distinction in the First

World War and was a member of Gabriele D'Annunzio's Fiume expedition. A fascist from very early on in the movement, Giuriati was a member of the Grand Council, a fascist deputy, and later the president of the Chamber. Giuriati would later serve as the secretary of the Fascist Party from 1930 to 1931.[18] At the end of his nine-month tour, Giuriati returned home and penned a comprehensive study of each nation that he had visited in Latin America and their potential value to the regime.

In the published version of this report, Giuriati noted with optimism the passionate patriotism he had found among the Italian collectivity in Argentina and was impressed with both the success that many had attained in their new country, as well as their loyalty and interest in the New Italy.[19] With Argentina in mind, Giuriati wrote that "instead of sending Latin America emigrants in disordered flocks, we should send them in pacific battalions to establish productive enterprises, disciplining our movement of demographic expansion to our incalculable advantage."[20] Giuriati concluded his observations by declaring that through the labor of its emigrants, "Italy must begin a wide-ranging policy in Latin America, following the example of ancient Rome, a constant inspirer . . . armed with workers who will break new grounds, constructing roads, and excavating mines, leveling fields. . . . The fruitful collaboration of [Italy with Argentina] will establish indestructible links between the Campidoglio, the citadel of Latin-ness, to the Latins beyond the sea."[21]

In his unpublished report, Giuriati was a bit more candid. He wrote that despite their strong numerical presence, Italian emigrants had in the past lost their identity in Argentina. To Giuriati the reasons for this "denationalization" were many: Argentine arrogance, emigrant ignorance, and of course liberal Italy's neglect of its compatriots. Giuriati described Argentines as fiercely proud of their country, haughty, and self-absorbed. Anxious to participate in Argentina's national life, emigrants from all over worked hard to assimilate: "'Soy argentino,' says the Italian, German, Turk, or Russian with pride, as if his adopted nation was worth abandoning his homeland without regret."[22] According to Giuriati, the emigrants themselves were also to blame. Arriving in Argentina at the turn of the century, "they were illiterate and ignorant of just about everything. They had no sense of the *patria* and were incapable of understanding it."[23] To Giuriati this was the fault of the liberal regime, for not only had the liberals failed to provide them with an adequate patriotic education, but their humiliating defeats in the international arena left their emigrants ashamed of their identity. In short, "they left without ever knowing their great *patria*, and would never know it."[24] For once these emigrants left Italy, Liberal institutions abroad did little to protect or educate them. However, in discussing the Italians in Argentina after the Great War and the advent of fascism, Giuriati seemed more optimistic. No longer the old emigrant ashamed of his identity, "the new Italo-Argentine veteran declared 'Go ahead and call me gringo; I know who I am and what I am worth.'"[25] For Giuriati this new spirit created possibilities for the regime in Argentina. Now was the time to act.

Rodolfo del Mineo, a member of Prince Umberto's delegation on the same voyage as Giuriati, further elaborated on the problem of assimilation in Argentina in a letter to the Foreign Ministry. He highlighted "our race's natural ability to adapt, the similarity of our language to Spanish, the willingness—unknown to Anglo-Saxons—of learning foreign languages, the fact that the children of Italians born in Argentina are legally considered citizens of the republic, and the hospitality of the country."[26] Del Mineo recommended a more active government intervention to counteract this state of affairs: "It is up to the Dante Alighieri and the Italian schools to propagate and more than anything defend the Italian language."[27] The president of a local section of the Società Nazionale Dante Alighieri echoed these sentiments, declaring, "We have to fight against this great country's natural attraction that more than any other foreign land has the power to absorb and assimilate young people, and our people more than any other is susceptible to this phenomenon."[28] Undeterred by the seemingly inevitable loss of Italian identity, the fascists vowed to fight against the natural tendency to assimilate.

The period from 1927 to 1936 was the high-water mark of Italian fascist interest in the South American republic.[29] Representatives of fascist Italy in Argentina acknowledged Italian immigrant assimilation into Argentine society while at the same time insisted that an aggressive fascist promotion of Italian culture and national identity abroad directed more generally to Argentine society could reverse this trend. One Italian diplomat wrote, "With rare exceptions, we consider a child with Italian parents born in Argentina as Italian, while they instead think of themselves as Argentine."[30] Others posited that emigrant ignorance of the New Italy regenerated by the fascist revolution explained this apparent desire to assimilate. As the teacher of the Italian school in La Plata explained, "Many children of our compatriots know Italy from their parents' descriptions, who, having emigrated many years ago, certainly know nothing of the Italy of today transformed and renewed by the war and by fascism."[31] According to this teacher, it was only through a more active and aggressive propaganda intervention through the schools that the regime could dispel these negative images of Italy, enhancing its prestige and influence in Argentina.

After his appointment to the post of Italian ambassador to Argentina in 1930, Count Bonifacio Pignatti traveled across the country and reported to the Foreign Ministry on the situation of Italians living in Argentina. According to Pignatti, things were indeed desperate: "Few children of Italians will ever admit their Italian origin. They are not only indifferent but hostile to everything Italian. . . . The children of Italians feel that they are Argentine to the very marrow of their bones. . . . They are therefore lost to us; they will never, under any circumstances, consider themselves Italian citizens."[32] For Pignatti, it would take "heroic" measures to reverse this trend: "If things continue the way they are going, in twenty or thirty years maximum, Italian influence in Argentina will be reduced to near zero."[33] Despite such bleak descriptions, Pignatti highlighted the important role the local Fasci and Scuole Italiane all'Estero were playing to stem the tide of assimilation. Like others, Pignatti was also not without his own ideas on how to improve conditions. He proposed a closer collaboration with Argentine officials, writing that "it is in our best interest to give the impression of renouncing our claims over the Italians that they are trying to assimilate," but only if they agree in return to "help us develop Italian cultural and language programs for the children of Italians born on Argentine soil so that they may come to respect and revere the *patria* of their origins."[34] Pignatti's suggestion begs the question not only of what Argentina would gain from such collaboration but also of what Italy would have to gain if it was sincere in renouncing claims over its emigrants. In highlighting the importance of advancing Italy's national project in Argentina, Pignatti also exposed the inherent problems involved in promoting that project in another sovereign state, namely, how to preserve Italian nationalism within another state that is at the same time attempting to assimilate its immigrants into its own national project. The two countries' national projects were inherently oppositional to one another, a fact lost on Italian propagandists, but one the Argentine government would be keenly aware of.

Not all reports to Rome on the situation in Argentina were as somber as Pignatti's. Augusto Mengiotti, captain of the Italian naval vessel *Alvise da Mosto*, reported to the Foreign Ministry that the situation was more favorable than it would appear. After visiting Italian community centers, the local Fascio headquarters, as well as Italian schools and Dopolavoro centers, Mengiotti reported that "my stay in Buenos Aires has left me with the sensation of fervid feelings of Italian-ness by our compatriots who live in this country, even those who have been away from the mother *patria* for many years."[35] Mengiotti did more than just visit with members of the Italian community. He also hobnobbed with Argentina's high society. His itinerary included polo games, golf tournaments, receptions at the prestigious Jockey Club, and even dinner on the president's yacht. In giving his impression of Argentina's elites, he reported that "Italians in this country enjoy much consideration, and Argentines are well disposed toward them."[36] The apparent receptiveness of Argentina's elites to Italian overtures in Mengiotti's account suggested that perhaps there were new avenues for the regime's promotion of its culture and national project by directing its efforts not only to members of the Italian community but also to Argentine society more generally. The idea was to target both the Italian community in Argentina as well as the Argentine general public in the hope of not only spreading Italian culture abroad but also strengthening Argentina's identification with Italy, creating both a stronger sense of Italian national identity among its emigrants as well as winning the admiration of the Argentine public as a whole.

Of all the intellectual figures of the fascist regime, Franco Ciarlantini lobbied the most energetically for this cultural promotion of Italy's national agenda. Ciarlantini's early life had followed the same trajectory as Mussolini's. A school teacher and active socialist journalist in the turn of the century, Ciarlantini left the party and become an interventionist in 1915, volunteering to fight in the war. After the war, he collaborated closely with Mussolini for *Il Popolo d'Italia*, officially joining the Fascist Party in 1923. During the 1920s he was a member of the Fascist Grand Council and a fascist deputy in parliament. Much of his work was devoted to promoting the fascist regime's cultural agenda.[37] As the editor-in-chief of *Augustea*, one of the regime's more prestigious cultural journals, Ciarlantini spoke often of the new cultural possibilities abroad created by the regime's national policies.[38]

After completing a tour of the South American republic to promote the diffusion of Italian books and the creation of Italian-language libraries, Ciarlantini penned his own thoughts on Argentina and its possibilities. In his *Viaggio in Argentina* and his editorials in *Augustea*, Ciarlantini spoke of Argentina as fertile ground for promoting the Italian national agenda abroad. The context for much of this talk was the first ever Mostra del Libro Italiano, a traveling exhibit of Italian books, which made its way to all of Argentina's major cities. In noting of the positive Argentine reception of the exhibit, Ciarlantini wrote that the diffusion of Italian books in Argentina "would greatly increase the spread of our language in the republic, which until now has not be adequately studied, for reasons which remain a paradox, since everyone understands the language and it is still spoken by the nearly three million of our compatriots who live there."[39] According to Ciarlantini, while Italian influences permeated Argentine society and the physical presence of Italians in the republic was unmistakable, something was not quite right: Argentine elites turned to France and Britain for their culture, and Italian immigrants in the nation seemed to have made little effort to promote, or even preserve, their Italian national identity.

Of the Italian immigrants in Argentina, Ciarlantini argued that much ground had been lost since "the demi-liberal governments never thought of cultivating our brother emigrants, by guaranteeing employment, obtaining land, preserving the mother language abroad, protecting their nationalism, or facilitating return to the *patria*. Nothing!"[40] Due to this neglect, these emigrants "know nothing about Dante, Michelangelo, or Galileo, and were not given any reason to be proud of their nationality."[41] This was beginning to change, however, thanks to the First World War and the advent of fascism: "The situation of Italians in Argentina today is absolutely different from that of before the Libyan War and the Great European War. . . . The victories on the Piave and Vittorio Veneto had a decisive impact."[42] Lest an opportunity be lost, much more work now had to be done to promote Italian language and culture in the community and strengthen its ties to the New Italy. To Ciarlantini, such should be the primary mission of Italian fascists in Argentina, to cultivate a new Italian national identity within the community.[43] In this endeavor, he further argued that the regime needed to articulate a culturally sophisticated version of Italy's national project in Argentina, explaining that "the first necessity above all else is to give to both the Argentines and the children of Italians a knowledge of Italy and of Italian life that goes beyond the image our emigration had provided." In short, "to replace the image of a proletarian nation that exported its people with that of a cultured Italy of learning and spiritual creation."[44]

Le Pagine delle Dante, the official magazine of the Società Nazionale Dante Alighieri, which since 1889 had been sponsoring Italian language and cultural courses throughout the world, often addressed the situation in Argentina and its potential. Upon completing a three-month tour of the country, the Italian novelist Mario Puccini contributed an article to *Le Pagine delle Dante*. In describing his experiences, he wrote, "I traveled, gave speeches, shook many hands, and looked many people in the eye. While I may forget some of the faces that I saw and confuse some of the hands I shook, I will never forget the sensation that Italy, so far away, was also so close."[45] According to Puccini, it was up to the Società Nazionale Dante Alighieri and the fascist regime to revive in its long-abandoned emigrant sons a love for the *patria* and restore their spiritual connections to Italy before "they are fatally lost forever."[46]

The noted Italian author Massimo Bontempelli, in a work based on his 1934 tour of South America titled *Noi, gli Aria: Interpretazioni sudamericane*, echoed many of the same concerns and aspirations. The spiritual state of Italian emigrants and their children troubled Bontempelli, who reported that everywhere he heard people declare, "I am an Argentine, son of Italians, while not one out of a hundred told me, I am an Italian, born in Argentina. . . . Even a ten year old boy, the son of thoroughly Italian parents who only spoke to him in Italian, would affirm—I am an Argentine."[47] He did notice that the Italian national project was bolstered by the prestige Italian culture was obtaining within Argentine society, commenting that, "Until yesterday, they looked to France for their culture . . . but now they are beginning to realize what we already have realized, that France no longer has anything to contribute to civilization. . . . They are therefore beginning to feel more and more that only the renewed Italy could foment spiritual renovation. This is the easiest, most friendly, and intense field for [our] fertile collaboration."[48] In the pages of Bontempelli's work, one can see new potential for inspiring a stronger sense of Italian national identity on a more cultural plain by reaching out not only to the community but also to the wider Argentine public.

Luigi Pirandello, one of Italy's most famed playwrights and novelists, also voiced support for the idea of promoting the Italian national project in Argentina. Pirandello throughout most of his life remained expressly apolitical. In 1923 he did, however, express admiration for Mussolini and joined the Fascist Party officially on September 19, 1924, at the height of the Matteotti scandal. From 1924 to 1926 Pirandello actively supported fascism and Mussolini's regime through a series of articles in fascist journals and in published interviews. After 1926 Pirandello privately expressed his ambivalence toward the regime and its suppression of individual liberty. He did, however, continue to publicly voice support for the Duce and continued to accept fascist honors and awards. In 1935 he defended Italy's invasion of Ethiopia and donated a number of gold personal effects, including his Nobel Prize medal, to the fascist war effort.[49] In his correspondence to the Italian Foreign Ministry, he often expressed interest in helping the regime promote Italian culture and language in Argentina. Traveling to the country in 1927 and again in 1936, Pirandello offered his services to the regime while touring with his theater company.[50] In talking of his experiences, he noted the nascent patriotism among members of the Italian community. In a speech in the city of Rosario, he declared, "As an Italian I am proud to find myself among you in this wonderful center of Italian activity that inspires and spreads love for the mother *patria*, its history, civilization, and art."[51] From Ciarlantini and Puccini to Bontempelli and Pirandello, major cultural figures in the fascist regime all understood Italian identity more broadly than the regime had previously. Given the undeniable presence of Italians in Argentina's society, there appeared to be an opportunity for the regime to direct its promotion of Italian national identity not only to the community but also to Argentine society more generally.

THE FASCI ITALIANI ALL'ESTERO IN ARGENTINA

In the early 1920s, Mussolini had high hopes for fascism's ability to infiltrate the Italian community in Argentina. He dispatched Ottavio Dinale, a party propagandist and the Fascist Party delegate for South America, to establish the Buenos Aires Fascio in 1923. Rome also subsidized the party's own newspaper in Buenos Aires, *Il Littore*.[52] Dinale's visit was, however, more successful in provoking street brawls than organizing a fascist network, and *Il Littore* enjoyed only a two-year run and very small circulation.[53] By the end of 1924, Bastianini could count 124 local Fasci in the United States of

America and Brazil, but only eight in Argentina.[54] Within Argentina the Fasci faced tremendous opposition not only from anarchists and socialists in the community, whose presence was quite large, but also from republicans and monarchists, whose opposition Italian officials attributed to Freemasonry. Although there was indeed a significant Freemason presence within the community, their numbers and role in opposing the regime has not been documented. A more likely explanation is the fact that the Italian community in Argentina was one of the oldest in the hemisphere with an already well-established network of community associations.[55] In areas where Italian immigrants were more recent arrivals, less organized, or in smaller numbers, the Fasci enjoyed more success due to the greater role they played in the community. This was true, for example, in other Latin American countries such as Peru and Mexico. Whatever the reason, the result was that the majority of the Italian community was ambivalent, if not openly hostile, to the Fasci's arrival on their shores.[56]

Upon learning of the existence of the Fasci within their state, Argentine officials also expressed concern that these Fasci were Italian agents provocateurs sent to stir up trouble in the Italian community and attack antifascists. Argentine police were also alarmed by the violence Fasci activities provoked and their paramilitary appearance. Ironically, the Fasci were more often the victims of violence, militant rhetoric notwithstanding. By 1930, despite their small number, members of the Argentine Fasci had more casualties, or "martyrs" as they called them, than any other country in the Americas.[57] Such was the state of affairs that all of the successful events the Fasci organized were confined to receptions held behind the closed doors of their halls, a sign that things did not go well when they dared venture out black shirted in public.[58]

In 1925 the Fasci in Argentina embarked on a new course of action. Following Mussolini's new directives, they shifted their focus from an aggressive and overtly political agenda to the mission of promoting and defending Italian identity in the republic. In January 1925 the regime found its man in Vittorio Valdani, naming him the new Fascist Party delegate in Argentina. An engineer by profession, Valdani had arrived in Argentina in 1899, becoming an important industrialist and prominent member of the Italian community.[59] Valdani joined the Fasci all'Estero in 1924 and remained a committed fascist to the end, becoming the republic of Saló's representative in Argentina in 1943 and accepting money from Nazi Germany to continue his work.[60]

Soon after his appointment, Valdani began to dismiss members of the Fasci, ensuring that those who remained, though few, were "good and of pure intentions."[61] In addition to personnel changes, Valdani realized that, given the conditions on the ground, the Fasci had to rethink their tactics. Fascism was, in Valdani words, "a school and a priesthood of which the Fasci are the temples."[62] Its mission abroad was "to enhance the image of the *patria*" by "earning the respect of friend and foe alike by the exemplary conduct of our members and by the faith that we openly profess."[63] In line with the regime's new approach abroad, Valdani's goal was to defend the regime against its many detractors in Argentina while giving his Fasci an air of respectability so that they appeared less threatening and its ideology more appealing. He worked to transform a poorly organized activist political movement into a respectable public relations organization for the regime. As part of this new program, he founded a fascist weekly, *Il Risveglio*, which served as the mouthpiece for the Italian Fascist Party in Buenos Aires, and campaigned against Italian community organizations opposed to fascism.[64]

In 1926 Valdani formed new local branches, this time in close coordination with consular officials in the area. In a speech given to his Fascio in September, he announced that "fascism is no longer a political movement, fascism today is the 'Religion of the *Patria*,'" and the new "program of the Fasci Italiani all'Estero is one of morality, faith, and the defense of patriotism."[65] These lines indicate a watershed moment in the regime's activities in Argentina. Its mission to spread the revolutionary fascist political ideology was now subordinate to the regime's emerging agenda to promote and defend an Italian national identity abroad.

Valdani's change in strategy is also demonstrated by his change in tactics. Aware of the difficult position of the organization in Argentina, Valdani ordered his men not to resort to violence, arguing that this would only play into the hands of its opponents and work against the fascist cause in the Americas. Instead he instructed the Fasci to win converts in the community by demonstrating their discipline, faith in the cause, and love of *patria*. Less overtly political and no longer as militant, Valdani had embraced the new national orientation of the Fasci all'Estero. By the end of 1927, things were coming together for the Fasci in Argentina; its more pragmatic, less internationalist agenda, which was developed in coordination with the Italian consulates, was beginning to show promise. These changes did not go unnoticed in Rome.

Upon taking control of the Fasci all'Estero in 1928, Piero Parini took a special interest in Argentina. In a report to Grandi, he identified Argentina, along with France, Belgium, Luxemburg, and Switzerland, as among the most challenging environments for the Fasci: "Their work is dangerous, full of uncertainty. They must work against the sentiments of much of the local population, against the abuse of power of local authorities, and against the bloody criminal acts of the *fuorusciti*, but [these Fasci] are firm in their convictions and their courage is admirable."[66] By 1930 many Italian antifascist exiles had indeed made their way to Argentina and were actively organizing the antifascist movement within the republic. According to Parini, the situation in Argentina was growing critical by the day. Before it was too late, he proposed that the Fasci redouble their efforts at winning over converts to Italy's national project abroad by targeting Italian youth, emphasizing educational programs, and supporting social and cultural initiatives. It was an approach that Parini suggested would successfully penetrate the community without provoking open confrontations with local authorities and antifascists.[67]

In December 1931 Parini embarked on a tour of South America, spending two months in Buenos Aires. In one of his first speeches to the Italian community, Parini acknowledged the failure of the regime's early efforts in the republic. Most of the Italians in Argentina had not welcomed fascism's extremist political ideology. To drive home this point, Parini quoted a letter from an old World War I comrade-in-arms who wrote, "Dear Parini, I have spent many years in this country after the war and I have followed everything that you have done and I have admired it, but if friendship unites us, democracy divides us."[68] According to Parini, this letter "opened up my eyes: that in 1931 an authentic veteran speaks of democracy to contradict an old comrade-in-arms is very strange. From this I can understand why the Italians in South America have not yet supported Fascism."[69] Fascism's virulently antidemocratic rhetoric had proven to be a liability in an Italian community that still valued democracy. For Parini, it was clear that a different, more nationalist, and less overtly political strategy was needed.

At the end of his visit to Argentina, Parini unveiled that new strategy for the republic. Speaking at a gathering of Italian fascists in Buenos Aires, he called on all Italians to exhibit "absolute agreement and unquestioned loyalty" to Mussolini's regime and commanded them to intensify their educational efforts by spreading the Italian language and nationalism throughout Argentina. With a focus more on national identity rather than politics, Parini ordered the Fasci to abstain from local politics and instead concentrate on "organized cultural actions" to demonstrate "the beauty of Italian culture, the product of thirty centuries of intellectual and historical growth."[70] Parini further commanded his followers to target the children of Italians living abroad, declaring that "it would be absurd, antinational, and antihistorical for a generation of children of Italians to deliberately forget Italy and not be proud of their Italian origin." It was up to fascist Italy's organizations in Argentina to "bring them close to the sources of Italian culture and Italian spirituality, to capture their hearts and minds so that they do not become the degenerate brats of a noble race."[71] To accomplish this goal, Parini called on the Fasci to expand their own youth programs and supervise the schools and cultural institutes not directly under the Italian regime's authority.[72] Parini's strategy was in line with the regime's new national project abroad and seemed to hold the greatest potential for success given the difficult situation on the ground in Argentina.

Parini's visit marked the final chapter in what remained of the infighting between intransigent fascists and the regime's representatives abroad. The new leader of the intransigent faction in Argentina was Steno Bolasco, an abrasive Fascist Party commissioner who had been active in the *squadristi* violence of fascism's early years and had supported Farinacci's extremist faction of the Fascist Party. In 1930 Giovanni Giuriati, recently made head of the PNF, pressured Parini to allow Bolasco to travel to Buenos Aires as a special party envoy. Giuriati was no doubt looking to consolidate his hold over the party by sending fascist dissidents like Bolasco as far away from Rome as possible. Despite his evaluation of Bolasco as "mentally unbalanced and lacking good sense," Parini acquiesced to Giuriati's request. It was a decision that he would soon regret.[73]

Upon his arrival in Buenos Aires, Bolasco mobilized what was left of the Bastianini-era activist fascists and immediately began to criticize both Valdani and Parini, declaring publicly that the Fasci all'Estero in Argentina, the Italian embassy, and Parini's DIES had all betrayed the fascist revolution. In a bid to spread fascism throughout the republic, Bolasco did not limit his actions to the Italian community. He joined forces with the Argentine right-wing Legion Cívica party and endorsed a program of violence and terror modeled after the fascist squads. He also funded a variety of local extremist fascist periodicals, not sanctioned by Valdani or the embassy, a clear violation of Mussolini's command to abstain from the internal politics of host nations. According to Parini, Bolasco's agitation undermined the regime's work in Argentina and created confusion and discord among Fascist Party members while also alarming the wider community. In March Parini finally arranged for Bolasco to be recalled to Italy after denouncing his actions in letters to Grandi as well as to Achille Starace, the new head of the PNF.[74] Bolasco's departure sent the message to other members of the party that discord would no longer be tolerated. It also made clear that the focus of the regime was now on promoting Italy's national project rather than its political agenda.

ITALY'S NATIONAL PROJECT THROUGH MEDIA

After Parini's appointment, fascist activities in Argentina moved from the streets to the pages of the Italian-language press. The Fasci Italiani all'Estero in its early form had failed, but it proved better suited to the new, more official nationalist propaganda role it was to play. Key to this new agenda was influencing public opinion in the Italian community. In 1930, with the support of the Italian embassy and under the supervision of Parini, Valdani founded the first fascist Italian-language daily, *Il Mattino d'Italia*. The newspaper would become the fascist regime's main print mouthpiece in Argentina. The Duce sent Mario Appelius, one of his most talented journalists, to Buenos Aires to serve as the editor-in-chief. Appelius had been a correspondent for Mussolini's *Il Popolo d'Italia*. According to a recent biography, Appelius was more devoted to adventure and amorous affairs than any particular ideology, but he was nevertheless one of fascist Italy's most effective propagandists.[75] He was as eloquent in his praise of fascism's ideals as he was vicious in his invectives against its detractors. He would become the famed radio voice of the regime during the Second World War.[76] While claiming to be free of outside influence, the obvious profascist bias of the paper made many suspect the regime's hand in its operations. Parini and the Italian embassy in Buenos Aires were in fact in frequent contact with Appelius but tried to maintain the illusion that the paper was in no way connected to them. In a telegram to Rome, Ambassador Pignatti clarified the regime's actual relationship to the paper by confirming his involvement and his contact with its editor, while at the same time stressing that the "the newspaper is run by its editor, free from any influence or control of Italian government authorities."[77] The very need to make this assertion, along with the close communication the newspaper had with officials in Rome, does however indicate that the Italian regime, through the embassy, Parini, and the editors Mussolini dispatched, were in fact in control of the paper's content.[78]

In a battle over readership, the upstart *Il Mattino* was in no position to challenge the oldest and most respected community newspaper, *La Patria degli Italiani*. Founded in 1876, *La Patria* throughout most of the 1920s had striven to stay above the political fray: it supported the Italian government but did not walk the Fascist Party line. Despite pressure from the embassy, it relied on a United States news service for all of its information on the regime and events in Italy. After Grandi and Parini began to concentrate their energies on the regime's image in the press, more and more pressure was put on the newspaper to adopt a profascist stance. This pressure had the effect of moving the paper more firmly into the antifascist camp. In December of 1929, an editorial in *La Patria* stressed the need for the Italian community to remain steadfast in the face of fascist pressure. In response *Il Legionario* charged the paper not only of antifascism but also of "anti-Italianism." It declared in a full front page editorial that "*La Patria* is no longer an Italian newspaper but an antifascist Argentine paper written in Italian."[79] *La Patria* responded by charging that fascism divided the Italian people and that *La Patria degli Italiani* is only "a rebel against abuse and bullying, and is for the defense of patriotic Italian emigrants and their search for the liberty that they have earned through their voluntary exile."[80] *Il Legionario* responded, insisting that the paper cannot be patriotic if it is against fascism, "because Fascism is the strongest and most complete expression of Italian patriotism."[81] Such were the opening salvos in a two-year confrontation between members of the fascist regime and the editorship of *La Patria degli Italiani*.

La Patria struck the first blows of 1931 when it broke a scandal that threatened to discredit Valdani's *Il Mattino d'Italia*. An anonymous informant in Italy provided the paper with evidence that Mario Appelius had abandoned his wife and young child in Alexandria and was currently living with his mistress, whom he now claimed was his real wife. Reports soon followed of criminal charges awaiting him from Egyptian officials.[82] The Italian embassy in Buenos Aires and the Fasci Italiani all'Estero scrambled to minimize the impact of the scandal, while ordering a top-secret investigation into who leaked the information. They concluded that the informant was actually a prominent fascist journalist, Ugo Imperatori, who had apparently leaked the story to get revenge after Appelius had refused to come to work for him. Just as more and more voices began to call for Appelius's resignation, Parini and Ambassador Pignatti struck back at *La Patria*. In a move that stunned the Italian community in Argentina, the Fasci Italiani all'Estero, through Valdani and other private investors, bought out *La Patria*'s creditors, taking control of the paper only to shut its offices down and channel the assets into *Il Mattino*.[83] To Parini this was the resounding victory that he had been hoping for, a victory for which he of course hastened to take all the credit. In reporting the affair to the Duce, Parini stressed that "it was *only* thanks to the tenacious and cunning actions of the ministry, including the Fasci Italiani all'Estero, that this battle was won."[84] Though no blood was spilled, it was the symbolic death of the community's oldest and most trusted voice. It was a pyrrhic victory that in the end damaged rather than improved the regime's image within the community. All could see the underhanded tactics that the fascists had resorted to in order to silence an opponent who had refused to be intimidated.[85]

After their takedown of *La Patria*, Ambassador Pignatti and Parini quickly lost patience with *Il Mattino*'s now scandalized editor. They insisted that he work more closely with them in disseminating Italian propaganda. Appelius resisted, exploiting the ambiguous relationship between the newspaper and the regime to assert his creative autonomy. His resistance to pressure from Parini, along with the deficit the newspaper was running and the highly publicized scandals around his personal affairs, soon led to his dismissal in 1932.[86] In March of the following year, Rome sent Michele Intaglietta to serve as the new editor-in-chief. A 1944 report from the postfascist Italian embassy in Buenos Aires that described his editorship of the newspaper characterized Intaglietta as "a real adventurer without scruples."[87] Intaglietta was in fact an accomplished propagandist for the regime who was sent to Buenos Aires by the Duce himself, who, in Intaglietta's own words, showered him with praise and encouragement upon his departure.[88] In a seventeen-page report to Valdani on his first year as editor, Intaglietta described his wholesale reorganization of the fascist daily. In his words, he "rapidly and violently removed with surgical precision all of the dishonest and dubiously committed personnel, while setting a serious and reserved tone so that everyone understood the system had changed."[89] In his report he was particularly critical of his predecessor, Mario Appelius, who had left the paper in debt and whose questionable private life had opened the journal up to criticism.[90] Aware that *Il Mattino* was intended to be much more than simply an Italian-language newspaper, he wrote that "as the most important fascist daily abroad it has a *political and propagandistic function* that must not be forgotten for even an instant."[91] To "accentuate the paper's fascist tone," *Il Mattino* reported on the accomplishments of the fascist regime in Italy filtered through the Italian Ministry of Propaganda, responded to fascism's detractors in Argentina, and "anonymously" collaborated with Argentine periodicals sympathetic to the movement.[92]

Under Intaglietta's stewardship, the functioning of the newspaper had changed, and its editorship after 1933 was even more closely aligned to the regime's agenda abroad. *Il Mattino* continued on throughout the 1930s with the added task of defending Italy's foreign policy in Ethiopia and Spain and would continue on into the war years backing the Axis Powers. Even after the fall of Mussolini in 1943, Intaglietta, now funded by the German Embassy, voiced ever more stridently a totalitarian fascist agenda.[93]

Historians Eugenia Scarzanella, Camilla Cattarulla, and Vanni Blengino have examined in detail different aspects of *Il Mattino d'Italia*'s propaganda initiatives under both Appelius and Intaglietta, highlighting how they attempted to appeal to the community and stressing the newspaper's centrality to the regime's overall effort to spread fascism and Italian identity in Argentina. To further propagandize the regime, for example, Intaglietta sponsored a referendum of support for the Duce through *Il Mattino*. The newspaper collected signatures from Italian immigrants throughout the region in order to demonstrate that the Italians of Latin America were fully behind the Duce. In March of 1934, he claimed to have obtained over one hundred thousand signatures from all over Latin America.[94] There is, however, no way to independently verify these figures. In a similar stunt to involve the community in the newspaper's propaganda, Intaglietta asked his readers to clip and answer a survey that asked, "What would you say if you had the chance to speak to the Duce?"[95] In its later investigation of fascist activities, the Argentine government recorded and saved over two hundred of these individual responses to *Il Mattino*'s query, a sign that members of the community did indeed participate in the paper's campaign, although probably not on the scale that Intaglietta had claimed.[96] Furthermore, in order to appeal to the broader Argentine public and make the propaganda seem less foreign, Argentine nationalist intellectuals were invited to contribute articles on fascism and the Italian regime.[97]

Intaglietta in his aforementioned 1934 report to Valdani also highlighted another of his accomplishments while editor, namely, the establishment of his own news service. In order to broaden the reach of his propaganda, Intaglietta inaugurated the Roma Press, a news service that provided daily information from the Italian embassy's telegraph, from its own correspondents in Rome, and later from the Ministry of Popular Culture.[98] The news wire and a number of articles were written in Spanish to appeal to Argentines.[99] Once established, Intaglietta received direct financial support from the Italian government in the form of a two thousand lire per month subsidy delivered through the Italian embassy, and enjoyed the "unconditional support" of Galeazzo Ciano, then secretary of the press and propaganda.[100] Its director, Tommaso Milani, reported to Rome that the mission of the Roma Press was to "make known the New Italy in all of its original thoughts and actions."[101] From 1935 on, its priority became supporting the Italian government's war in Ethiopia and responding to its condemnation by the League of Nations, as foreign affairs monopolized its coverage.[102] Throughout the 1930s, the Roma Press was distributing on average three thousand articles, news reports, and photographs per trimester.[103] It also sponsored radio transmissions, buying airtime from Radio Excelsior. It broadcast news from Italy in both Italian and Spanish on a daily basis and also a transmitted a variety of Italian musical and cultural programming on the weekend, an indication that the regime's nationalist cultural project also figured prominently in its message.[104]

In 1936 Italian antifascists founded their own news service in Argentina, the Italpress. With its head office in Buenos Aires, and correspondents operating out of Paris, the new press agency not only challenged fascist Italy's control over information, it also confused many Latin American subscribers who mistakenly thought that the Italpress had replaced the Roma Press as the Italian regime's press agency in the region.[105] From 1936 onward, interest in the Roma Press news services waned—not, however, because of the efforts of their antifascist nemesis, but instead because of changing world events, in particular the Spanish Civil War, Nazi aggression in Europe, and the looming world war.[106] By the end of the 1930s, on the recommendation the Italian embassy in Argentina, the regime formed its own government press agency, which made use of the Stefani news wire and took over the Roma Press's offices.[107]

In addition to his newspaper and its news service subsidiary, Intaglietta was also well aware of the importance of film in propagandizing Italy's national project. To that end, he organized the distribution of Luce newsreels and documentaries throughout Argentina during the 1930s. These films were projected in local Italian consulates, Fasci meeting halls, and Dopolavoro centers. Intaglietta also negotiated contracts to have the newsreels projected in commercial Argentine theaters. This effort was by and large unsuccessful, however, since Luce could not compete with Hollywood powerhouses Fox, Metro, and Paramount, who distributed weekly Movietone newsreels free of charge as part of their film packages.[108] Together, all of these media outlets saturated the Italian community with its national project abroad. They furthermore provided a clear public platform from which to proclaim the new Italian national discourse.

FASCIST ITALY'S CULTURAL ORGANIZATIONS IN ARGENTINA

Although the political activism of the Fasci all'Estero may have provoked the most reactions among members of the community, and *Il Mattino d'Italia* certainly served as fascist Italy's mouthpiece in Argentina, the key to Mussolini's nationalization strategy was the regime's cultural organizations abroad. Less abrasive and overtly political, these organizations targeted the children of emigrants and focused almost exclusively on the project of re-creating the Italian nation within Argentina.

Parini recognized that were Italy's ambitious project of redefining national identity abroad to have any hope of success, it would have to instill in the next generation of children born outside of Italy both the beliefs and values of the regime as well as with love and pride for the New Italy. Just as the regime emphasized indoctrinating its youth at home, influencing the children of emigrants was fundamental to its attempts at reshaping Italian national identity in Argentina. In November of 1928, Mussolini ordered Italian representatives abroad to pay special attention to the Italian youth movement, directing them to assist the Fasci Italiani all'Estero in organizing Balilla sections and youth programs.[109] In a circular to consular officials, Parini likewise stressed the pressing need to organize Italian youth abroad "to keep alive their connection to Italy and prevent them from falling prey to the powerful foreign influences around them." Aware of the negative reactions that the Fasci Italiani all'Estero had provoked by wearing their black shirts in public, Parini instructed the foreign sections of Balilla to choose a slightly different style of uniform and in some cases to even go by a different name, such as "Young Explorers," rather than Balilla. He made clear, however, that this was only for show, explaining that "in substance these societies are not and must not be anything other than genuine sections of the Opera Nazionale Balilla (ONB)." It was a thin camouflage, just enough to avoid being shut down by the local authorities while at the same time making fascist Italy's presence in foreign nations unmistakable.[110] To increase membership in the Balilla, members of the local Fasci were required to register their children, and all children in Italian schools abroad, both those run by the government and those subsidized by the regime, were also required to sign up.[111]

Throughout the 1930s, Balilla members figured prominently in the public events and ceremonies of the Fasci Italiani all'Estero and Dopolavoro in Argentina. Whether serving as the color guard or leading the audience in Giovinezza, Balilla activities were often mentioned in local newspapers and reports to Rome.

In 1932 Parini began a summer camp program for foreign-born Italian children enrolled in the Balilla. Every year around four thousand children spent their summer vacation in fascist summer camps in Italy. At the most famous of these camps, Campo Mussolini, children spent the summer months fraternizing and training with Italian sections of the Balilla, all the while being indoctrinated in the values of the fascist regime.[112] In full fascist regalia, the summer camps were disturbingly reminiscent of military basic training, as young Balilla buglers sounded the call to attention and Avanguardisti trained with rifle and bayonet.[113] Their vacation ended with a September tour of Rome and the modern architectural marvels of fascist Italy. The highlight of the trip was an audience with the Duce himself at Palazzo Venezia. Pictures from these events show the young "Italians Abroad" parading in uniform down the Via Imperiale and as captivated crowds for one of Il Duce's typically animated speeches.[114] Though the actual numbers of participants were relatively modest, the summer program's true value to the regime was as a propaganda device: photos from the summer camps figured prominently in all fascist publications abroad, not only monopolizing *Il Legionario*'s summer issues but also finding their way into the Italian emigrant presses as well as mainstream foreign newspapers.

Few of the fascist youths in Argentina attended these much-publicized summer camps for the simple reason that Italy's summer was Argentina's winter and children were still in school. Since these children could not come to the Italian summer camps, the Italian summer camps came to them. In 1933 the Italian consulate in Cordoba founded fascist Italy's first-ever summer camp in South America. In January and February, one hundred children of Italian descent attended the camp, which was located in the sierras around Cordoba. According to all reports, the experiment was a success, and the Italian ambassador, upon inspecting the camp, recommended that each of the Italian consulates in Argentina found one of their own.[115] The idea caught on, and by 1935 three camps were fully operational in Argentina, located in Cordoba, Mendoza, and Bahia Blanca, and others were soon established in neighboring Uruguay and Brazil. The activities of the camps followed the exact same guidelines as those in Italy, though as had been prescribed, the children wore slightly different uniforms. Photos from the camps show students in military formation, sounding roll call, marching in step, and giving the fascist salute to the Italian flag.[116] In its April 1935 issue, *Il Legionario* featured a full-length glossy exposé of the camps and their activities, boasting that they instilled in their young members fascist discipline, obedience, martial valor, and love of the *patria*. For it was only thanks to the fascist regime that "Italy, which is so far away on a map, is now so close to the children's hearts." It was metaphorically as if "one of Italy's borders came alive and miraculously flew over the ocean to the distant lands of Argentina, Uruguay, and Brazil, allowing young children the chance to breathe in Italian air and feel its spirit."[117]

On August 18, 1937, thirty-seven Italian children, members of the fascist Avanguardisti and Piccole Italiane, disembarked in Buenos Aires from the ship *Augustus*. It was their last stop on a South American propaganda cruise organized by the DIES and the high-water mark of fascist Italy's youth propaganda in the South American republic. Describing the large cheering crowds of both Argentines and Italians who came to meet the Avanguardisti, the Italian ambassador reported that the experience "has left Argentines as well as our compatriots the most authentic image of the renewed Italy."[118] Ten years earlier, such a cruise had not been possible. Martin Franklin, the Italian ambassador in 1927, had voiced his fears of bad press, Argentine government opposition, and possibly violent public protest.[119] The 1937 visit was therefore a small victory for the regime and an indication that much had changed from the street brawls of the early 1920s.

Along with the ONB, Parini also imported to Argentina another popular fascist Italian cultural initiative from home, the Opera Nazionale Dopolavoro. Under the supervision of the Italian consulates, local fascist sections established Dopolavoro centers throughout Argentina. Its activities seemed to be one of the few successful initiatives associated with the Fasci Italiani all'Estero. This initiative especially took off under Parini's supervision. During the 1930s requests for Italian books, feature films from Italy, Luce newsreels, and other propaganda materials flooded the secretary general's office and later the Ministry of Popular Culture, as did newspaper clippings and reports of successful lecture series on Italian culture and the fascist regime.[120] According to historians Marco Pluviano and Irene Guerrini, the Dopolavoro enjoyed more success than other fascist initiatives in Latin America thanks to its more subtle political agenda and the variety of its social-cultural programs.[121] Indeed, even the most pessimistic reports on the experiences of Fasci Italiani all'Estero in Argentina acknowledged the positive work of the Dopolavoro and recommended that it expand its activities.[122]

The fascist Italian organizations operating in Argentina gained an important ally in their work when the regime back in Rome took over the Società Nazionale Dante Alighieri. Within Argentina, the Dante Alighieri had eight centers of activity, operated nine Italian-language schools, and housed a twenty-housand-volume Italian-language library in Buenos Aires. In addition to their courses, the society organized trips to Italy, arranged classical music and opera concerts, and held art exhibitions. It also invited prominent Italian figures to give a series of lectures in their halls. In 1933, for example, Massimo Bontempelli lectured on Italian history and literature and Gino Arias on fascist law and economics.[123] Not all of the Dante Alighieri's members in Argentina were happy with the new fascist orientation of their society. Many left in protest and formed their own rival, Nuova Società Dante Alighieri.[124] During the late 1930s, much to the frustration of the regime, the Nuova Dante competed against and often undermined or discredited the activities of the official society in Argentina.[125]

THE SCUOLE ITALIANE ALL'ESTERO IN ARGENTINA

In the late 1930s, all of the regime's aforementioned organizations and initiatives in Argentina found some form of expression in the Scuole Italiane all'Estero, the Italian school system abroad. Within Argentina, they were more than simply another organization taken over by the regime; they were also the central point of intersection for its other initiatives. Many of these schools were organized and run by members of the local Fascist Party sections, others were operated by the Dante Alighieri, all of the school children were enrolled in the ONB, and Dopolavoro events made use of the classrooms after school. The importance of the regime's propaganda through the schools was also not lost on Argentine officials, for it was this initiative that would ultimately alarm the Argentine government and lead to the suppression of many of the fascist activities.[126] A close examination of the schools' functioning and their experiences in Argentina is therefore essential to understanding Italy's nationalization project in Argentina.

Although the schools abroad did enjoy some success in other parts of the world, the case of Argentina was more troubling for the regime. The reports on the conditions of schools in Argentina that flooded the now centralized Direzione Generale delle Scuole all'Estero soon dampened much of the regime's early enthusiasm. In addition to the all-too-common complaint of insufficient funding, consular officials and leaders of Italian organizations in Argentina stressed the need for greater supervision and more efficient dispersal of subsidies. Unlike the schools in North Africa, which were run directly by the Italian government through their consulates, most of the schools in Argentina were subsidized schools, run by the Italian associations, the Società Nazionale Dante Alighieri, or Catholic religious orders. These schools were supervised but not directly controlled by the Italian consulates in Argentina, making it difficult to ensure that the regime's new directives were being followed. According to the Italian Consul in Cordoba, "there are many schools in this consular district, but very few that do more than just use the word 'Italian' in their name."[127] In a similar vein, the Italian consul in Rosario wrote, "I watch with justifiable worry the scholastic issue in general in Argentina, but my other duties, which overwhelm me with work, prevent me from keeping these schools under closer supervision."[128] Members of the community also noted the inability of consular officials to supervise the schools well, with one remarking, "the consular agents, overwhelmed with urgent diplomatic affairs, cannot find the time and do not always have the required competence to oversee, direct, and administrate scientifically and conscientiously these scholastic institutions."[129] Consular officials were further frustrated by their inability to influence the functioning of unsubsidized Italian schools. As one remarked, "a new Italian subsidy would give me the opportunity and in a way the *right* to make frequent visits to the schools to ensure that the programs are developed properly."[130]

Members of the local Fasci and DIES officials in Rome blamed the consular officials themselves for the schools' woes. They saw the diplomatic corps as a remnant of the liberal regime, not fully committed to the new fascist ideological program abroad. The director of personnel for the schools complained, "There are consular agents who have thirty years of uninterrupted service in the Americas—How could they possibly represent the Italy of Vittorio Veneto and Mussolini, these poor devils who are part of the Italy when from Mantua to Udine there was not even enough polenta for people to eat in the winter."[131] Whatever the reasons—distance, lack of funding, overwork, incompetence, or lack of commitment—all agreed that the schools were not promoting the new national agenda.

Italian consuls and fascist officials were particularly bothered by the subsidized schools run by Catholic religious orders. In Argentina nearly half of the schools offering courses in Italian language and culture were run by the Salesian Society and its sister order, the Daughters of Mary Help of Christians. Founded by John Bosco in 1857, the order emphasized works of charity for poor and abandoned children as well as the education of young boys for a life in the priesthood. The Salesian Society established schools in Argentina as early as 1876 and was one of the Catholic Church's most influential orders among Italian immigrants in Argentina. While most of these schools were in fact run by priests of Italian origin and although Italian culture and language instruction were emphasized, they clearly had a different mission and ideological agenda. Just as the regime was negotiating compromises with the Catholic Church at home, it was forced to rely in part on this network of Catholic schools to help promote its language and cultural instruction, not however without some misgivings. Grandi instructed his ambassadors to pay special attention to the religious missionary schools in their reports to Rome.[132] In response, consular officials, while lauding the instruction of Italian within the schools, insisted that they were of little or no value in promoting the national agenda of the regime.[133] The Italian consul in Mendoza, in fact, suggested that the government suspend its subsidy, explaining that "the Salesians' efforts have certainly been beneficial, especially since they are in part made up of good Italians and can turn to local institutions and committees; however, their promotion of Italian-ness is very limited. I therefore do not think we should give them financial assistance, but instead send them Italian textbooks and scholastic material." According to this official, funds should be diverted to the establishment of a government-run school better equipped for promoting Italy's new national agenda.[134]

Italian officials were similarly frustrated with subsidized schools run by the local Italian community. The regime's relationship with the association Pro-Schola during the 1920s was emblematic of this problem. The Pro-Schola was a scholastic association run by the Italian community in Buenos Aires that organized and for the most part funded the ten major nonreligious Italian schools in Buenos Aires. Founded in 1868 by the Società Mutuo Soccorso, its mission was to provide a free rudimentary education to children of Italian workers. Relying almost entirely on donations from prominent members of the community, as well as on an Italian government subsidy, the association's schools were controlled by an elected committee.[135] The Pro-Schola committee resisted the new fascist reorientation of the schools' mission and refused to swear a fascist oath of allegiance. In a 1925 letter to the Italian ambassador, the Pro-Schola committee insisted that fundamental to the schools' success and the unity of its various supporting associations was their founding statute, which "affirms perennial loyalty to the distant *patria*, while avoiding any discussion of politics or religion."[136] Throughout the 1920s, the Italian embassy put more and more pressure on the Pro-Schola committee to support the fascist agenda, at one point even suspending its Italian government subsidy. Finally, the regime had its way, and in 1928 the members of Pro-Schola who opposed fascism left in protest. It was a small victory for the regime, although not without consequence since it led to a drop in enrollment and the closure of seven out of its ten schools.[137]

Other Italian schools did more than resist fascist overtures and directly opposed the regime. Three schools in particular, Italia Unita, Edmondo de Amicis, and Tito Luciani, provided an antifascist Italian educational alternative. As the consul of La Plata lamented, "for the past three years the Italian schools in this district have been taken over by members of the antifascist group Società Italia Unita, which after eliminating all of their competent instructors has transformed the classrooms into hotbeds of antinational propaganda."[138] Challenging fascist claims over Italian identity, the main antifascist newspaper of Buenos Aires, *L'Italia del Popolo*, reported that these schools "demonstrated to the fascists the Italian-ness of free Italians without Judas's thirty silver coins [the Italian government subsidy] and have with enthusiasm countered the fascists' supposedly exclusive patrimony over Italian identity."[139]

Parini used his cadre of fascist teachers armed with fascist textbooks to spearhead his reorganization of the Scuole Italiane all'Estero in Argentina. He established fifteen new government schools during the 1930s. In each of these schools, located from Cordoba to Bahia Blanca, from Rosario to Mendoza, fascist teacher-agents working with members of the local *fascio* took control of the local Italian schools' day-to-day operations. In some places, like Bahia Blanca, the new teacher-agents took over old community-run schools. In other places, they established new schools, as were the cases in Mendoza and Cordoba. In Buenos Aires the Pro-Schola maintained control over its schools, but its committee, now purged of its antifascist members, left much of their schools' functioning to the five teacher-agents assigned to them. The largest Italian school system in Argentina, the Dante Alighieri schools in Rosario de Santa Fé, frustrated Parini to no end. The teacher-agents under his authority often came into conflict with Felice Felicioni, who as head of the Dante Alighieri felt that he had control over the schools' operation. Despite his personal feud with Felicioni, Parini acknowledged that the schools in Rosario were a model of success. Beyond a primary education and Italian language instruction, these schools advanced the regime's propaganda initiatives, hosting Dopolavoro and Balilla activities as well as disseminating Italian propaganda material, often through the students, into the community.

By the end of the 1930s, the schools had become effective, well-coordinated vehicles for the regime's promotion of the New Italy. In 1939, with twenty-three teacher-agents assigned to Argentina and government funding totaling 1,643,765 lire, the number of students officially enrolled in government controlled schools totaled 3,374, with nearly twice as many students involved in after school activities, a 47 percent increase from 1930.[140] This increase demonstrated the greater commitment on the part of the regime to developing and expanding the school system, although given an Italian immigrant population in Argentina of over a million, these numbers are by no means impressive.

CONCLUSION

Membership in all the Italian regime's organizations in Argentina numbered in the hundreds and in the best of times thousands—far from impressive given the size of the Italian population. Although these organizations did little to mobilize large numbers in the Italian community, the Fasci Italiani all'Estero, Dopolavoro, and Balilla did succeed in attracting attention to the regime and played key roles in disseminating propaganda material. In this regard *Il Mattino d'Italia* and the Roma Press were especially important vehicles of propaganda for the regime, both the products of a collaborative effort on the part of the local Fasci and the regime's institutions in Rome.

Italian fascists had arrived in Argentina soon after Mussolini took power but accomplished little during the 1920s and were instead plagued by a contradictory and ill-defined agenda, a confusing organizational structure, and competing personalities. By the late 1930s, thanks in large part to the reorganization of the regime's efforts abroad while under Parini and the reorientation of the Fasci in Argentina by Valdani, the fascists developed a better-coordinated and more coherent organizational apparatus in the republic. By the 1930s, the regime shifted focus more narrowly on promoting the Italian national project among its emigrants and fighting against their natural pull towards assimilation.

In order to better understand and evaluate the full significance of the regime's national project in Argentina, it is essential to closely analyze the actual content of propaganda within Argentina. The literature produced by the organizations and propagandists discussed above provide a striking image of how the regime sought to redefine the Italian nation abroad by incorporating Italian expatriates back into the national project.[141] This propaganda also sheds light on how the Italian national project is transformed once it arrives in Argentina. Once received in Argentina, this propaganda took on new meanings, and the Italian national project became something fundamentally different from what the regime intended. The next chapter examines the message of this changing national agenda in Argentina before going on to analyze the debates that it engendered within the Italian community as well as among the Argentine general public and political establishment.

NOTES

1. The historiography on fascist activities in Argentina has greatly increased over the past few years. Ronald C. Newton was the first to provide a narrative overview of both Italian fascist activities in Argentina as well as community reactions and responses. See Ronald C. Newton, "*Ducini, Prominenti, Antifascisti*: Italian Fascism and the Italo-Argentine Collectivity, 1922–1945," *Americas* 51, no. 1 (1994): 41–66. More recent scholarship has focused narrowly on specific aspects or episodes in the Italian fascist project. Loris Zanetti in "I Fasci in Argentina negli anni trenta," in *Il Fascismo e gli emigrati: La parabola dei Fasci italiani all'estero (1920–1943)*, ed. Emilio Franzina and Matteo Sanfilippo, (Rome: Laterza, 2003) 140–151, sketches the Fasci Italiani all'Estero's activities in Argentina in the 1930s, downplaying Italy's interest in Argentina and its importance and impact. Eugenia Scarzanella, Vanni Blengino, and Camilla Catarulla, in Eugenia Scarzanella, ed., *Fascisti in Sud America* (Florence: Le Lettere, 2005), highlight different aspects of the regime's activities, focusing on *Il Mattino d'Italia*. In this chapter I also analyze *Il Mattino d'Italia* along with its related Archivio Centrale dello Stato archival documents, but draw different conclusions from that evidence. Rather than

viewing the newspaper as a fascist community mouthpiece, I see it instead as simply another vehicle used by the regime to disseminate its propaganda, and I place less importance on Vittorio Valdani's influence on the newspaper.

2. Luigi de Rosa, "L'emigrazione italiana in Argentina: Un bilancio," in *L'Italia nella società Argentina : Contributi sull'emigrazione italiana in Argentina*, ed. Fernando Devoto and Gianfausto Rosoli (Rome: Centro Studi Emigrazione, 1988), 77.

3. Arnd Schneider, *Futures Lost: Nostalgia and Identity among Italian Immigrants in Argentina* (New York: Peter Lang, 2000), 313.

4. Ibid., 315.

5. David Rock, *Argentina, 1516–1987* (Berkeley: University of California Press, 1987), 139.

6. James Scobie, *Revolution on the Pampas: A Social History of Argentine Wheat, 1860–1910* (Austin: University of Texas Press, 1964).

7. María Inés Barbero and Susana Felder, "El rol de los italianos en el nacimento y desarrollo de las asociaciones empresarias en la Argentina," in Devoto and Rosoli, *L'Italia nella società Argentina*, 140.

8. Ibid., 144–45.

9. Rock, *Argentina*, 192, 224.

10. Schneider, *Futures Lost*, 317.

11. Samuel L. Bailey, "The Italians and Organized Labor in the United States and Argentina: 1880–1910," *International Migration Review* 1, no. 3 (1967): 56–66.

12. Ibid.

13. Ludovico Incisa Di Camerana, *L'Argentina, gli Italiani, e l'Italia: Un'altro destino* (Milan: Servizi Promozioni Attività Internazionali, 1998), 388.

14. Emilio Gentile ("L'emigrazione italiana in Argentina nella politica di espansione del nazionalismo e del fascismo," *Storia Contemporanea* 17, no. 3 [1986]: 355–96) was the first to focus specifically on the allure of Argentina to both Italian nationalists and fascists, followed by Alessandra Ruberti ("Il fascismo e l'emigrazione italiana in Argentina nella stampa di Regime (1922–1930)," *Affari Sociali Internazionali* 20, no. 3 [1992]: 107–16). Like Gentile, this section also discusses the reports to Rome on Argentina as a potential area of fascist penetration; however, in contrast to Gentile, who argues that the regime's interest waned after 1926, I argue here that its interest continued well into the 1930s.

15. Giovanni Borsella, *L'emigrante italiano e l'Argentina* (Milan: Fratelli Treves, 1925), 107.

16. Ibid., 15.

17. Ibid., 18.

18. *Dizionario biografico degli Italiani* (Rome: Istituto della Enciclopedia Italiana, 1960–), 57:120–22.

19. Giovanni Battista Giuriati, *La crociera italiana nell'America Latina* (Rome: Arti Grafiche Affini Roma, 1925), 9–10.

20. Ibid., 13.

21. Ibid., 19.

22. Giovanni Giuriati, "Studio dei paesi dell'America Latina," Fondo Giovanni Giuriati, pp. 521–39, Archivio Storico della Camera dei Deputati (hereafter cited in notes as ASCD). Gentile, "L'emigrazione italiana," also provides an analysis of the Giuriati archive; although, in contrast to my study, he views Giuriati's assessment of Argentina as more pessimistic overall. I am in fact indebted to Gentile for suggesting that I visit this archive.

23. Giuriati, "Studio dei paesi dell'America Latina," Fondo Giovanni Giuriati, p. 523, ACSD.

24. Ibid., 530.

25. Ibid., 532.

26. Rodolfo del Mineo, Tenente di Vascello, Bordo, September 6, 1924, Archivio Scuole (1923–1928), file 634, Archivio Storico del Ministero degli Affari Esteri (hereafter cited in notes as ASMAE).

27. Ibid.

28. President of Dante Alighieri committee of Rufino A. Baretti, 1930, Archivio Scuole (1929–1935), file 778, ASMAE.

29. Disappointing results in Argentina along with world political events would shift the regime's focus away from its programs directed toward Argentina. From 1936 onward the regime would focus primarily on defending its foreign policies and image abroad, not just in Argentina but all over the world.

30. Consul in Cordoba to Ministry of Foreign Affairs, September 15, 1933, Archivio Scuole (1929–1935), file 779, ASMAE.

31. Carlo Guaschino, "Relazione didattica sull'anno scolastico 1928," La Plata, December 10, 1928, Archivio Scuole (1929–1935), file 779, ASMAE.

32. Pignatti to Direzione Generale degli Italiani all'Estero, July 5, 1930, Inventario della Serie Affari Politici (1919–1930), file 808, ASMAE.

33. Ibid.

34. Ibid.

35. Augusto Mengotti to the Naval Ministry, November 18, 1932, Le Carte del Gabinetto del Ministro e della Segretaria Generale dal 1923 al 1943, file 821, ASMAE.

36. Ibid.

37. *Dizionario biografico degli Italiani* (Rome: Istituto della Enciclopedia Italiana, 1960–), 25:217–18.

38. Both Gentile in "L'emigrazione italiana" and Frederico Finchelstein in *Transatlantic Fascism: Ideology, Violence, and the Sacred in Argentina and Italy, 1919–1945* (Durham, NC: Duke University Press, 2010) highlight the centrality of Ciarlantini in advocating for greater Italian involvement in Argentina.

39. Franco Ciarlantini, "Poeti del Argentina," *Augustea*, October 31, 1927.

40. Franco Ciarlantini, *Viaggio in Argentina* (Milan: Edizioni Alpes, 1929), 196.

41. Ibid., 201.

42. Ibid., 195–96.

43. Ciarlantini, "Italia e Argentina," *Augustea*, January 31, 1930.

44. Ciarlantini, *Viaggio in Argentina*, 218.

45. Mario Puccini, "La 'Dante' nell'America Latina," *Le Pagine delle Dante*, November–December, 1936.

46. Ibid.

47. Massimo Bontempelli, *Noi, gli Aria: Interpretazioni sudamericane*, ed. Sebastiano Martelli (Palermo: Sellerio, 1994), 72–73.

48. Ibid., 78.

49. Gaspare Giudice, *Pirandello: A Biography* (London: Oxford University Press, 1975), 143–65.

50. Luigi Pirandello to Ministry of Foreign Affairs, February 11, 1936, Argentina, Inventario della Serie Affari Politici (1931–1945), file 11, ASMAE.

51. Pirandello, "Pel teatro e per la lingua d'Italia in Argentina," *La pagine delle Dante*, no. 4 (1927): 61.

52. Newton, "*Ducini, Prominenti, Antifascisti*," 46; Gentile, "L'emigrazione italiana," 379.

53. Gentile, "L'Emigrazione italiana," 389.

54. Luca de Caprariis, "'Fascism for Export?' The Rise and Eclipse of the Fasci Italiani all'Estero," *Journal of Contemporary History* 35, no. 2 (April 2000): 158.

55. Ibid., 158.

56. Italian community responses to fascism and the antifascist movement in Argentina are examined in detail in chapter 5.

57. "Caduti in terra straniera per il Fascismo (1923–1933)," included in Piero Parini, *Italiani per il Mondo* (Milan: Mondadori, 1935), 87–93.

58. Reports from the Argentine Fasci in Vita dei Fasci, *Il Legionario*, 1925.

59. Cornelio di Marzio, "Pro-memoria per il Duce," September 15, 1927, Carte Cornelio di Marzio, file 47, Archivio Centrale dello Stato (hereafter cites in notes as ACS).

60. Italian Ambassador to Foreign Ministry, December 19, 1944, Argentina, Inventario della Serie Affari Politici (1931–1945), file 40, ASAME. Scarzanella in *Fascisti in Sud America* offers an excellent and thorough biographical sketch of Vittorio Valdani.

61. Vittorio Valdani, "Vita dei Fasci, Argentina," *Il Legionario*, May 2, 1925. See Vita dei Fasci, Argentina sections from January to October 1925 for the names of those dismissed.
62. Ibid.
63. Ibid.
64. Cornelio di Marzio, "Pro-Memoria per Il Duce," September 13, 1927, Carte Cornelio di Marzio, file 47, ACS.
65. Vittorio Valdani, "Vita dei Fasci, Argentina," *Il Legionario*, October 2, 1926.
66. Parini to Grandi, October 7, 1930, Le Carte del Gabinetto del Ministro e della Segretaria Generale dal 1923 al 1943, file 821-4, ASMAE.
67. Ibid.
68. Piero Parini, speech given in Buenos Aires, December 24, 1931, appearing in *Il Giornale d'Italia*, December 25, 1931.
69. Ibid.
70. Piero Parini, "I problemi delle collettività italiane nel sud-america," *Il Legionario*, February 20, 1932.
71. Ibid.
72. Ibid.
73. Parini to Achille Starace, March 16, 1932; Parini to Grandi, March 16, 1932; Le Carte del Gabinetto del Ministro e della Segretaria Generale dal 1923 al 1943, file 819, ASMAE.
74. Ibid.
75. Livio Sposito, *Mal d'avventura* (Milan: Sperling and Kupfer, 2002).
76. Ibid.
77. Pignatti to Foreign Ministry, February 5, 1931, Argentina, Inventario della Serie Affari Politici (1931–1945), file 3, ASMAE.
78. Scarzella emphasizes instead Valdani's role in the newspaper in *Fascisti in Sud America*.
79. "Parole Serene agli italiani dell'Argentina," *Il Legionario*, January 11, 1930.
80. "Giudizi romani che ci riguardano," *La Patria degli Italiani*, January 13, 1930.
81. "Peccati di orgoglio, "*Il Legionario*, January 25, 1930.
82. Telegrams from Pignatti to the Foreign Ministry from July through December 1931, Argentina, Inventario della Serie Affari Politici (1931–1945), file 3, ASMAE.
83. Pignatti to Foreign Ministry, December 16, 1931, Argentina, Inventario della Serie Affari Politici (1931–1945), file 3, ASMAE.
84. Parini to Pellegrino Ghighi, November 19, 1931, Le Carte del Gabinetto del Ministro e della Segretaria Generale dal 1923 al 1943, file 821-4, ASMAE.
85. Pantaleone Sergi, "Fascismo e antifascismo nella stampa italiana in Argentina: Cosí fu spenta 'la Patria degli Italiani,'" *Altreitalie* 42 (2007): 4–44, details the last days of *La Patria* and its conflict with *Il Mattino d'Italia*. The perspective of the Italian community on this affair will be explored in detail in chapter 5.
86. Italian Embassy in Buenos Aires to Parini, August 31, 1932, Argentina, Inventario della Serie Affari Politici (1931–1945), file 3, ASMAE.
87. Italian Ambassador to Foreign Ministry, December 19, 1944, Argentina, Inventario della Serie Affari Politici (1931–1945), file 40, ASAME.
88. Michele Intaglietta to Vittorio Valdani, March 30, 1934, Buenos Aires, Ministero della Cultura Popolare (hereafter cites in notes as Minculpop) Direzione Servizi della Propaganda, file 4, ACS.
89. Ibid., sheet 3.
90. Ibid., sheet 4.
91. Ibid.
92. Ibid.
93. Italian Ambassador to Foreign Ministry, December 19, 1944, Argentina, Inventario della Serie Affari Politici (1931–1945), file 40, ASAME.
94. Scarzanella, *Fascisti in Sud America*, 160. These figures are also found on page 6 of Michele Intaglietta's aforementioned report to Valdani, March 30, 1934, Buenos Aires, Minculpop Direzione Servizi della Propaganda, file 4, ACS.

95. An interesting analysis of these responses is found in Camilla Cattarulla, "Cosa direste a Mussolini se aveste occasione di parlargli? Un inchiesta de 'Il Mattino d'Italia,'" in Scarzanella, *Fascisti in Sud America*, 175–203.

96. Comisión Investigadora de Actividades Anti-Argentinas, box 22.3–23.2, record 15, Archivo del Congreso de la Nación (ACN).

97. Vanni Blengino, "La marcia su Buenos Aires ('Il Mattino d'Italia')," in Scarzanella, *Fascisti in Sud America*, 205–34, examines the contributions to *Il Mattino d'Italia* of these Argentine nationalist intellectuals.

98. Intaglietta to Valdani, March 30, 1934, Buenos Aires, Minculpop Direzione Servizi della Propaganda, file 4, sheet 8, ACS.

99. See Finchelstein, *Transatlantic Fascism*, for an examination of the relationship between the Roma Press and the Argentine Right.

100. Italian Embassy in Buenos Aires to Foreign Ministry, April 10, 1934, Minculpop Direzione Servizi della Propaganda, file 4, ACS.

101. Milani to Eugenio Coselschi, January 2, 1935, Minculpop Direzione Servizi della Propaganda, file 4, ACS.

102. "Elenco degli articoli preparati da questa direzione generale in lingua spanuola e publicati nella stampa sud-americana, per intessamento della 'Roma Press,' durante el mes di gennaio," Minculpop Direzione Servizi della Propaganda, file 4, ACS.

103. Milani, "Relazione della Roma Press per il trimestre luglio-agosto-settembre," October 1936, Minculpop Direzione Servizi della Propaganda, file 4, ACS.

104. Milani to Ciano, April 12, 1934, Minculpop Direzione Servizi della Propaganda, file 4, ACS.

105. Milani to Ministry of Press and Propaganda, December 15, 1936, Minculpop Direzione Servizi della Propaganda, file 4, ACS.

106. Milani, "Relazione della Roma Press per il trimestre luglio-agosto-settembre," October 1936, Minculpop Direzione Servizi della Propaganda, file 4, ACS.

107. Ministry of Popular Culture, "Appunto per la direzione generale per la stampa all'estero," August 26, 1937, Minculpop Direzione Servizi della Propaganda, file 8, ACS.

108. Direzione Generale per i Servizi della Propaganda to Luce, March 8, 1938, Minculpop Direzione Servizi della Propaganda, file 8, ACS.

109. Mussolini to Italian embassies, November 5, 1928, Le Carte del Gabinetto del Ministro e della Segretaria Generale dal 1923 al 1943, file 821-4, ASMAE.

110. Grandi to Mussolini, Parini to Italian embassies and Balilla, undated, 1932, Le Carte del Gabinetto del Ministro e della Segretaria Generale dal 1923 al 1943, file 821-4, ASMAE.

111. Ibid.

112. Parini, "Appunto per S.E. Capo del Governo," August 26, 1934, Le Carte del Gabinetto del Ministro e della Segretaria Generale dal 1923 al 1943, file 820, ASMAE. For an analysis of the overall experience of the regime's summer camps and other youth activities for Italian children abroad, see Pretelli, *Fascismo e gli italiani*.

113. *Il Legionario* photos 1936–1939.

114. Ibid.

115. Antonio Garaviglia to Mussolini, November 16, 1933, and "Appunto per il Gabinetto di SE Ministro," January 9, 1934, Le Carte del Gabinetto del Ministro e della Segretaria Generale dal 1923 al 1943, file 820, ASMAE.

116. "Le Colonie Estive Italiane nel Sud-America," *Il Legionario*, April 15, 1935.

117. Ibid.

118. Italian embassy, Buenos Aires, to Ministry of Foreign Affairs, "Crociera Sud Americana dell'ONB per Anno XV," September 1, 1937, Argentina, Inventario della Serie Affari Politici (1931–1945), file 18, ASMAE.

119. Martin to Foreign Ministry, Inventario della Serie Affari Politici (1919–1930), file 807, ASMAE.

120. See, for example, Luigi Bakunin, Secretary of the Fasci of Cordoba, to the Secretary General, June 8, 1935, Archivio Scuole (1929–1935), file 779, ASMAE.

121. Marco Pluviano and Irene Guerrini, "L'Opera Nazionale Dopolavoro in Sud America," *Studi Emigrazione* 32, no. 119 (1995): 518–37.

122. Pignatti to the Foreign Ministry, January 23, 1931, Argentina, Inventario della Serie Affari Politici (1931–1945), file 3, ASMAE. There are also numerous reports on Dopolavoro events in the pages of *Il Legionario*.

123. Felice Felicioni to Mussolini, "Relazione del Presidente della Società Nazionale 'Dante Alighieri,'" January 1934, Minculpop, Gabinetto, file 91, ACS.

124. Letter of Torquato di Tela, April 23, 1937, Inventario degli Archivi Microfilmati delle Associazioni Italiane in Argentina, role 89, ASMAE.

125. The work of the Nuova Dante Alighieri will be examined in depth in chapter 5.

126. I mention the Argentine government's reaction here to illustrate the importance of the schools. I examine the issue of Argentina's response to the schools and the regimes' other initiatives at length in chapter 6.

127. R. Consul, Cordoba to Foreign Minister, March 6, 1930, Archivio Scuole (1929–1935), file 779, ASMAE.

128. Bruno Gemelli, Italian Consul Rosario di Santa Fe, "Relazione scuole provincia di Santa Fe 1928," July 13, 1929, Archivio Scuole (1929–1935), file 780, ASMAE.

129. Executive Committee of Pro-Schola Buenos Aires to the Ministry of Foreign Affairs, April 4, 1922, Archivio Scuole (1923–1928), file 634, ASMAE.

130. Consul in Cordoba to Foreign Minister, March 6, 1930, Archivio Scuole (1929–1935), file 779, ASMAE.

131. Tonucci to Parini, "Relazione del Ufficcio Personale," Rome, March 29, 1932, Archivio Scuole (1929–1935), file 776, ASMAE.

132. Dino Grandi to R. R. Agents, "Circolare Riservata," undated, Archivio Scuole (1929–1935), file 776, ASMAE.

133. Paolo de Simone, R. Consul in La Plata, to Foreign Minister, May 13, 1933, Archivio Scuole (1929–1935), file 779, ASMAE.

134. Consul in Mendoza to Italian Ambassador, Buenos Aires, January 22, 1932, Archivio Scuole (1929–1935), file 778, ASMAE.

135. Augusto Torelli to Ciro Trablaza, May 17, 1924, Le Carte del Gabinetto del Ministero e della Segretaria Generale dal 1923 al 1943, file 624, ASMAE.

136. The Scholastic Commission Pro-Schola to Ambassador Count Aldovarndi Marescotti di Viano, April 29, 1925, Archivio Scuole (1923–1928), file 634, ASMAE.

137. Torelli to Trabalza, September 11, 1924, Archivio Scuole (1923–1928), file 634, ASMAE.

138. The antifascist movement in Argentina and its other forms of resistance to the regime's initiatives will be further explored in chapter 5. R. Consul in La Plata Romolo Bertuccioli, February 12, 1930, Archivio Scuole (1929–1935), file 780, ASMAE.

139. Un Vecchio Socio, "Le scuole italiane non Fascistizzate," *L'Italia del Popolo*, December 8, 1932.

140. Italian Ambassador in Buenos Aires to Foreign Ministry, "Instituzioni scolastiche in Argentina," Buenos Aires, October 21, 1939, DGRC Archivio Scuole (1936–1945), file 58, ASMAE.

141. Comisión Investigadora de Actividades Antiargentinas, *Despacho e informe*, Buenos Aires, 1942.

Chapter Four

An Italian National Identity in Argentina

Covered in dust in the basement files of the Archivo del Congreso de la Nación in Buenos Aires, in the midst of evidence for the Congressional Investigation on Anti-Argentine Activities, lies a curious little book. It is a pocket-sized handbook on how to be a good Italian fascist abroad, and but one of many striking examples of a wide range of books and other materials that articulate the messages underlying all of the Italian regime's activities in Argentina.[1] From Luce films and radio broadcasts to books, lectures, and exhibits, much of this propaganda offers highly suggestive, albeit fragmentary, glimpses at the content of the regime's overall project abroad. These materials promoted all aspects of the regime, everything from highlighting the great cultural achievements of Italian civilization and celebrating the new Italy renovated by fascism to defending the regime's wars in Ethiopia and Spain and proclaiming fascism's universal struggle against liberalism and bolshevism.

Throughout all of the material, one theme predominated over the others: that of spreading the Italian national project abroad. This was especially the case in the materials targeting Italian immigrants in Argentina, which attempted to instill devotion to the *patria* by extolling the virtues as well as the privileges of being an "Italian living abroad." The propaganda further contended that emigrants were still an integral part of the Italian nation and could play an invaluable role in the "New Italy" of the fascist era. These materials help us answer the question of how a nation defines its identity abroad. They allow us to analyze how the content of a national project changes when it is exported to another nation-state. Some of these changes were authored by the regime themselves in other cases the new Argentine context in which the Italian national project arrived altered the meaning of that content.

A useful way to understand how these national messages are received differently in Argentina is to think of the Italian national propaganda as a form of culture being consumed in Argentina. As David Forgacs has explained, "the term cultural consumption may be used not only for products that are 'cultural' in the narrow sense of the word (paintings, music, television programmes, etc.) but also more broadly for the consumption of symbols or meanings of the most diverse kinds."[2] The way in which that culture is consumed, the meanings that it is ascribed, and the ability to contest or critique its messages depend on the consumer's socioeconomic and educational background. Another key variant, especially for this study, is the location where the consumer lives along with the cultural assumptions of that society.[3] For example, an American television sitcom when viewed in Latin America or the Middle East will take on entirely different meanings than its producers back in the United States had intended. As with other forms of cultural consumption, Italy's national project abroad looks different and is embedded with different meaning when it is viewed within Argentina.

Among the varied types of propaganda materials sent to Argentina, one of the clearest articulations of the Italian national project is found in the textbooks of the Scuole Italiane all'Estero adopted by the schools in Argentina. These works targeted the children of Italian emigrants throughout the world between the ages of six to twelve and consisted in a five-year program of elementary study. The textbooks were a standard series distributed to the Italian schools in Argentina as well other countries. These textbooks provide a glimpse into the Italian national project abroad, while the lesson plans, curricula, and Italian consular reports from each of the major Italian schools in Argentina illustrate how the Italian fascist teachers used that content to nationalize the children of Italians living in Argentina.

There is a growing interest among historians in the field on the fascist regime's textbooks in the context of indoctrinating Italian children abroad with an ideology similar to the one the regime was teaching at home.[4] Historians who have examined the content of the Italian schools abroad have identified many of the textbooks' defining themes, including preserving Italian language and culture, resisting assimilation, nostalgia for the homeland, pride in Italy's cultural heritage, and of course, support and devotion to Mussolini and the fascist regime.[5] When examined in an Argentine context, however, these themes are reshaped and take on different meanings once they come in contact and compete with Argentina's own national themes. Beyond describing the content of these textbooks and the school curricula within Argentina, this chapter focuses on the implications that this content had on the Italian national discourse within Argentina and, more generally, what these differences tell us about the changing dynamics of a state-sponsored national identity when that identity is being instilled inside of another nation-state.

As a close reading of the textbooks will demonstrate, the national project as it was expressed in Argentina represented a fundamentally different concept of the Italian nation and national belonging than both its program at home as well as it program in other national settings. In some instances the changes to the messages were made by members of the regime in a conscious effort to tailor their national project to the Italian experience in Argentina. In other cases, the simple act of presenting the same national text but to a different audience in a different context changed its meaning.[6] What is a patriotic program designed to inspire loyalty to the state in one context becomes a seditious agenda undercutting loyalty to a state in another context. Argentine responses to the Italian national discourse examined here would in fact confirm the treacherous character of a national project when it operates within another state's national context.

PROPAGANDA'S MANY VARIED FORMS

Propaganda materials sent by the Ministry of Press and Propaganda and later the Ministry of Popular Culture cast a wide net, targeting not only the Italian community but also the Argentine general public. Everything from Italian fascist magazines to Luce newsreels and feature films found their way into the South American republic. Journal subscriptions requested by the Italian embassy for the purpose of propaganda included *Rassegna Italiana, Gerarchia, Nuova Antologia, Il Diritto del Lavoro, Biografia Fascista,* and *Il Legionario*—in short, official journals of the regime's cultural, social, and political programs.[7] The embassy also ordered several books and pamphlets on fascist doctrine and the regime's accomplishments, for example, *Lo Stato Corporativo* and *La Dottrina del Fascismo* by Benito Mussolini, and works by various authors on the "new" Italian worker, the Opera Nazionale Dopolavoro, fascist youth and the Balilla, the social work of the Assistenza e Previdenza, and the role of women under fascism and the "protection" of motherhood and childhood. The embassy requested between one hundred and five hundred copies of each book, both in the original Italian as well as in Spanish translation.[8]

In addition to regular shipments of Luce newsreels, some 129 propaganda films were also sent to Argentina, including titles such as *Camicia Nera* and *Marcia su Roma*, depicting the fascist "revolution"; *Alle Madri d'Italia* and *Per la Protezione della Stripe*, on the subject of motherhood and childbearing; and *Decennalia*, celebrating the accomplishments of the regime's first ten years. The most popular films, judging by the number of times requested and places shown, depicted Italy's First World War victory; titles included *La Diana del Piave, Guerra Nostra,* and *Vittorio Veneto*.[9] According to the director of the Alianza Cinematográfica Italo-Argentina, these films were the most effective form of propaganda, completing the dual function of "correcting the false impressions foreigners have of our *patria* and its regime, while also igniting a greater love of the *patria* in the hearts of the millions of Italian residents here, who can now take pride in being children of a great mother, who has restored them to their proper place in the world."[10] These films were shown in Dopolavoro centers throughout Argentina and were also made available to commercial movie theatres.[11]

For much of the 1930s, propaganda requests to Rome from the Italian embassy emphasized the need for cultural rather than overtly political propaganda for Argentine public consumption. The failure of the Fasci all'Estero's political activism of the 1920s, along with the adverse reactions that the blatant Nazi propaganda campaign was provoking in the 1930s, convinced the representatives of the regime that the best strategy was to win people over through cultural propaganda, only later working in the political message. In discussing the diffusion of propaganda on the Argentine radio waves, the Italian ambassador explained, "To make our propaganda the most effective, and to have the greatest possibility of penetrating the community, it must be of an artistic-cultural nature." Over time, "the political message would appear as a direct corollary, a spontaneous and natural outgrowth of the cultural."[12] Along these lines, the Italian embassy told Rome to tone down the political propaganda sent to the Argentine press, suggesting instead variety pieces, "like for example, Marconi, or Argentine celebrities in our country, or anything about soccer." Other propaganda items for the general public included news on arts and leisure, Italian aviation and navigation, celebrity gossip, archaeological discoveries, and religious festivals.[13]

Beyond the more general goal of creating a favorable view of the regime and its actions abroad, a significant amount of material specifically targeted the Italian community. The goal underlying this effort was to promote Mussolini's national project abroad in order to attract community support for the fascist regime and direct participation in its efforts. Throughout the 1930s, Piero Parini offered glimpses of his interpretation of the regime's national mission abroad in speeches, articles, and interviews in fascist periodicals. Included as evidence of anti-Argentine activities, Parini's 1937 pocket manual *Norme di vita fascista all'estero* was the most final and complete articulation of how he ultimately defined the Italian national identity abroad. It is a handbook on the life an Italian fascist must lead while living in foreign lands.[14]

No longer the forgotten humble laborer of the past, the new Italian abroad, Parini proclaimed, was now the proud member of a "superior civilization."[15] According to Parini, Mussolini, the man "who in his infallible genius has ensured Italy's triumph in the world," remade the Italian emigrant in his image: "Mussolini, the first Italian abroad, has given the Italian abroad his unmistakable features."[16] To Parini, Italians abroad were an "aristocracy," the heirs and custodians of Italian culture: "every Italian must remember that they have flowing through their veins the blood of a race that has given the world the greatest civilization under the sun."[17] Their birthright was, however, only an invitation to become Italian; to be a true Italian abroad was a privilege that had to be earned, a choice that one had to make.

If Mussolini and the fascist revolution gave the Italian abroad a new sense of pride, these Italians now had an obligation to serve the regime and earn the new honor and respect bestowed upon them. "Italy in the name of her living and her dead commands you to be worthy to love her, honor her, and serve her with all of your heart in peace and in war, now and forever!"[18] To be an Italian abroad meant to live the fascist lifestyle and believe in the values of the regime: "Mussolini's Italian who lives beyond Italy's borders is like all of the Italians living inside of the kingdom: he is a citizen, a soldier, and a worker; his personal life must be a model and a mirror of the traditional values perfected and refined by the Fascist education."[19] In short, "he must make the foreigner say in admiration: Here are the Italians of Mussolini!"[20] Parini further commanded Italians abroad to identify themselves first and foremost as Italians, speak Italian, and forget their regional divisions, thinking only of the "nation, the regime, and the family."[21]

Parini's pamphlet also exposes the inherent tension that continued to exist within the regime's program abroad, namely, the entanglement of fascism's internationalist political agenda with its national project. For although Parini reiterated Mussolini's command to abstain from the politics of host countries, he went on to explain that "fascism is not spiritually neutral: it must be on one side of the barricade or the other. The modern world is polarized by two political and religious conceptions of social, national, individual life: there can never be an agreement or truce between fascism and bolshevism."[22] Therefore, according to Parini, "wherever the Bolshevik menace threatens religious principles and political systems similar to those of fascism, the Italian abroad must collaborate, honestly and frankly, to defend those principles."[23] This line is but another example of how the regime conflated being Italian with supporting fascism. It actually undercuts the rest of the pamphlet's national agenda, which highlights instead the importance of the Italian race, civilization, and language.

Taken together, Parini's instructions to Italians abroad encapsulate many of the defining features of fascist Italy's concept of the Italian national identity abroad. What are common features of most national projects at home—

for example, loyalty and devotion to the nation and speaking the national language—take on a radical new meaning when exported abroad since following these instructions necessarily means resisting the national culture of the host nation. The fact that this national identity must operate outside of the confines of the nation also explains why Parini defined that identity as participatory. As Parini explained, one must actively strive to become an Italian abroad and maintain and defend that identity in a hostile environment where the natural inclination is to assimilate. That Parini's Italian abroad is by nature fascist adds an additional ideational component to how the regime defined its national identity abroad. More than just an ethnic-racial conceptualization, to be an Italian abroad additionally meant sharing values and ideals of the fascist political movement.

Argentine investigators underlined in red a passage on page seventeen of Parini's pamphlet. The investigators must have considered it to be especially important since it is the only underlined passage in the book. The passage describes the fascist regime's "vast network of institutions abroad, from the Case Italiane to the Scuole all'Estero."[24] It was in fact the Italian schools that seemed to threaten Argentina's national sovereignty the most.[25] Like national projects within a nation-state, success depended on the state's ability to instill its national identity on the next generation. Parini did not simply target Italian emigrants; he went after their children as well.

All of the features of the fascist Italian national project abroad outlined in Parini's manual were in fact incorporated into the schoolbooks sent to the Italian elementary schools in Argentina. In commissioning these books, the Direzione degli Italiani all'Estero e Scuole (DIES) laid out the goals and agenda that the texts were to promote. They were to "fully adhere to the spirit and actions of the regime" and serve as "secure bulwarks in the conservation and defense of Italian identity around the world."[26] Given the varied locations in which these texts would be used, this posed an especially difficult challenge because they were told not "to offend the political and religious sensibilities of the [foreign] states."[27] This is in fact a very problematic directive since the very project of promoting a national project inside another nation-state could not, by definition, avoid offending the host nations. Prominent contributors to the textbooks included the historian Gioacchino Volpe and the regime's most prized modernist artist, Mario Sironi, while the bulk of the elementary school primers were authored by Giuseppe Fanciulli and Clementina Bagagli, with illustrations by Angelo della Torre. Published from 1929 to 1934, these texts were sent by the DIES both to schools in Argentina directly run by the Italian government as well as to other schools there that taught Italian.[28]

For any nation, school textbooks, especially those funded by the government, provide an excellent opportunity to examine how a state articulates its national project as well as how it attempts to instill this patriotic vision on its young citizens. A close analysis of these Italian texts abroad highlights the peculiarities of Mussolini's national project in Argentina. In celebrating Italian holidays, pledging allegiance and devotion to the nation, and recounting a patriotic narrative of Italian history, these books shared much in common with other nation's educational projects—that is, with one significant difference, namely that these books were used in schools operated in other nation-states and competed with alternative national narratives. The foreign Argentine context in which this national narrative was articulated led to a number of alterations to that project, alterations that do nothing less than recast Italy's national identity. For example, the Italian identity expressed in the fascist literature in Argentina is participatory; implied in the textbooks is that young students must actively *become* Italian, choosing Italy over the country in which they are living. At home the nation-state does not have to compete with other national projects for the hearts and minds of its young, and youth are not asked to choose one nation over another. They are simply born and raised into one. Furthermore, removed from its ethnic-cultural national context, the national identity abroad expressed by the regime is actually much more ideational than the one expressed at home in that to be an Italian means to believe in and share the values of the Italian fascist regime. This concept of a national project actually does not look that dissimilar to New World national projects, which have always relied on a shared set of ideals more that an ethno-cultural identity.

The actual national imagery and symbolism used by the regime in the construction of that national project also take on new and at times conflicting meanings when projected into an Argentine public space. Evidence of this alternative conceptualization of Italian national identity is most striking in the schoolbooks directed toward first and second graders in Argentina. These books wasted little time unveiling their national project to students. Patriotic messages interspersed throughout the textbooks are present in colorful drawings of city and country life, the Italian names of animals, and the retelling of popular fables. One such drawing depicts a young boy embracing a map of Italy and declaring, "Italy, my land, I love you very much! We all love you!" while another describing King Victor Emmanuel III declares, "Long live the King of Italy! Long live my king!"[29] These messages, on the surface seemingly innocent and benign, actually had quite subversive implications. Even though these children are living and in most cases were born in Argentina, the textbooks are telling them that their true loyalty is to Italy, "my land," and to Victor Emmanuel, "my king." In other words, despite their place of birth, they were Italian first and foremost and must love and be loyal to their Italian *patria*. No mention is made of being loyal to their new Argentine nation.

When first grade students turned to page forty-four of their reader, they found the drawing of a six-year old boy, dressed in a Balilla uniform giving a fascist salute. The text reads: "God help Italy now and forever. Help me, O Lord, become a good Italian."[30] A short passage and simple image, but filled with meaning. The passage implies a participatory sense of identity: one was not simply born an Italian but by his actions made the conscious decision to "become" one. Furthermore, the image accompanying the text makes unmistakably clear that being a good Italian meant being a good fascist. This passage and many others like it demonstrate that the fascist writers were attempting something far different from simply fostering a nostalgic love for the distant *patria*. Despite the inconvenient fact that these students were living in Argentina, they are told that they should identify themselves as Italians, and as Italians they were obligated to faithfully obey and support the fascist regime. It is upon this identification of fascism with Italian national identity that the regime's entire project rested. This perhaps explains why from a very early age, implicitly as well as explicitly, these works associated the two identities.

One of the implications, whether intended or not, of this conflation of Italian national identity with fascism is that it was not enough to simply be ethnically or culturally Italian, although that was without a doubt also a requirement. Children instead must additionally identify with and embody the values of the regime in order to be considered Italian. These values included discipline, obedience, self-sacrifice, and most of all, love and devotion to the distant *patria* and allegiance to fascism's tenets. "Even you, little Italians far away from the *patria* but closer than others to your father's heart, must work and struggle every day to become better and grow up strong, honest, and hardworking: to become Italians worthy of our great *patria*."[31] The first and second grade texts emphasize that to be an Italian abroad meant to be obedient and disciplined. The children in the books always knew their "place" and always "did their duty." The second grade text explains that a good child must learn to obey in order to be able to command. Self-disciplined, he must "command his mouth to be quiet when told; command his ears to listen to his mommy and his teacher; and command his eyes to focus on his work and studies."[32] Even the girls, "who are not as strong as the boys," were disciplined and understood how to obey commands, "completing difficult exercises without ever tiring or complaining."[33]

On page eighty-nine of the first grade reader, the image of Il Duce's austere face made its appearance, with the text reading, "All Italian children love Mussolini, the Duce who leads the New Italy and works tirelessly for the good of the *patria*."[34] And Mussolini in turn loved all children: "He loves them because children are the most beautiful hope for Italy; if they grow up strong, hardworking, and good, Italy will also be strong, powerful, and happy."[35] No introduction to fascism would be complete without the Duce, and by the printing of these texts the cult of Mussolini as the embodiment of the Italian nation had become a well-established trope in the propaganda. His life had already achieved mythological status, and the texts made a point of identifying Mussolini with all Italians at home and abroad.[36]

Both the first and second grade textbooks also introduced children to the symbolism and ideology of the regime midway through the books by describing Italy's official symbol: the fascist bundle. "*Il fascio littorio* is the symbol of fascist Italy. The united and tied rods signify concord, union, and love. The axe signifies courage and strength. Under this symbol unified and disciplined Italians work for the greatness of the *patria*."[37] To be a member of the *patria*, you must be disciplined and obedient to the regime, for there is no room for discord in the New Italy. The second grade reader expanded upon this definition of the *fasci*, asking, in an attempt at the philosophical, "What could be weaker than a thin reed that meekly bends with the slightest breeze? But many reeds tightly tied together form a strong *fascio* as tough as steel."[38] In its simplistic way, this passage alluded to the idea of the anti-individualist corporate state, so common in fascist propaganda, for "only the union and harmony of all citizens creates the strength and power of a people. For this reason the fascist bundle was chosen as the symbol of the new Italy."[39] This discussion of the *fascio* also suggested that, more than a mere political regime, fascism *was* Italy's ideological and moral system, which shaped an Italian's life and informed one's worldview. The *fascio* must by extension be accepted an integral Italian national symbol.[40] The *fascio* is, however, a perfect example of a symbol whose meaning can be contested when outside of its national context. In Argentina, as in other New World republics, the *fascio* is instead associated with the republican traditions emerging from the French Revolution. What is an almost innocuous symbol of the fascist dictatorship within Italy is not necessarily the case in another national context.

To become Italian, the texts exhorted children to join the Balilla, Italy's fascist youth organization. For example, one of the young protagonists of the second grade reader, Mimmo, "signed up to become a Balilla . . . but Mimmo knows that to be a true Balilla it is not enough to just wear the uniform and march in step with the other children. He knows that a Balilla, even when he is not wearing the uniform, is a small soldier of Italy."[41] Even at six years of age, the message was clear: youth should be devoted to becoming Italy's soldiers of tomorrow. When they are old enough, they will be able to go to Italy to serve in the Italian army, just like Mimmo's friend Aldo, "who is happy and smiling. He will go across the mountains and over the seas to Italy to become a soldier for two years."[42] Of the many passages on this theme within the texts, perhaps the most revealing is a song written by Giuseppe Fanciulli, found in a first grade songbook specifically for children abroad, titled "The Little Soldiers." The lyrics of this song did not simply depict Italian children as the future soldiers of Italy, but instead specifically targeted Italian children abroad, calling on them to serve the nation.[43]

After learning the basic values and requirements to becoming good Italians abroad, the children were now ready to play a role in the New Italy. The idea of a boy's patriotic duty to serve in the military is fundamental to all state-sponsored educational systems since the nineteenth century. However, in the case of the schools in Argentina, this is problematic. While the children reading the books may or may not have been Italian citizens, many were certainly Argentine citizens and obligated to serve in Argentina's military. The textbooks needed to explain why the children should serve in their Italian rather than Argentine *patria*. The fact that they do not in any way address this issue not only weakens its appeal to the children, it also further highlights the subversive nature of its project within Argentina.

The more advanced texts for the third, fourth, and fifth grades expanded upon the themes of Italians abroad as part of the *patria* and the obligation of Italians abroad to devote their lives to the regime. "More glorious pages in the history of Italy are still yet to be written, other goals are still to be conquered," concluded the third grade history text. "It is on you, children, the soldiers and citizens of tomorrow, to write these pages and accomplish those goals. Italy looks lovingly upon you, wants you, and waits for you."[44] This appeal further reminds children that it is not enough to call themselves Italian. They must choose to actively participate in that national identity.

In *Sole d'Italia*, the fifth grade reader, Parini retold the history of Rome's founding, highlighting his readership's connection to Rome's glorious past. According to Parini, this connection in blood and in spirit to their Roman ancestry came in turn with an obligation to return to the new fascist Rome.

> I want to teach you a motto in Latin that should become the motto of all young Italians abroad, so dear to the Duce's heart. The motto is: ROMA REDIT—REDI ROMA, which means "Rome returns—Return to Rome." . . . The second part is an invitation to you, young Italians abroad. RETURN TO ROME! Return to the great mother that will protect you and always welcome you in her arms![45]

The message is unequivocal: the children of emigrants, though far away, remained integral to the *patria*; therefore, like their little brethren across the sea, they too had to devote themselves to the *patria* and prepare to fight and struggle for its greatness.

Emigrants were to be as loyal to their *patria* as they were hardworking. "Emigrants live very different lives, but they all share one thing in common: a desperate love for the distant Patria."[46] Aware that these Italians were not living within the national territory, the textbooks indicate that to be an Italian abroad meant that they had to actively defend their nationality from any other national project in its way. As if to will it so, textbooks depicted Italian emigrant communities as bastions of the Italian nation abroad: "Italians [abroad], save for rare exceptions, never adapt, never lose their national characteristics, never change their customs, and never feel alone or isolated in a foreign land."[47] For rather than assimilating, emigrants remained Italian and remained as much a part of Italian national life as if they were in Italy. For according to these texts, the nation where they lived was not consequential, a fact that would most certainly not be missed by Argentine authorities reading these texts.

Short exemplary stories of Italians abroad expressing their deep devotion to the *patria* abound in the school texts. "Una Canzone Gratis," found in Orazio Pedrazzi's *I nostri fratelli lontani*, is perhaps the most obvious of these tales. It is the story of three Italian immigrants living in New York who came to America when they were young children but whose "love of their country never diminished in their hearts."[48] In 1915 they answered the *patria*'s call to arms and prepared to depart for Italy. Fearful that they might "die in exile" if their ship sank before reaching their beloved homeland, they approached the great tenor Enrico Caruso and asked him to sing some Neapolitan songs for them before they departed, so that, "if we must die, it would be as if we had spent one day in Naples."[49] Moved to tears by the young men's love of country, Caruso agreed to give them a special free performance. On that night he performed the greatest concert of his life. In the end, only one of the young men saw Italy again, for tragically, right as they approached the Bay of Naples, their ship was torpedoed.[50] This example of heroism by Italian immigrants who volunteered to fight for the *patria* in the Great War was the image of choice to the fascist writers, at once demonstrating courage and martial valor as well as a love of the distant *patria*.

Unlike most domestic national projects, the authors of these books were aware that their national project had to compete with other national projects. While still in school and living in a foreign land, children, the schoolbooks instructed, were to choose Italy over those other national projects and resist at all costs being corrupted by foreign national agendas. The story of a young Italian boy forced to attend a French school in Tunisia, also found in *I nostri fratelli lontani* best captures this theme. Threatened by the strong Italian presence in their colony and disturbed by the great success of the Italian schools, sinister French officials shut down the schools. "What did the French think?" asked the author. "They believed that Italian children were weak and would easily abandon their *patria* in order to become French." For the French, like other foreign governments around the world, "want to forcefully remove our children's Italian spirit and convert them into foreigners, to make them forget the glories of their country, the memories of their fathers, the language of their parents, the sweet memory of their distant land, to make them bastardized strangers."[51] But the Italian school children remained steadfast and defiant, vowing "to remain Italian at all costs."[52] The young protagonist of the story was quiet and disdainfully proud, only responding to his new French teacher when necessary. Then one day, after the teacher read aloud a passage from a French geography book that insulted the *patria*, calling it a land of poverty and criminals, the boy could stand no more and exploded: "And we are supposed to study these books, and learn this filthy slander about our country!" he declared, throwing the book at the teacher's head.[53] Just short of explicitly instructing students to challenge their host nations' authority, this tale sent a clear signal that they were duty bound to protect and defend the good name of Italy by resisting any form of assimilation and foreign indoctrination. It is a wonderfully ironic message since the Italian schools abroad had a national agenda no less propagandistic than the one so criticized in the story. The Italian agenda within Argentina was in fact even more insidious since, unlike the French in Tunisia, it was being promoted outside of its political jurisdiction.

The same Giuseppe Fanciulli, the author of the fascist songbook discussed above, also penned a two-volume work on religious instruction, a virtual gospel according to fascism.[54] Linking religion with the state, he declared that "the true Christian is not a slave to pleasure and material interests; he is loyal, devoted to his family, and ready to serve the *patria* with all of his strength."[55] Fanciulli also manipulated passages from the Bible and lives of saints to reinforce obedience to the Italian nation. To fascists, "Render unto Caesar that which is Caesar's" meant that it was Jesus' command to loyally obey the "new" Roman Empire; and Saint Paul's letter to the Romans reminded students that "all authority comes from God, and the existing authorities are instituted by him. Anyone who rebels against authority is resisting a divine institution." Lest the message of obedience not be clear, Fanciulli went on to tell his young readers that "the true Christian knows that pain is necessary, as is suffering, but not rebellion."[56] Of course, this did not mean obedience to just *any* civil authority, for obedience was reserved for the *patria* and its institutions. It is a distinction driven home by the fascist exposition of the Fourth Commandment: "Honor thy mother and father. Following this commandment means that beyond our mothers and fathers we must also love, respect, and obey *our superiors*, which in our religious life means the pope, the bishop, and the priest; and in our civil life means the king, the head of the government, and all who represent them."[57] Notice that this quote makes no mention of honoring and obeying the civil authority of whichever country the young reader lives in, but instead specifically says to be loyal to King Victor Emmanuel III; the head of government, which was Mussolini's official title; and all who represented them—in other words, members of the Italian regime. Although Christian teachings have often been used to teach obedience to secular power, few in the modern era explicitly equated devotion to the state with devotion to God. It is also especially rare to find an exhortation to obey the secular authorities of a nation different from the one in which the reader was living. This is significant. By commanding children in Argentina to obey the authorities of Italy rather than those of Argentina, the Italian fascists were themselves violating Saint Paul's command.

Fanciulli went on to explain that the true Christian was "the best son, the best brother, the best soldier, the best citizen."[58] It could not have been otherwise since "the soldier of Christ is also the perfect soldier of the *patria* in times of peace and times of war."[59] Fanciulli went so far as to compare joining the Italian army to being confirmed a Christian. "Every faith, every great idea, has need of soldiers." Confirmation initiated "soldiers of Christ" ready to defend Jesus' "celestial *patria*," just as the youth of Italy trained, learned to follow military orders, and "arm[ed] themselves to defend the *patria* and offer to sacrifice their lives."[60] Discipline, obedience, and self-sacrifice thus were the gospel according to the Italian regime, with the Christian message of peace and love lost in fascist bellicosity.

"His great heart," Fanciulli wrote of Saint Francis, "while it longed for the celestial *patria*, also beat with love for the terrestrial *patria*."[61] From Saint Benedict to Saint John Bosco, the texts also used the lives of the saints to promote the Italian agenda. Not the humble servants of God with whom we may be familiar, the fascist versions of the saints were marked by a "will" to achieve great things. Bold and audacious, their will to achieve made them the "holiest of all saints," as well as apostles of the *patria*. As Mussolini himself explained in his entry for Saint Francis in a fifth grade text, "The followers of Saint Francis were both missionaries of Christ and missionaries of Italian-ness. . . . Where we find the splendid and humble works accomplished in the name of the saint we find there the mark of our *patria*."[62] Along with Saint Francis, Catherine of Siena "devoted herself to both the Church and the *patria*," never mind that the Italian nation as such did not exist in her age. The texts also recognized John Bosco's Salesian brothers, who ran many of the schools in Argentina, for their work promoting Italian-ness abroad, and for serving the *patria* as much as God.[63] Not only were the greatest saints of the Church Italian, but since to be Italian necessarily meant to be a fascist, these saints also embodied the values of the fascist regime.[64] Taken together, the religious messages of these books in fact tell us much about the national liturgy of the fascist regime, one of history's most striking examples of the abuse of sacred imagery to promote a secular agenda. To them, to be a good Christian meant you must also be a good Italian and, therefore, a good fascist: obedient, disciplined, and willing to fight and die for your distant country.

As is true of many state-sponsored national programs, the schoolbooks abroad also manipulated Italy's national narrative to promote their concept of the Italian nation. In these works, the fascist regime was at once a return to the glory of ancient Rome and the consummation of the virtues of the Risorgimento. Of Rome's rise to greatness Parini wrote, "Those poor peasants and shepherds who lived along the banks of the Tiber were men of will. They were strong and courageous in battle and had a will of steel that sustained their daring. The secret of their fortune and the immortality of Rome lies in that small word: *will*."[65] Two thousand years later, the will to power and courage to achieve returned to Italy in the person of Il Duce, since "Mussolini's will is a Roman's will, and fascism signifies the return of Rome."[66] Rome's heritage becomes another example of a contested national image when read in Argentina's national space. Many nations have identified themselves as the spiritual heirs of Rome's past glory. The problem with ancient Rome as a national icon is that it is can be, and has been, co-opted by many different nations and political movements. In many significant ways, all of Western civilization can lay legitimate claim to Rome. For example, both France and Britain had already identified their empires with imperial Rome.[67] More significantly, the Roman Republic served as a model for all of the New World democracies that came out of the enlightenment. Such was the case with Argentina. Argentina's own national narrative, rather than highlighting Roman imperialism, identified instead with Rome's republican political virtues, the cornerstone of modern democracy.

Next to Rome, the Risorgimento and its heroes figured prominently in this Italian national narrative. The young readers did not, however, learn about Mazzini's republican ideals or Garibaldi's concern for the poor and downtrodden. Instead, they read of daring individuals who sacrificed themselves for the nation. Visionaries, these heroes died before seeing the culmination of their great endeavor, which was only truly completed by the fascist "revolution," referred to by Volpe as "the New Risorgimento." Accordingly, fascist squads were a new Giovine Italia, filled with the same youthful enthusiasm of Mazzini's movement. Aware of his sacred role in completing the Risorgimento, Mussolini took on the mantel of Garibaldi, solemnly proclaiming that "the Blackshirts are continuing and perfecting the work of the Redshirts."[68] Garibaldi in particular is a problematic icon for fascism's national project since he is also a key figure in Argentina's own national narrative. Garibaldi's struggle for justice against tyranny in the Pampas is an alternative and equally compelling image of the "Hero of Two Worlds." As will be shown, the fascist image of Garibaldi described here simply would not resonate as well as its competing Argentine image in the Italian community.

The First World War, as fascism's foundational myth, of course occupied an inordinate amount of space in just about all of the texts. Schoolbooks devoted entire chapters to First World War martyrs, all of whom before their deaths movingly declared their love for the *patria*. Nazario Sauro's letter to his wife and child before facing an Austrian firing squad was the most often cited example of martyr prose. To his wife he wrote, "I die happy to have done my duty as an Italian. . . . Teach our children that their father was an Italian first, then a father, and then a citizen," and to his son he wrote, "Swear in the name of the Patria . . . that you will always be Italian, no matter where you go and above all else."[69] This last line, "no matter where you go," is of special importance as a message to the children in the schools in Argentina. It was a voice from the grave reminding them that, however far away they may be, they were still Italians. Tailoring their work to schools abroad, the authors made clear that Italians emigrants also did their patriotic duty during the war and could participate fully in the devotion to First World War martyrs and pay homage to the tomb of the Unknown Soldier, a soldier who according to Gioacchino Volpe may have even been born in the Americas and, if so, was no less an Italian than if he had been born in Italy, since "he carries the name of all soldiers living and dead." And "Honoring him means honoring all those who fought and suffered in the war."[70] Even the first and second grade readers introduced their students to the sacrifices made by their fathers during the Great War. Students read about the "Altar of the Patria" and learned that scars were "glorious badges of honor carried by your fathers who fought heroically for the *patria*, as you too will someday."[71] In fact, as early as the second grade, students were told of their obligation to become Italians worthy of the First World War's great martyrs.[72]

In describing the fascist movement and seizure of power, schoolbooks abroad blamed the liberal regime and socialist "subversives" for ruining the fruits of Italy's victory. For Volpe, the fascists were not a motley group of disaffected youths and war veterans who used violence and intimidation to destabilize the countryside, but instead the heroic movement of the Italian nation itself led by Italy's "greatest sons."[73] According to the narrative, the fascists not only validated the great patriotic sacrifices of the World War I martyrs but were joined by the spirits of the fallen comrades in their movement to save the nation: "It was as if the living and the dead returned to live together and the living listened to the words of the dead."[74] In other words, fascism had transcended party politics and became the nation itself: "Soon Italy was redirected toward the ideals that had inspired our martyrs, and Italy and fascism became one and the same."[75] No longer just a struggle against subversives, it was now a national struggle against "the Italians of disorder, of forgetfulness, of cowardice: the fight against Italians who no longer want to be Italians."[76] By equating fascism with Italian identity, these passages again made explicit that only the true Italian was a fascist. The myth of the so-called mutilated victory, that the war was won in the trenches by the soldiers but lost by the liberal regime at the peace conference, was one of the most effective and enduring tropes of the fascist regime in Italy, as was fascism's co-optation of Italy's victory in the war.[77] Outside of Italy, however, that narrative was not in the mainstream. The war and its destruction dominated the international press, so much so that it inspired the founding of the League of Nations and a number of international peace accords. This is but another example of a narrative being read differently when operating within a contested space in which it must compete with alternative narratives.

Mussolini's bold and decisive March on Rome was, of course, how the historical narratives explained his seizure of power. No mention was made of the political power-brokering arrangement that actually occurred before the so-called march, and the king was not the indecisive and ambivalent monarch who acquiesced to Mussolini's appointment, but instead, "[seeing] in the Blackshirts the strength that would save Italy, [he] called on Mussolini and entrusted him with the government."[78] As Volpe's work concludes, "After the March on Rome, the people now have the freedom to work and enjoy the fruits of their labor, to worship God publicly, to celebrate the victory, to feel Italian."[79]

In addition to the battle of the grain, protection of maternity, public works, and youth programs, the third grade text emphasized the fascist regime's special work abroad: protecting and honoring the millions of Italians living in other countries.[80] For as Parini himself declared in another text, "Il Duce watches over all Italians, and no one is closer to the Duce than you who seem so far away"[81] No longer abandoned to their fates, these emigrants, textbooks announced, under the fascist regime, were now considered an integral part of the Italian nation.[82] Much more than simply celebrating the accomplishments of Italian emigrants, these texts reincorporated them into Italy's national project. In the words of Volpe, "Their work has served others and has served Italy."[83] The schoolbooks depicted Italian emigrants as muscular, daring, and disciplined soldiers of labor rather than impoverished workers in search of a better life. One such illustration, titled "Emigration," showed a column of powerfully built men plowing a field, with helmets on their heads and rifles over their shoulders; another showed an Italian emigrant standing on top of the world, flanked by an eagle, driving a shovel deep into the globe.[84] Italians abroad were soldiers conquering the world in the name of the *patria* with their labor.[85] The work of Italian immigrants in Argentina figured prominently in these sections. One text declared that if a map was drawn indicating Italian labor, "all of Argentina from Chaco to the Tierra del Fuego, from the Andes to the River Plate, would be painted in a color that the key would indicate represents: The Work of Italians!"[86] The not-so-subtle implication here is that Argentina was more Italian than perhaps any other nation in the hemisphere.

Just as Italians within Italy worked for the greater good of the *patria*, Mussolini "wants Italians living abroad to participate with the rest of us, sharing the labor and the pains and the joys of other Italians, so that everyone will be tied together into one strong *fascio*."[87] The schools abroad have educated them well and allowed them to participate in the glories of the new Rome. In return, they had to defend the *patria* and it institutions abroad while preparing themselves for the return home when called to arms. With youth and the molding of a new generation of Italians central to the regime's education initiative, no ink was spared in exhorting young Italians abroad to follow the Duce. "You are the dawn of life, you are the hope of the *patria*, above all else the army of tomorrow."[88]

Taken together, the fascist textbooks sent abroad articulated a clear nationalization program, one that focused on redefining Italian identity to incorporate Italian emigrants and their children within the orbit of Italy. Evidence from the Italian embassy in Buenos Aires, the Argentine Department of Education, and later the Commission on Anti-Argentine Activities all confirm that the texts discussed above were sent to many of the schools in Argentina. The question still remains how these texts were adapted to the situations on the ground and to what extent each of the Italian schools in Argentina incorporated the fascist Italian message into their lessons.

ITALY'S NATIONAL PROJECT IN THE ITALIAN SCHOOLS IN ARGENTINA

In spreading this fascist Italian national identity through the schools a delicate balance had to be struck so as not to offend host government officials, whose approval was necessary to ensure the prestige of schools and maintain enrollment, while achieving its mission of promoting a foreign national project within a sovereign state. For this reason Mussolini stressed that "subsidized primary and secondary schools must obtain parity with local government schools, as well as adhere to local rules, laws, and requirements so that their degrees will be recognized and of equal value to those of the local government."[89] According to Mussolini, this was especially important for the schools in South America, where due to the high number and proportion of Italians living in those nations it was possible for Italian schools to potentially provide the children of Italian immigrants with a complete education to, in the words of Mussolini, "serve not only their practical needs, but no less importantly instill in them the ideals of the distant *patria*."[90] The goals of attaining parity and local government recognition of the schools' diplomas, while at the same time instilling in their students loyalty to Italy, were however inherently contradictory, a contradiction that would ultimately seal the fate of the fascist Italian schools in Argentina.

Although it is impossible to know exactly what went on within the classroom walls, we can get a good sense of how the teachers in these schools attempted to promote the fascist agenda by examining the lesson plans and reports on the schools activities, which were sent both to Rome as well as to the Department of Education in Argentina. What follows below is a brief panorama of the lessons and programs of study from each of the major Italian schools in Argentina, with an analysis of how they did (or did not) incorporate the Italian national project into their schools.

The Italian elementary school XXI Aprile, in the interior city of Mendoza, run by the local Fascio, was perhaps one of the most ideologically driven of the schools in Argentina. Founded in 1932 with a DIES subsidy, the school was originally named the Scuola del Fascio but was renamed the Scuole XXI Aprile in 1934, no doubt to avoid offending Argentine sensibilities by such an overtly political affiliation.[91] The elementary school boasted 180 students in its inaugural year and 250 the following. Connected to the elementary school were two nursery schools with over seventy children and run by six teachers, all members of the Fascio, who volunteered to work without compensation.[92] Described by the consul there as "the first truly Italian school in Mendoza," its mission was one of "intensive cultural and spiritual propaganda."[93] The 1932 arrival of Amarillide Avoli, one of the newly appointed teacher-agents, bolstered the Fasci's initiative. In addition to teaching, Avoli supervised evening programs for adults and Italian after-school activities. The DIES also supplied textbooks as well as fascist uniforms for the students.[94]

While not the largest of the Italian schools, and located some distance from the capital, the school's close affiliation with the Fascist Party and its direct supervision by the DIES make its activities probably the closest semblance of what the regime was attempting to achieve through its educational program in Argentina. Its programs also demonstrate the ever-present tension between achieving equivalency to Argentine government standards and promoting an Italian national agenda. Aware of the difficulty of such a task, Trevisan Ferruccio, the school's principal, in a speech to the community explained, "Everyone must be convinced that the school, which teaches Spanish as well as Italian, is completing the delicate task of rapprochement and Italo-Argentine understanding."[95] To that end, Ferruccio explained that its goal was to instill "unlimited devotion to our *patria* as well as to the Argentine *patria*, indivisible in our thoughts and hearts, bonded by blood, labor, and civilization."[96] The problem is how to show "unlimited" devotion to two different nations: one would have to have priority over the other, and as the school's curricula would show, Italy far overshadowed Argentina.

Unlike the rhetoric for public consumption, the school's curricula and lesson plans, both those sent back to Rome as well as those shown to Argentine inspectors, clearly emphasized a fascist Italian education.[97] "A very large amount of time is given to fascist culture; because the students are so young, the teacher never misses an opportunity to make them feel proud to be Italian and to be grateful that they are able to attend an Italian school."[98] The 1938 report to Rome highlighted its patriotic and fascist mission: "With enthusiasm and energy, not an opportunity is missed by the teacher to make sure that the students are kept abreast of life in the distant *patria*, and of its ever increasing power in all areas thanks to the enlivening impulse of fascism."[99] Daily rituals included the singing of Giovinezza (the Fascist Party anthem) and the Royal March, while important dates on the fascist calendar, such as April 21 (Rome's founding), May 9 (the declaration of the empire in Ethiopia), and May 24 (Italy's entrance into World War I) were observed with parades and solemn ceremonies.[100] From this brief look at the school's activities, it is quite evident that the Italian national agenda ultimately trumped any concern for offending Argentine sensibilities, an emphasis that would not be without consequences by the late 1930s. Argentine government inspectors would, in fact, later use the very same lesson plans as damning evidence in their crackdown on the Italian schools.

The schools established by the Fascio in Mendoza, though small, were of great ideological interest to the regime. The schools in Buenos Aires, however, in terms of both numbers and visibility, were a higher priority. By 1928 the schools run by the Pro-Schola committee reached a low point as the ten original schools were reduced to three and student enrollment dropped to 250. During this period the schools reorganized and came to be dominated by fascists within the community, as the nonfascist associations and contributors withdrew their support. Now under an ideologically more fascist administration, a new Italian subsidy and the arrival of five teacher-agents, armed with the new school books, revitalized the three remaining schools: Margherita di Savoia, Principe Umberto, and Gabriele D'Annunzio.[101] In 1934 the Pro-Schola added a new school, La Boca, named after the city's colorful Italian neighborhood.[102] Under Parini's close supervision, enrollment rose from 259 in 1931 to 1,017 in 1935, peaking at 1,643 students in 1939.[103]

Along with increased enrollment, the teacher-agents attempted to both promote the Italian regime's national project abroad as well as attain Argentine government recognition. In the annual state exams administered by the Argentine Department of Education, over 95 percent of the Italian schools' students passed their exams and were promoted to the next grade. Pro-Schola school reports also highlight the much improved Italian instruction, thanks in large part to the teacher-agents assigned to the schools along with the new subsidies and Italian texts.[104] Many of the schools' students were exposed to fascist propaganda through the Balilla, which had 229 boys enrolled, and the Piccole Italiane, which counted 164 members. During a typical school day, students listened to weekly Italian government radio broadcasts, were given the photographs of fascist "martyrs" to pray for, and observed Italian fascist holidays, October 28 (celebrating the fascist March on Rome), first among them.[105] Although the Argentine school inspectors up until 1938 rated Pro-Schola's overall performance as "satisfactory," the schools' programmatic emphasis on fascist Italy and Italian language instruction over Spanish and the history of Argentina did not go without notice.[106]

The Istituto Medio Italiano of Buenos Aires was perhaps the most important school established in the city during this period. Founded in 1934, the much-awaited Italian secondary school counted sixty-three students in its inaugural year. Vincenzo Tasco, head of the local Fascio, enthusiastically recounted that

> the prestige of the school has already been affirmed; the families of the students are faithfully following us; the students are glowing with enthusiasm; the community is beginning to awaken; one already speaks about the school with satisfaction; there had been many who looked on with indifference, if not hostility, ready perhaps to throw stones, but who have now been won over by the seriousness of our organization. This modest, small school will soon become a great beacon of Italian-ness.[107]

With a less overtly political agenda compared to the elementary school program, the school emphasized the instruction of Italian and Latin language and culture, along with meeting the other secondary school requirements of the Argentine Department of Education. There is no evidence that any of the fascist messages found in the elementary school texts made their way into the secondary school's curriculum. In 1935 the principal of one of the most prestigious Argentine secondary schools, the Colegio Buenos Aires, associated with the University of Buenos Aires, asked the school to provide a special series of courses in Latin and Italian for its own students. This request bolstered the school's quest for prestige, a move that according to the school's director, Professor Zama, "assured our school's fate"; since "[Colegio] Buenos Aires is attended by the children of Argentina's best families, the sympathy and credit that we will attain from this milieu will be of great benefit."[108] Unlike many of the elementary schools being established and reorganized, the Istituto Medio and its accords with the Argentine school was, in Parini's words, "of capital importance," offering the best possibility of influencing the native Argentine community and further expanding Italy's cultural mission.[109]

The experiences of the nearby schools within the province of Buenos Aires, which were under the direct supervision of the Italian Consulate in La Plata, are also indicative of the fascist changes to the Italian school program during the 1930s. Within this jurisdiction, the Italian consulate and the local Fascio established seven new schools. The Scuola Italiana Vittorio Emanuele III in La Plata, the Istituto Culturale Umberto di Savoia in Bahia Blanca, and the Scuola Italiana in Avellaneda were the largest of these schools, each averaging over 150 students per year. In addition to primary education, these schools offered cultural lectures for adults, Balilla and Dopolavoro activities, as well as evening classes in Italian run by members of the local Fascio. Courses were taught in both Spanish and Italian in an attempt to gain Argentine government recognition of the schools' degrees, but an emphasis on fascist Italian national culture was readily apparent. As the principal of the school in La Plata explained, "Of nationalist and fascist propaganda, I can tell you that propaganda is the principle aim of our instruction, which is being slowly, slowly revealed, with tact so as to not irritate the sensibilities of our students, not all of whom are children of Italians."[110]

Although the extent to which these reports accurately reflect what was going on in the classroom cannot be determined, a look at the Scuola Vittorio Emanuele III's program of study at the very least reveals how it attempted to propagate a fascist Italian national agenda. Its curricula for grades one through five included lessons on the regime's accomplishments: "the history of fascism from its origins to the seizure of power," "the new constitutional organs of the Italian state," "the corporative system and the labor charter," "the battle of the grain," "the rural movement," "demographic politics and the protection of maternity and infancy," and "the youth movement and the Dopolavoro." Other topics in the curricula were tailored to the experience of the regime abroad, stressing the organization and mission of the Fascist Party abroad and the importance of Italians living around the world.[111]

By 1938, as Argentine government officials began to suspect the school's political mission, topics related to Argentina were carefully mixed into "patriotic education" lesson plans. Within these lessons, however, focus on the Italian regime remained unapologetically preeminent. The third grade curriculum, for example, began with a discussion of Argentina and its heroes, followed by a discussion of "our heroes" and the greatness of Rome, and concluded with a discussion of the great "salvation" of the Italian nation: the Duce. As the teacher explained, "I try by all means possible to complete the mission that I have been assigned: to instill in the children a great love for Italy, and a great love for our DUCE; I teach them to always trust in the DUCE's motto "Persevere to succeed" because He has always trusted in this motto and He has always won."[112] In his evaluation of how students responded to such teaching, the Consul of La Plata observed that "the children have demonstrated an exact knowledge of the work of the regime. . . . In simple and spontaneous remarks they have expressed affectionate admiration of the *patria* of their parents. . . . In the hearts and minds of these children is a vast and disciplined Italy that is making great strides under the guidance of the Duce."[113] By 1937 the principal of the school in La Plata boasted an enrollment of over 250 students, filling the school to capacity and managing to fully incorporate the school's texts into the curriculum while simultaneously obtaining Argentine governmental recognition of the school's degrees.[114]

At the southern end of the province of Buenos Aires in the city of Bahia Blanca, the regime took under its control another new school, Umberto di Savoia, established by the Italo-Argentine Institute of Culture. With a smaller and less affluent Italian population compared to La Plata, the teachers of this school had a much harder time attracting students and implementing the new Italian curriculum. Andrea Di Silvestri, one of the fascist teacher-agents who closely collaborated with the local Fascio, increased the school's enrollment from 30 in 1934 to 141 students by 1937.[115] In attempting at integrating the texts sent from the DIES into its program, Di Silvestri remarked that he tried his best to instill "a knowledge of the history, the glory, the beauty of our *patria*, and of fascist achievements; in a word, to strengthen [the students'] conscious of Italian-ness."[116] The Italian community of Bahia Blanca, however, was largely indifferent and unsupportive of the school's initiatives. Di Silvestri reported to Rome that pessimism, ignorance, fear, and assimilation were to blame for low enrollment.[117] To gain more support, Di Silvestri developed programs to reach out into the community and improve the regime's image among the local inhabitants. To this end, he projected monthly newsreel films from Italy as part of an after-school program and offered evening lectures open to the public on topics that included "the sociological work of fascism," "the ideals of the fascist youth," "Mussolini and his victory over time and man," "the spirit of Rome in the new Fascist Empire," and "new generations of Italians."[118] The school also invited guest speakers from Buenos Aires, such as the author Arturo Isnaldi, who lectured on "Italy, the cradle of Latin-ness and creator of modern thought."[119] By 1937 Di Silvestri reported that thanks to the active support of the DIES and the local Fascio, the school had made exceptional progress given the "moral and material difficulties" that the situation in Bahia Blanca presented, imploring the DIES "not to lose faith in the future of this far-away little school, where everyone is working in the name of Italy and the Duce."[120]

The Italian regime encountered even more problems attempting to establish a school in the province of Cordoba, northwest of Buenos Aires. As late as 1933, no school had been established, though the prospect of one was much debated. According to a local Italian teacher, with residents who were second- or even third-generation Argentines, "The establishment of a purely Italian school would be a moral, intellectual, and material fiasco. *Moral* because the students and parents of the students would never renounce their love and patriotic feelings toward Argentina."[121] An agent sent by the Italian ambassador in Buenos Aires argued instead that it was in fact *only* through the establishment of an Italian school that, "we could stop the process of spiritual submersion that little by little is subduing the Italians who have long resided here. [Through the schools] we could correct false impressions and rescue many souls that in a few more years will be irredeemably lost for our cause."[122] Such words capture perfectly the conviction of many fascists that assimilation was a process that could be reversed almost by mere force of will. The Italian consulate did establish a school in Cordoba, by 1939 counting 180 students. However, it never enjoyed the success or prestige of the other regions, as reports from the consulate often noted its poor organization, lack of funding, and sparse community support.[123]

"The dwarf has been transformed into a giant!" commented Rosario's schools director in 1932 on the development of one of the most important Italian schools in Argentina: the Scuola Dante Alighieri of Rosario.[124] The six schools run by the Società Nazionale Dante Alighieri in Rosario de Santa Fé became a model of success. In his report on the schools' activities, the Italian consul, Bruno Gemelli, boasted impressive results. With a teaching staff that was "disciplined, concerned with self-improvement, obedient, and always attentive to its mission . . . the number of students registered, in attendance, and being promoted is clear evidence that the school is in full development and on the rise, thanks to the teachers and the DIES." Gemelli argued that these schools "served their mission well," citing that it was one of few private foreign schools to have nearly all students in the fourth, fifth, and sixth grades levels pass the Argentine certification exams and advance on to higher Argentine education. Most importantly, teachers of these schools "not only teach the specified material, but also organize lectures and conferences to reawaken within the students and their relatives who participate in the gatherings affection and admiration for our great *patria.*"[125] With the infusion of a forty thousand lire government subsidy and the arrival of five teacher-agents, enrollment steadily increased throughout the 1930s, peaking at 669 registered students in 1937, with 553 students enrolled in its after-school programs.[126]

The Dante Alighieri school of Rosario emphasized much of the same Italian propaganda as the other schools: celebrating fascist holidays, coordinating fascist youth sections, as well as showcasing the achievements of the fascist regime. The teachers in Rosario sought to integrate fascist Italian political propaganda across its curriculum.[127] Fourth grade students read and discussed a passage that focused on the themes of "God, the *patria*, the family, the Italian family in the *patria* and abroad in the thoughts and desires of Mussolini."[128] In religion class, after discussing the Ten Commandments, the teacher moved on to the topic of "a young fascist's education. The values of strength and goodness, and the Duce's love of all Italian children: those near and those far away." For a recitation course, the students recited the "Ten Commandments of the Balilla," which closed with the command to "thank God every day that he has made you an Italian and a fascist."[129] The curricula from Rosario also emphasize the regime's importance to Italians living in Argentina. In discussing the Roman Empire, a fourth grade lesson stresses the commonality of "Latin peoples" throughout the world who are the "proud descendents of Rome," while a geography lesson highlighted the "exclusive" role of Italians in the settlement and development of Argentina.[130] Most importantly of all, lessons stressed the regime's renewed interest in Italians living abroad: "For Italians abroad, Rome has returned to its imperial glory, returned with the rumble of Italian motors on land, sea, and air, to bring its light to its distant children, filling their hearts with pride and profound love for the distant *patria*."[131]

The teachers of Rosario also used the students themselves as vehicles of the regime's national project to the wider community through the publication of a school magazine, *La Scuola Viva*. Poetry and writings supposedly from the students themselves expressed love for the *patria* and the fascist regime. Take, for example, "La Bandiera," written by a fifth grader:

> How beautiful the Italian flag is! When I see it I salute it, holding my cap in respect because I remember my distant *patria*. On May 24 the Italian flag along with that of Argentina waved above the school's balcony. Upon leaving I asked my mother to buy me an Italian flag and she agreed. I came home, ran straight to my room, and placed it in the middle of a flower vase. I am happy to be Italian, and my flag will always fly in my house.[132]

Another student memorialized the death of three fascist aviators who had "conquered new triumphs for Italy," commenting that the news of their deaths "left a painful impression in the distant *patria*, and also in Italians who live far from the native soil. . . . As an Italian, I follow with love and pride the happy events of my country, while I am also moved emotionally by its misfortunes."[133]

By the late 1930s, as the Italian regime was receiving increasingly bad press in Argentine newspapers for both the Ethiopian War and the Spanish Civil War, the teachers in Rosario instituted class discussions geared toward current events. Students discussed and translated into Italian the articles, which were then "clarified" and put in the perspective of "Fascism's Idea, which must give humanity a new direction." The teacher then instructed students to go home and explain to their families and friends how to interpret the current events.[134]

The teachers of each of the schools claimed that they were careful to adapt their programs to the schools' Argentine context in order to ensure enrollment and government recognition. These attempts, however, were clumsy and disingenuous, and even in the best of cases could not mask entirely the underlying Italian national agenda. In just about every case, some version of the fascist national message was incorporated into the school's activities. As will be later shown, this fascist-patriotic agenda, however diluted or disguised by its other programs, would eventually be viewed by Argentine school inspectors as a dangerous violation of their national sovereignty.

CONCLUSION

Taken as a whole, the Italian propaganda in Argentina sought not only to instill the ideals of fascism and loyalty to the *patria*; its goal was nothing short of creating a new Italian person abroad who adapted to life outside of the *patria*. This "Italian abroad" was to be strong and courageous, desperately devoted to the *patria*—the distant *patria* that he longed for, that he hoped to make proud, that he was willing to die for. This nationalization project was especially pronounced in the textbooks and curricula of the Scuole Italiane all'Estero found within Argentina. These books attempted to nationalize the children of Italian immigrants in Argentina, reincorporating them into the Italian nation by instilling in them the values and ideals of the New Italy.

This nationalization project, however, entered a contested national space when it crossed into Argentina. Its discourse on the Italian nation did not have the hegemonic power it enjoyed back in Italy, where children were forced to study with the state school system and were not, at least publicly, exposed to alternative national narratives. Instead, within Argentina this national narrative was but one of many within the Italian Argentine public sphere. Many members of the Italian community in Argentina would not accept fascism's claims over Italian identity and challenged the fascist propaganda, revealing their own conceptualization of their Italian national identity as well as their place in Argentine society. The Argentine government similarly would not sit by and allow the regime to continually promote an agenda that threatened to undermine its own national and political identities. It was only a matter of time before Argentine authorities would recognize the seditious nature of this propaganda and have the fascist regime's organizations shut down.

NOTES

1. The book was Piero Parini's *Norme di vita fascista all'estero* (Verona: A. Mondadori, 1937). It will be analyzed below.
2. David Forgacs, "Cultural Consumption, 1940s to 1990s," in *Italian Cultural Studies: An Introduction* ed. David Forgacs and Robert Lumley (New York: Oxford University Press, 1996), 273.
3. Ibid., 274.
4. Three historians have examined the Scuole Italiane all'Estero, during the fascist period. Giorgio Floriani, *Scuole italiane all'estero: Cento anni di storia* (Rome: A. Armando Editore, 1974), provides a general history that analyses the changing laws and decrees during the schools' history without examining the schools' content or experiences in individual countries. Claudia Baldoli, *Exporting Fascism: Italian Fascists and Britain's Italians in the 1930s* (Oxford: Berg 2003), and "I Fasci italiani all'estero e l'educazione degli italiani in Gran Bretagna (1932–1934)," *Studi Emigrazione* 36, no. 134 (1999): 243–81, both study the experiences of fascist-era Italian schools in Great Britain. Baldoli makes similar use of the Scuole Italiane

all'Estero archival records, and her arguments parallel my own, but for the case of Great Britain. Most recently, Matteo Pretelli, *Il fascismo e gli italiani all'estero* (Bologna: Clueb, 2010), also includes a chapter on fascist youth organizations and the Scuole Italiani all'Estero throughout the world. Also see his work for another analysis of the content of the school textbooks sent abroad with a focus on the school's curricula in the United States. For the education program in Italy, see Emilio Gentile, *The Sacralization of Politics in Fascist Italy* (Cambridge, MA: Harvard University Press, 1996), and Tracy H. Koon, *Believe, Obey, Fight: Political Socialization of Youth in Fascist Italy, 1922–1943* (Chapel Hill: University of North Carolina Press, 1985), 74–83.

5. Two works that have specifically dealt with these themes within the schools abroad are Baldoli, *Exporting Fascism*, and Pretelli, *Il fascismo e gli italiani all'estero*.

6. In analyzing the content and scope of fascist Italy's national project through the textual and visual analysis of its propaganda abroad, this chapter is informed by recent cultural approaches Italian fascism. Ruth Ben-Ghiat, *Fascist Modernities: Italy, 1922–1945* (Berkeley: University of California Press, 2001), for example, uses modernist cultural productions in film and literature to understand how intellectuals under fascism created and articulated fascist identities, while Claudio Fogu, *The Historic Imaginary: Politics of History in Fascist Italy* (Toronto: University of Toronto Press, 2003), focuses on fascist representations of history communicated through exhibitions and media, as does Emily Braun with the visuals arts in "The Visual Arts: Modernism and Fascism," in *Liberal and Fascist Italy: 1900–1945*, ed. Adrian Lyttelton, 196–215 (Oxford: Oxford University Press, 2002).

7. Italian Embassy in Buenos Aires to the Ministry of Popular Culture, December 19, 1937, Ministero della Cultura Popolare (hereafter cited in notes as Minculpop) Direzione Servizi della Propaganda, file 7, Archivio Centrale dello Stato (hereafter cited in notes as ACS).

8. Italian Embassy in Buenos Aires, various book orders, Minculpop Direzione Servizi della Propaganda, file 7, ACS.

9. Raffaele Mancini to Mussolini, "Memoriale su un progetto di lavoro per l'affermazione della cinematografia italiana in Argentina," Minculpop Direzione Servizi della Propaganda, file 4, ACS.

10. Ibid.

11. Film shipments found in Minculpop Direzione Generale Propaganda, Nuclei di propaganda in Italia e all'Estero (NUPIE), file 16, ACS.

12. Italian Embassy in Argentina to Ministry of Popular Culture, "La radio in Argentina possiblità della propaganda italiana," January 1, 1940, Minculpop Reports (1922–1945), file 18, ASC.

13. Arlotta to Foreign Ministry, "Propaganda attraverso la stampa locale," April 28, 1934, Minculpop Direzione Servizi della Propaganda, file 4, ACS. For an excellent analysis of Italian propaganda directed toward Argentines with a focus on Argentine nationalism, see Federico Finchelstein, *Transatlantic Fascism: Ideology, Violence, and the Sacred in Argentina and Italy, 1919–1945* (Durham, NC: Duke University Press, 2010).

14. , Parini, *Norme di vita fascista all'estero*. Although the pamphlet is only attributed to "Segreteria generale dei fasci all'estero," based on the writing style and content of the document, I am confident in Parini's authorship. Matteo Pretelli in *Il fascismo e gli italiani all'estero* identifies this work as one of the key texts produced by the Direzione degli Italiani all'Estero.

15. Parini, *Norme di vita fascista all'estero*, 22.
16. Ibid., 29.
17. Ibid.
18. Ibid., 35.
19. Ibid., 15.
20. Ibid., 14.
21. Ibid., 21.
22. Ibid., 12.
23. Ibid., 13.
24. Ibid., 17.
25. The Argentine investigation will be discussed in detail in chapter 6.

26. DIES Undersecretary of Schools to Parini, June 6, 1930, Le Carte del Gabinetto del Ministero e della Segretaria Generale dal 1923 al 1943, file 821-4, Archivio Storico del Ministero degli Affari Esteri (hereafter cited in notes as ASMAE).
27. Ibid.
28. "Le nostre scuole d'oltre confine," *Diritti della Scuola*, Rome, July 15, 1933.
29. Clemetina Bagagli, ed., *Letture classe prima: Scuole italiane all'estero* (Rome: Librería dello Stato, 1933), 21, 41.
30. Ibid., 44.
31. Clementina Bagagli, ed., *Letture classe seconda: Scuole italiane all'estero* (Rome: Librería dello Stato, 1932), 91.
32. Ibid., 16–17.
33. Ibid., 106.
34. Bagagli, *Letture classe prima*, 89.
35. Ibid.
36. Bagagli, *Letture classe seconda*, 91.
37. Bagagli, *Letture classe prima*, 88.
38. Bagagli, *Letture classe seconda*, 89.
39. Ibid.
40. This interpretation is informed by the works of Emilio Gentile, including *The Sacralization of Politics in Fascist Italy*.
41. Bagagli, *Letture classe seconda*, 95.
42. Bagagli, *Letture classe prima*, 36.
43. Giuseppe Fanciulli, *Canzoncine italiane* (Rome: Librería dello Stato, 1931), 15–17.
44. Scuole italiane all'estero, *Il libro della III classe elementare: Storia, geografia, aritmetica* (Verona: A. Mondadori, 1933), 87.
45. Piero Parini, "Roma Ritorna—Ritorna a Roma," in Scuole Italiane all'Estero, *Sole d'Italia: Letture Classe V* (Rome: Librería dello Stato, 1934), 48.
46. Orazio Pedrazzi, *I nostri fratelli lontani* (Rome: Segreteria Generale dei Fasci all'Estero, 1929), 12.
47. Ibid., 63.
48. Ibid., 66.
49. Ibid., 68.
50. Ibid., 69.
51. Ibid., 19.
52. Ibid., 20.
53. Ibid., 23–24.
54. This treatment of religion and spiritual devotion confirms Gentile's characterization of fascism as a political religion that borrowed freely from Christian religious imagery and ritual. See Gentile, *Sacralization of Politics*.
55. Fanciulli, *Letture di religione per le Scuole Elementare Italiane all'Estero*, vol. 2 (Verona: A. Mondadori, 1934), 153.
56. Ibid.
57. Ibid., 30–31.
58. Ibid., 154.
59. Ibid., 85.
60. Ibid., 84.
61. Ibid., 121.
62. Benito Mussolini, "San Francesco," in Scuole Italiane all'Estero, *Sole d'Italia*, 79.
63. Fanciulli, *Letture di religione*, 147.
64. Parini, "Prefazione," in Scuole Italiane all'Estero, *Sole d'Italia*.
65. Parini, "Roma Ritorna—Ritorna a Roma," in Scuole Italiane all'Estero, *Sole d'Italia*, 48.
66. Ibid.
67. Adrian Lyttelton, "Creating a National Past: History, Myth, and Image in the Risorgimento," in *Making and Remaking Italy: The Cultivation of National Identity around the Risorgimento*, ed. Albert Russell Ascoli and Krystyna Von Henneberg (Oxford: Berg, 2001), 31-44.

68. Gioacchino Volpe, *I fatti degli Italiani e dell'Italia: Letture storiche*, Scuole Italiane all'Estero (Verona: A. Mondadori, 1932), 334. The expanded second edition of Volpe's history is titled *Il Risorgimento dell'Italia* (Rome: Direzione Italiane all'Estero, 1934).

69. Nazario Sauro, "Testimento," in Scuole Italiane all'Estero, *Sole d'Italia, 72*; Scuole Italiane all'Estero, *Il libro della III classe elementare*, 72.

70. Volpe, *I fatti degli Italiani*, 321.

71. Ibid.

72. Ibid., 18.

73. Ibid., 325.

74. Ibid., 321.

75. Scuole Italiane all'Estero, *Il libro della III classe elementare*, 84.

76. Volpe, *I fatti degli Italiani*, 320.

77. See James H. Burgywn, *The Legend of the Mutilated Victory: Italy, the Great War, and the Paris Peace Conference, 1915–1919* (Westport, CT: Greenword Press, 1992).

78. Scuole Italiane all'Estero, *Il libro della III classe elementare*, 86.

79. Volpe, *I fatti degli Italiani*, 327.

80. Scuole Italiane all'Estero, *Il libro della III classe elementare*, 87.

81. Piero Parini, "Prefazione," in Scuole Italiane all'Estero, *Sole d'Italia*.

82. Scuole Italiane all'Estero, *Storia e geografia per la IV classe elementare* (Verona: A. Mondadori, 1938), 213.

83. Volpe, *I fatti degli Italiani*, 269–72.

84. Pedrazzi, *I nostri fratelli lontani*, cover and p. 8.

85. Scuole Italiane all'Estero, *Storia e geografia*, 213.

86. Luigi Barzini, "Il lavoro italiano nell'Argentina," in Scuole Italiane all'Estero, *Sole d'Italia*, 187.

87. Volpe, *I fatti degli Italiani*, 353.

88. Benito Mussolini, "Ai giovani avanguardisti," in Scuole Italiane all'Estero, *Sole d'Italia*, 130.

89. Benito Mussolini, "Scuole sussidite, Istruzione Circolare no. 1 riservatissima," Rome, January 10, 1925, Archivio Scuole (1923–1928), file 634, ASMAE.

90. Ibid.

91. Piero Balducci, Fasci Italiane in Mendoza, to Orazio Laorca, Italian Consul in Mendoza, December 12, 1934, Archivio Scuole (1929–1935), file 780, ASMAE.

92. R. Consul in Mendoza to Parini, June 20, 1932, Archivio Scuole (1929–1935), file 778, ASMAE.

93. R. Consul in Mendoza to Parini, March 1933, Archivio Scuole (1929–1935), file 778, ASMAE.

94. Trevisan Ferruccio, "Relazione della Scuola Italiana XXI Aprile," March 1, 1938, DGRC Archivio Scuole (1936–1945), file 58, ASMAE.

95. Ibid.

96. Ibid.

97. Lesson plans sent by the fascist Italian schools to Argentine state inspectors, although lacking some of the fascist bravado found in the reports to Rome, did clearly place emphasis on subject matter related to fascist Italy. See, for example, "Programa," sent by Silvia Doglia of the Pro-Schola to the Argentine Inspector General of Private Schools on July 3, 1939, Fondo del Ministerio de Educación, 1939:28, Archivo General de la Nación Intermedios (hereafter sited in notes as AGNI).

98. Avoli, "Relazione finale della Scuola Italiana 'XXI Aprile' in Mendoza," 1936, DGRC Archivio Scuole (1936–1945), file 57, ASMAE.

99. Avoli to DIES, June 22, 1938, DGRC Archivio Scuole (1936–1945), file 57, ASMAE.

100. Ibid.

101. Associazione Italian Pro-Schola, "Cenni riassuntivi sull'origine e sull'andamento delle scuole Italiane in Buenos Aires," 1933, Archivio Scuole (1929–1935), file 778, ASMAE.

102. "Gli sviluppi della Pro-Schola e la sua fusione con la Dante Alighieri," *Il Mattino d'Italia*, September 25, 1934; Ambassador in Buenos Aires to Foreign Minister, "Instituzioni Scholastiche in Argentina," October 25, 1939, DGRC Archivio Scuole (1936–1945), file 58, ASMAE.
103. Ibid.
104. Association Pro-Schola, "Relazione Finale," December 30, 1933, Archivio Scuole (1929–1935), file 778, ASMAE.
105. Ibid.
106. Benito F. Vaccarezza, Argentine Inspector General of Private Schools, *Inspeccion general de escuelas particulares da cuenta de los programas de enseñanza del idioma italiano que se imparten en las escuelas dependientes de la asociación italiana Pro-Schola*, "Expediente 15461-I 139," Fondo del Ministerio de Educación, 1939:28, AGNI.
107. Tasco to Parini, May 17, 1935, Archivio Scuole (1929–1935), file 778, ASMAE.
108. Ibid.
109. Parini to Tasco, June 13, 1935, Archivio Scuole (1929–1935), file 778, ASMAE.
110. G. Rosso to Direzione Generale Scuole Italiane all'Estero, La Plata, December 21, 1934, Archivio Scuole (1929–1935), file 779, ASMAE.
111. Vincenzo Cucinetti, "Prima Relazione Scolastica," La Plata, April 21, 1937, DGRC Archivio Scuole (1936–1945), file 57, ASMAE.
112. Irma Traversa, "Programma Particolaregiata della classe terza anno scolastico 1938," La Plata, 1938, DGRC Archivio Scuole (1936–1945), file 57, ASMAE.
113. Consul in La Plata to DIES, December 13, 1939, DGRC Archivio Scuole (1936–1945), file 57, ASMAE.
114. Cucinetti, "Prima Relazione Scolastica," La Plata, April 21, 1937, DGRC Archivio Scuole (1936–1945), file 57, ASMAE.
115. "Bahia Blanca," 1935, DGRC Archivio Scuole (1936–1945), file 58, ASMAE.
116. Ibid.
117. Di Silvestro, Istituto Italo-Argentino di Cultura Umberto di Savoia, "Relazione sul funzionamento delle scuole italiane," May 3, 1937, DGRC Archivio Scuole (1936–1945), file 57, ASMAE.
118. Di Silvestro, "Relazione finale sull'Andamento delle Scuole," December 14, 1937, DGRC Archivio Scuole (1936–1945), file 57, ASMAE.
119. "Gotitas," *El Atlantico*, August 16, 1935.
120. Di Silvestro, May 3, 1937, DGRC Archivio Scuole (1936–1945), file 57, ASMAE.
121. De Navazquez to Raimondo Carbonelli, September 1, 1933, Archivio Scuole (1929–1935), file 779, ASMAE.
122. Ferruccio Agosti to Mario Arlotta, November 13, 1933, Archivio Scuole (1929–1935), file 779, ASMAE.
123. Ambassador in Buenos Aires to Foreign Ministry, "Instituzioni scolastichi in Argentina," October 21, 1939, Buenos Aires; Cesare Afeltra to Foreign Ministry, December 1, 1937, Cordoba, DGRC Archivio Scuole (1936–1945), file 57, ASMAE.
124. Director Società Dante Alighieri in Rosario to Bruno Gemelli, July 25, 1932, Archivio Scuole (1929–1935), file 780, ASMAE.
125. Bruno Gemelli, "Cattedra di Lingua e Letteratura Italiana, Relazione anno 1930," ASMAE, Archivio Scuole (1929-1935) b. 778.
126. Mario Miglietta to DIES, December 31, 1937, DGRC Archivio Scuole (1936–1945), file 58, ASMAE.
127. Director of the Dante Alighieri of Rosario to DIES, December 29, 1931, Archivio Scuole (1929–1935), file 780, ASMAE.
128. "Programma Didattico della Scuola Dante Alighieri, Rosario, 1934," Archivio Scuole 1929–1935, file 780, ASMAE.
129. Ibid.; Scilla de Glauco, ed., *La Nuova Italia* (New York: Nikolas Press, 1939) 101.
130. "Programma Didattico della Scuola Dante Alighieri, Rosario, 1934," Archivio Scuole 1929–1935, file 780, ASMAE.
131. Ibid.

132. Armando Quadrio (3a B.), *La Scuola Viva, Rivista degli Alunni della Scuola "Dante Alighieri" di Rosario* 5, September 1929.

133. Carradori Alfonso (6a Classe), *La Scuola Viva, Rivista degli Alunni della Scuola "Dante Alighieri" di Rosario* 7, April 1931.

134. Mario Miglietta, Scolastic Director in Rosario to DIES, December 31, 1937, DGRC Archivio Scuole (1936–1945), file 58, ASMAE.

Chapter Five

The Nation Abroad Responds

Piero Parini must have been confident after reorganizing the fascist regime's efforts abroad and setting some of Italy's most talented propagandists to work promoting the "New Italy" in Argentina. While he undoubtedly expected some resistance to his efforts from the community, he could not have anticipated the intense debate his efforts would provoke. Both pro- and anti-fascist members of the Italian community actively challenged the new Italian identity abroad that the fascist regime had constructed, engaging instead in their own lively debate over what it meant to be "an Italian living abroad." It was a debate that at once affirmed the existence of an Italian national consciousness in Argentina while at the same time undermined the regime's supposed control over "the nation abroad."

Perhaps the most significant difference between a national project at home compared to one abroad involves the nation-state's ability to control its national discourse. Most successful nations in the modern era have managed to instill from above their version of the national project, which they inculcate through schools, the military, other state institutions, as well as state-sponsored initiatives. Once outside of the nation-state, operating within a relatively free public space, the government has no hegemonic control over its national discourse, leaving it open to be challenged, if not completely reimagined, from below. Unlike with a national project promoted by a government within its borders, the Italian state had no way of controlling how its message was received. Under the fascist regime in Italy, it was difficult to openly challenge the propaganda with which the regime bombarded the public on a daily basis. Argentina, however, was far away from the coercive mechanisms of the nation-state. The missionaries of fascist Italy abroad could only proselytize, unable to force the conversion of Italian communities.

In Argentina and elsewhere, the Italian regime also had to compete with members an international antifascist movement composed of Italian political exiles known as *fuorusciti*. The *fuorusciti* who arrived in Argentina presented the community with an alternative vision of Italian identity, one based on liberty and justice, an identity replete with its own set of symbols, historical myths, and images. Historians who have studied fascism and antifascism in Argentina and elsewhere have done well in highlighting how both the fascists and antifascists created competing definitions of Italian identity in opposition to one another. In each case their political opponents were cast as "anti-Italians," against which "true" Italians were defined. Over the past two decades, historians have in fact focused more and more attention on the Italian community's responses to fascism in Argentina. Historians who have treated this question generally frame their analysis in terms of fascism and antifascism, measuring the extent to which fascism penetrated the community as well as the antifascist response.[1]

The question of Italian national identity in Argentina during the period, however, is much more complex than one of two oppositional systems of Italian identity, fascist and antifascist. Free to accept or reject the propaganda arriving on their shores, members of the community responded to both the fascist and antifascist message by revealing their own original notions of national identity as well as their complex relationships to both Italy and Argentina. By looking at the question of how Italian national identity is conceived of and contested abroad, this chapter breaks down the fascist/antifascist dichotomy. It will show that both pro- and antifascist members of the community created their own notions of the Italian nation abroad that transcended the political debate of the day. The community's various articulations of the Italian nation were fundamentally different from both the fascist and antifascist models and were informed more by the democratic values and beliefs of Argentina's own national narrative.

As Italians continued to advance socially and integrate themselves politically into their new nation, the socioeconomic context of the community in Argentina during the 1930s informed the debate over Italian identity and fascism. For historians of Italian emigration, these social concerns were in fact far more relevant than the politics of the day. Fernando Devoto, for example, after providing a good overview of fascist and antifascist activities in Argentina in his recent history of the community goes on to explain that, "beyond the polemics between fascists and anti-fascists . . . the interwar years were characterized by other phenomena that had more of an effect on the lives of Italians and their descendants."[2] These two concerns were not, however, mutually exclusive. The one influenced the other in the construction of a collective identity, confirming Eric Hobsbawm's contention that "national consciousness cannot be separated from the acquisition of other forms of social of social political consciousness."[3] Ultimately, both the Italian fascists and *fuorusciti* alike would come to realize that Italian identity in Argentina was more complex than either group had imagined. What neither group fully appreciated was the fact that Italian national debate reached the community at a time when Italian immigrants and their children, long excluded from Argentina's national life, were beginning to integrate themselves in their new nation's social and political landscape. In the end, it was the Argentine social-cultural context that would shape the way in which the members of the Italian community formulated their own concept of the Italian nation abroad.

THE ALTERNATIVE ITALY IMAGINED BY FASCIST SUPPORTERS

Many prominent members of the Italian community in Argentina voiced their support for the fascist regime in Italy and identified themselves as fascists, with some more ideologically committed than others. Their understanding of fascism's program was, however, different from that of the regime, as was their concept of Italian identity. Rather than simply accepting the regime's constellation of symbolic national imagery, myths, and historic narrative, those sympathetic to fascism instead attached it to their own existing national iconography. The result was a fundamentally different imagined community based on a distinctive set of national values. Fascism, even within Italy, meant different things to different people depending on their political background, ideological commitment, and motivation for supporting the regime. In this instance, these discrepancies also tell us much about the different values and concerns of Italians living as immigrants in Argentina and go a long way toward explaining why Piero Parini and the Italian embassy had trouble establishing their national programs in the South American republic.[4]

Arsensio Guido Buffarini, the president of the Federazione Generale delle Società Italiane nell'Argentina and self-appointed spokesman for the Italian community, was among the first prominent members of the community to gravitate toward the regime. Born in 1866, Buffarini was a medical doctor who immigrated to Argentina in 1895. An active member of the Italian community from his arrival, Buffarini was a board member of numerous Italian associations and president of the Società Nazionale Dante Alighieri in Buenos Aires from 1917 to 1921. Buffarini's face, sporting his unmistakable gray beard, can be found in just about every photograph of community events. Before the fascist seizure of power, Buffarini long advocated for the defense of Italian culture and the spread of Italian literature, and supported

Italy's First World War effort and Francesco Saverio Nitti's recovery fund after the war. In 1919 Buffarini was named the president of the Federazione, an institution founded in 1912 that regulated the activities of 457 Italian community associations in Argentina and included 260,000 members. Continuing as president throughout the fascist period, Buffarini often voiced his support for the regime's initiatives.[5] He returned regularly to Italy, making much of his audiences with the king and the Duce. During his 1926 visit, Buffarini presented Mussolini with a gold medal from "the Italians of Argentina" in honor of "fascism's great work of national regeneration, from which the emigrant workers of our Latin republic have drawn strength and inspiration."[6] Much to the fascists' dismay, his support for the regime was in fact mostly in the form of symbolic gestures, like dedicating statues in honor of the regime and praising Mussolini's work at community banquets, while doing little of substance.

Lured into the fascist camp by the promise of awards, titles, and recognitions, Buffarini often vied with the regime's representatives for recognition from Rome. Styling himself as an intermediary between the fascist regime and the community, Buffarini saw it as a personal affront when the Italian embassy did not consult with him, while at the same time he tried to promote his own initiatives without the embassy's support. This shameless self-promoting, along with his inability (or unwillingness) to rally the community around the regime, was a source of constant frustration in Rome. Italian Ambassador Count Bonifacio Pignatti described Buffarini in a 1930 telegram to Parini as "one of those people who gravitate around the Italian authorities, but who do not like it when those authorities hinder their penchant for showing off." Referring to Buffarini as "second rate," Parini suggested that the ambassador should not waste time on such individuals.[7] Foreign Ministry notes for Dino Grandi summed up these impressions with the following: "Commendatore Buffarini has been described in numerous reports from the Italian embassy and consulate in Buenos Aires as a very vain person, without much following in the community."[8]

There may be some truth to these fascist characterizations. Proud of his illustrious title of Cavaliere di Gran Croce della Corona d'Italia, Buffarini certainly loved the limelight and was often pictured wearing a chest full of honorary medals and awards. He even had a seven-hundred-page book published in his honor in 1931 that included all of his speeches as well as laudatory newspaper clippings and praise-filled correspondence.[9] Nevertheless, as head of the Federazione, Buffarini was indeed a very influential member of the community, and a look at his speeches and writings suggests that the fascist regime was frustrated by more than just his vanity.

When speaking of Mussolini and the fascist state, Buffarini chose to avoid any discussion of fascist ideology, often simply praising the regime for making Italy a great nation. In 1926 the Argentine daily *La Nación* interviewed Buffarini upon his return from Rome. Reporters asked him if he thought the fascist program was antidemocratic and whether he thought the fascist system could really resolve the problems facing Europe. Avoiding political debate, Buffarini chose instead to simply reply by "expressing his admiration for the resurgence of the kingdom under Mussolini's direction."[10] Maintaining what he described as an "apolitical patriotism," Buffarini directed his Federazione members to follow his lead and put politics aside by supporting whatever government was in power in Italy. He explained, "We must recognize the constituted governments that represent Italy in the presence of other nations, support them, and respect them, because by doing so we are showing our support and respect for Italy."[11] This type of support suggests that Buffarini was not an ideologically committed fascist but instead chose to support the regime only out of what he perceived to be his patriotic duty. Thus while undoubtedly an Italian abroad, Buffarini was not the "new" Italian abroad of the regime since fascism was an integral component to that identity.

Unlike the fascist regime, which aggressively propagandized a fascist Italian national identity abroad, Buffarini supported the regime in hopes that this would enhance the image of Italian immigrants in Argentina. He often stressed the need for Argentine and Italian cooperation and mutual respect, revealing his sense of a dual identity and divided loyalty. "Our organization's work has always been to show love and great tenderness for the distant *patria* as well as affectionate respect for the *patria* that hosts us."[12] After establishing deep roots in Argentina, Buffarini considered it as much his home as Italy. In a 1925 interview for *La Razón*, he admitted as much: "I have lived in Argentina for thirty-one years, and my affection for this county is so strong that when I am in Italy I am dominated by a strong desire to return."[13] Argentina had become for Buffarini a "second *patria*," as valid as his first: "The government of this hospitable country has always recognized our loyalty and the productivity of our labor."[14] Never wavering in his profession of loyalty to Argentina, Buffarini was as anxious to visit with the presidents of Argentina as he was to meet with the Duce, and he delivered speeches at Argentine patriotic celebrations as well as Italian events. Thus while undoubtedly loyal to Italy, Buffarini identified himself as something other than simply an "Italian living abroad." He clearly did not fit the mold of the regime's fascist Italian emigrant, who was supposed to resist assimilation and favor the Italian regime over all others.

Buffarini similarly envisioned Italy's relationship with Argentina as one of mutual exchange rather than of Italian national penetration. Buffarini asserted that both Italy and Argentina were the products of nineteenth-century revolutions and that the labor of Italian workers had made both nations beacons of modern civilization. For Buffarini, this shared history tied the two peoples' national destinies together. It is only by this logic that we can understand why a supposed fascist argued on several occasions that Italy should honor two Argentine patriots: Manuel Belgrano, the son of an Italian merchant and Argentine founding father, and Bartolomé Mitre, an important Argentine liberal statesman and italophile.[15] For Buffarini, the two symbolized Italian influences on the establishment of Argentina's democratic society, a manifestation of the way in which the two peoples shaped one another's national histories. These two historical figures, in Buffarini's mind, were a perfect representation of the mutual respect and admiration between the two peoples. Immaterial to Buffarini was the fact that the two leaders promoted a liberal democratic ideology that the fascist regime vehemently opposed. Such sentiments, undoubtedly shared by many other immigrants within the community, worked at cross-purposes with the regime's agenda. Buffarini strove to integrate Italians into Argentina at a time when the fascists were attempting to preserve and strengthen an Italian identity abroad apart from the host country's nationality. Although Buffarini's support for the regime was undoubtedly welcomed, the nature of that support did very little to advance the regime's more ambitious national program.

Folco Testena, pseudonym of Comunardo Braccialarghe, was another prominent fascist sympathizer within the community who, like Buffarini, often frustrated fascist officials with his own sense of an Italian national identity. Born in 1875 as the son of a militant member of the First International, Testena grew up an anarchist. He immigrated to Argentina in 1906 and began his journalistic career as an editor for *La Patria degli Italiani*. In 1917 he founded the radical republican paper *L'Italia del Popolo*. He was as well known in Argentine literary circles as he was in the Italian-language press. A prolific writer, poet, and translator, he is most famous for his Italian translation of *Martín Fierro*.[16] In the early 1920s Testena converted to fascism, leaving *L'Italia del Popolo* to become the editor-in-chief of another major Italian-language newspaper, *Il Giornale d'Italia*. In 1931 he turned what had been a patriotic-monarchist daily into an expressly profascist paper, declaring that "we will follow with love and care the grandiose political and economic phenomenon that is renovating our country and placing it once again at the head of all nations."[17] Testena also shared the regime's preoccupation with preserving Italian identity in Argentina. He explained, "We want our compatriots to have a greater love and passion for the defense and diffusion of our language and Italian thoughts in this land. . . . We believe that the problem of language, of schools, and of acquiring books is of the utmost importance for us Italians in Argentina."[18] On this issue Testena saw eye to eye with the regime; on many others he would not.

In a series of open letters to Piero Parini during the latter's visit to Argentina from December 1931 to January 1932, Testena harangued Parini and challenged his characterizations of the Italian community in Argentina, openly questioning the wisdom of his strategies while offering the fascist minister unsolicited advice and criticism. These editorials provide invaluable insights into how an Italo-Argentine responded to the fascist propaganda initiative and asserted his own distinct concept of an Italian national identity abroad.

In the first of these letters, Testena criticized Parini's heavy-handed tactics in reorganizing the regime's efforts in Argentina. He suggested that he take better advantage of the existing community organizations rather than importing new ones from Italy.[19] Testena went on to warn Parini that he had thus far been relying on incapable Italian officials and members of the community, "who can only succeed in causing new damage to our name and the Italian culture we want to defend."[20] Fiercely independent and unwilling to follow Mussolini's maxim to "obey without questioning," Testena insisted that Italians were individuals who by their very nature should be free to think for themselves. He responded to Parini's criticism of the Buenos Aires Fascio for its disunity, declaring, "We Italians are the most tenaciously individualist people on the earth. This can be and sometimes is damaging; however, this Italian pride in oneself and consciousness is also beautiful. Without this 'I' we would have never had that glorious and terrible Renaissance, which was only thanks to a miraculous flowering of our individuality."[21] These lines suggest that underlying Testena's critique of Parini's strategy was a fundamentally different concept of Italian national identity.

Testena's Italian national identity abroad was intrinsically democratic in spite of its fascist affiliation. Unwilling to accept Parini's claim that fascism was not compatible with a democratic civil society, Testena responded that "they [Italians in Argentina] have not given their support only because they do not know that democracy is 'a government by the people and for the people' and that the fascist experiment does not change this in substance, only in name and in form."[22] In an odd attempt to reconcile fascism's authoritarian structure with liberal democracy, Testena went on to explain that "the word democracy simply means that one should not be obligated to obey someone else who is without qualifications, without ability, without a right to command."[23] What is interesting here is that Testena is himself openly questioning Parini's authority. Perhaps he thought that Parini was "without right to command," or perhaps, without acknowledging it, he believed in the open debate afforded by a democracy. Even as a fascist sympathizer, Testena's independent stances on a wide array of issues demonstrates an implicit belief in the free exchange of ideas inherent to a democratic public sphere. It is a sign that while many Italo-Argentines chose to identify themselves with the Italian regime, they also considered free expression an important part of their identity as Italians abroad.

"How can Parini claim it to be 'perfectly useless' for fascists and Italians to interest themselves in internal Argentine politics?" Testena asked, "perplexed" by Parini's command for Italians to abstain from local politics.[24] Testena asserted that "it is unquestionably dangerous for Italy and for the

Italians living here to remain completely alienated from this country's public life." Especially since "our commercial development and our salaries depend on political decisions made here, as does the future of our children. . . . Here we have made our hearths, here our children have been born, here everyone has made their fortune or has the hope of making one."[25] For Testena, the unique identity of the Italian community in Argentina should be used to the advantage of the regime. "We Italians in Argentina are something different; in our interests, sympathies, and identity, we are Italo-Argentine."[26] Instead of resisting assimilation, as Parini had commanded, Testena insisted that the Italian community's value to the regime was in fact its assimilation into the Argentine nation since, "in Argentina, no Italian feels like a foreigner. For a German or a Frenchman to interest themselves in Argentine politics could be seen as interfering and would be inopportune, as it would likewise seem for an Italian in transit without any connections to this country."[27] In other words the regime's efforts were entirely misguided. Rather than trying to artificially impose and defend a new Italian identity abroad, the regime should instead use the communities' existing transnational identity as a way of influencing Argentine politics.

According to Testena, it was in fact Parini's disregard for the sociopolitical situation of Italians in Argentina that accounts for the "level of incomprehension" that existed between the community and the fascist regime. Testena went on to suggest that the regime should promote a revolutionary social as well as nationalist agenda that advanced the needs of Italian workers in Argentina. By 1931 Italian fascism was anything but revolutionary, and there is nothing to suggest it would ever consider such a strategy. The fact that Testena would even suggest it is a telling sign that his understanding of fascism was quite different from that of the regime. In highlighting the fascist regime's disregard for the social realities of the Italian immigrants, Testena exposed one of the limitations of a national project outside of the nation-state. With their livelihoods dependent on Argentina, Italian immigrants simply would not support an agenda, nationalist or otherwise, that threatened their socioeconomic well-being.

"The vast majority of us do not have other links with Italy other than that of pride, nor other obligations other that the duties imposed by the voice of our blood."[28] According to Testena, Parini and the regime were wrong both in their directives toward Italians in Argentina as well in their characterizations of the Italian community. They not only failed to appreciate the ways in which the lives of these Italo-Argentines were already fully immersed in Argentine society, but they also undervalued the Italian patriotism within the community. For Testena, the patriotism of Italians abroad is in fact valuable precisely because it was not motivated by self-interest. As he explained, "Our patriotism is of a superior quality, because it is spontaneous and genuine, 24-karat gold. . . . The governments of Rome have never realized that we Italians in Argentina . . . are the model of Italian patriotism, exactly because we have remained loyal in thought and in spirit to the distant *patria*, of which we ask nothing, always ready to give."[29] In stating that identification with Italy and Italian patriotism was a free choice rather than an obligation, Testena also implied that the Italians in Argentina were something different from the blindly devoted and obedient "Italians abroad" of the propaganda.

Testena felt it was his right to disagree openly with officials sent by the regime and to reject policies emanating from Rome. He also felt free to interpret Italian national identity in his own way to suit his own values and beliefs. His polemical style and challenging of fascist authorities would not have been tolerated by the fascist regime within Italy. Even in Argentina, the Italian embassy was less than thrilled with his defiantly independent stance on fascist policy and took steps to discredit it. The embassy-sponsored daily *Il Mattino d'Italia* went so far as to accuse Testena of stealing its subscribers and advised its readers that *Il Mattino* was the only official and truly Italian voice in the community.[30]

Testena's preoccupation with the loss of individual liberty and the threat fascism posed to democracy would be the overriding theme in one of the most fascinating books produced within the community in favor of the Italian regime: Goffredo Marchetti's *Risposte di buon senso alle principali obbiezioni che si fanno all'estero contro il fascismo*.[31] Marchetti was an industrial engineer from Rome who married into one of the La Plata Italian community's most respected families. A nationalist turned fascist in 1921, Marchetti attempted to put to ease many of the fears within the Argentine community brought on by Mussolini's increasingly violent rhetoric and aggressive foreign policies. Each section of the book begins with an "objection" made against fascism, followed by Marchetti's response. Making fascist ideology palatable to a democratic audience abroad was no small task: over half of the objections and responses involved fascism's opposition to democracy and individual liberty. Marchetti went to great lengths to convince his readers that fascist Italy was not a repressive dictatorship based on violence and coercion, but instead a widely popular regime based on the principles of justice and humanity, with violence only a last resort, not a tactic of choice.

"Fascism is a true, authentic, and crystalline democracy."[32] Making use of one particular trope in the Italian fascist rhetorical repertoire, Marchetti insisted that the fascist regime was a truer democracy than the so-called liberal parliamentarian democracies. Its officials were devoted public servants disinterested in self-promotion and motivated by the good of the nation. "The Duce of fascism and all of the high *gerarchi* are in constant direct contact with the people through massive public assemblies." More than simply staged events, these crowds *were* the Italian people, and Mussolini was their devoted servant, interpreting and dutifully carrying out what was best for the nation.[33] Despite overwhelming evidence to the contrary, Marchetti insisted that Italians within Italy still had individual liberty and the freedom to voice opposition: "In the fascist regime, all opinions can be expressed, and all forms of criticism can be made, but only in an appropriate forum, by a competent body, and by qualified persons."[34] This restricted freedom of expression was the only way to "protect" a democracy from abuse, unlike "those so-called democracies, where everything is permitted to anyone. Where anyone can propagate the most absurd and pernicious theories, deceive the public."[35] Following this logic, what was seen as repression was instead simply ensuring that citizens act responsibly and protecting the public from damaging ideas.

Beyond simply casting fascist Italy as an idyllic democracy, Marchetti also catered to a readership in the Americas by likening Mussolini and the fascist movement to the fathers of the American republics, who, like Mussolini, were forced to resort to violence and to violate international laws in order to free their nations from oppression.[36] On more than one occasion, Marchetti went so far as to equate Mussolini's actions with those of George Washington, another great father of his own country, explaining that "the moment may arrive in which an act of rebellion is as necessary and as noble in its goals as George Washington's act of rebellion that led to the founding of the United States of America."[37] Drawing the analogy even further, Marchetti argued that Mussolini's invasion of Ethiopia and defiance of the League of Nations was analogous to Washington's revolution: in both cases people were victimized by an imperialistic Great Britain and fought to defend their nation's rightful place in the world.[38]

Fascism, an ideology of "social justice" and democracy; Mussolini, the George Washington of his people; fascist Italy, not a dictatorship but a beloved regime in the service of "humanity and progress": such is Marchetti's Italy. Even though Mussolini did indeed portray Italy as a victim in his speeches prior to Ethiopia's invasion as well as on occasion define fascist Italy in terms of a "true democracy," on the whole the emphasis placed by Marchetti on these themes distorted the image of fascist Italy being projected by Mussolini and members of the regime at the time. The difference between Marchetti's pamphlet and the Italian propaganda produced in Rome was therefore more of a question of focus and selection rather than content. It was in fact Marchetti's overriding preoccupation with defining Mussolini's Italy as a free and open democracy in the same tradition as American republics that distorted the image of the fascist regime. It is a distortion that suggests that democratic values, in contrast to the regime's propaganda, were a fundamental component to Italian immigrant identities.

Hailed for its "modest simplicity" if not entirely accurate characterizations, a copy of the book was sent by the Italian embassy in Buenos Aires to the Ministry of Popular Culture in Rome, suggesting that the it could be put to good use as a propaganda piece since "it can reach the minds of many

impatient readers, who would not be able to handle a more eleva
The fact that such a work would be recommended for wide circu
indication that by 1940 the fascist regime was more preoccupied
ing public opinion abroad than ideological consistency.

These three prominent supporters of the fascist Italian regime had much in common. Each took it upon himself to interpret Italian national identity to fit his own ideological sensibilities; each wrote in favor of a democratic civil society and individual liberty; and perhaps most important of all, each was anxious to be accepted into the fabric of Argentine society. This preoccupation demonstrates a sense of an Italian national identity abroad distinct from the model advanced in the fascist propaganda, which had encouraged its followers to maintain their own identity apart from the host nation.

Unlike the "official" Italian fascist national narrative disseminated by the regime, these community sympathizers created their own narrative replete with their own symbolic imagery. Mussolini was placed in an unlikely pantheon of iconic figures that included Manuel Belgrano, Bartolomé Mitre, and even George Washington, each of whom were identified as fathers of their countries who valued democracy and individual freedom. By placing Mussolini in this context, they created a new and distinctively Italian Argentine narrative of fascism and its place in Italian history.

It is perhaps Buffarini's depiction of Garibaldi, one of the most iconic images of Italian national identity, that provides the most telling illustration of how these fascist sympathizers imagined a collective identity different from the fascist model. Depicted in a drawing in his collected writings as shaking Garibaldi's hand, Buffarini identified himself with the Italian patriot and claimed to be following in the his footsteps when he immigrated to South America.[40] Garibaldi was the embodiment of his own transnational identity and an iconic figure used along with Christopher Columbus and Manuel Belgrano to assimilate his Italian identity with Argentina's national narrative. For Buffarini, Garibaldi was not the nationalist forerunner of Mussolini's fascist "revolution," which completed the work of the Risorgimento, but instead, "Garibaldi is the representative of the glory of Italian emigration."[41] For Buffarini, Garibaldi's value lay in the fact that this great Italian, through his revolutionary struggles for liberty and democracy on the River Plate, had contributed to the making of modern Argentina, and in so doing validated the Italian presence in the Argentine nation, as well as embodied a set of democratic ideals that both Italians and Argentines held in common.[42] Buffarini, in short, made the Garibaldi icon his own, identifying the Risorgimento leader with the Italian immigrant community. It is this narrative use of the Garibaldi mythology that speaks to the divide between fascist sympathizers in the community and the Italian regime.

Chapter 5

ITALIAN *FUORUSCITI* IN ARGENTINA

The fascists were not the only ones who spoke to Italian communities abroad and promoted an Italian national identity outside of the nation. Italian antifascist exiles, known as *fuorusciti*, traveled around the world from country to country speaking out against the brutality of the fascist regime and organizing resistance from abroad. Italian officials abroad monitored their every step, sending meticulous reports to the Italian political police back home, but unable to silence these opponents of fascism while they remained abroad. Pages and pages of these police dossiers, now housed in the Archivio Centrale dello Stato, enable us to retrace the *fuorusciti's* steps. From Paris and New York to Rio de Janeiro and Montevideo, the *fuorusciti* played a pivotal role in presenting immigrants with an alternative image of Italian national identity.

These *fuorusciti* used their own collection of national iconography and imagery to argue that fascism was a perversion of Italy's true national character, whose origins lay not in the martial authoritarianism of ancient Rome, nor in the fascist new man born in the trenches of the First World War, but in the universal humanism of the Renaissance and the democratic idealism of Mazzini and Garibaldi. To be a true Italian abroad, therefore, meant to espouse these values in opposition to the fascist model.

The *fuorusciti* were a heterogeneous collection of individuals, including monarchists, Catholics, socialists, anarchists, communists, liberals, and republicans. They were united mainly in their hatred of the fascist regime and lacked organizational coherence. Although many moved in intellectual circles and had much more influence within academic institutions rather than among the masses, the *fuorusciti* who made their way to the republics of South America tended to be of a more radical bent politically and made an especially strong effort to appeal to the Italian immigrant masses.[43] While most antifascist exiles wrote only of the crimes and injustices perpetrated by the fascist regime, those operating in Argentina, Uruguay, and Brazil also wrote on the social and political conditions within the Italian communities in which they lived and coordinated their activities with local Italian associations.[44] They also collaborated with their South American political counterparts, translating important texts by prominent Italian socialists and anarchists into Spanish, supporting the local radical press, and speaking directly on the dangers of fascist ideology to the working classes of South America.[45]

Many important antifascists passed through South America during their period in exile. The special importance of the Italian community in Argentina was as apparent to the antifascists as it was to the fascists, well aware of the high number of Italians living in the republic as well as the attention that the Italian regime was giving them.[46] From young firebrands like the violent anarchist Severino di Giovanni to elderly statesmen of the fallen liberal regime like the socialist leader Arturo Labriola, Argentina became a meeting place for antifascists of all stripes. These *fuorusciti* leaders made up their own distinct group that was interwoven into the political landscape of the wider Italian community in Argentina. Collaborating with and living among the Italians of Argentina, many of the *fuorusciti* became much more a part of the communities in which they worked than the agents and officials the fascist regime was dispatching from Rome.[47]

Domenico Gasperini was one of the first Italian *fuorusciti* leaders to actively organize the antifascist movement in Argentina. The Italian police files on his subversive activities date all the way back to 1905. A revolutionary socialist since that time, Gasperini was an active member of the party, operating in Italy and across the border in France right up through the early 1920s. It was during this time that he was reportedly a guest of Angelica Balabanoff in Paris.[48] Balabanoff was an active leader and inspirational figure in the Italian revolutionary socialist movement since the turn of the century; she had also been one of Mussolini's lovers when he was still a young socialist agitator.[49] According to Italian police reports, Balabanoff's monetary and moral support had strengthened Gasperini's "rigid revolutionary socialist tendencies."[50]

In 1928 the Italian Consulate in Buenos Aires alerted Italian police of Gasperini's presence in Argentina, reporting that he had become the secretary of the Federazione Socialista Italiana nell'Argentina as well as the head of the Alleanza Anti-fascista Italiana. Actively involved in the revolutionary socialist movement in Argentina, Gasperini was for a time editor of the socialist daily *La Vanguardia* and was involved in Argentina's socialist as well as Italian antifascist associations. In the early 1930s he published two of his own papers: the weekly *Italia Libre* devoted to the antifascist cause, and the biweekly *Italia Proletaria* focused on Italian revolutionary socialism. After a brief retreat from political activism in the face of virulent criticism from rival socialist factions, Gasperini continued from 1931 as the leader of the Italian revolutionary Socialist Party. As the 1930s progressed, he began to work more closely with other antifascist parties, shocking Italian police by his overtures toward prominent anarchists. Gasperini also coordinated nonpartisan committees to commemorate Giacomo Matteotti, to oppose the Italian invasion of Ethiopia, and to support the Popular Front in Spain. A report from the Italian consulate in his police file dated September 10, 1939, sums up his activities during these years most succinctly: "Gasperini is still in residence in Argentina, and is as firm as ever both in his socialist convictions as well as in his aversion to fascism, which he continues to work against. He still participates in every public antifascist demonstration, never failing to deliver his typically venomous words."[51]

Gasperini's organizational work and leadership role made him a key figure among the Italian antifascists living in Argentina, but fellow socialist leader Francesco Frola, thanks to his speechwriting and prolific publishing, was perhaps the best known of all the *fuorusciti* who made Latin America their base. Frola spent the majority of his years in exile in Brazil and later Mexico, but left his mark on Argentina as well. Chased from the Italian Parliament and assaulted by Blackshirt squads during Mussolini's swift and brutal repression of the opposition in the wake of the Matteotti Crisis, the former socialist deputy first began his antifascist activities in Paris in 1925. The following year he relocated to Brazil, where he lived precariously, harassed at every turn by fascist agents. In 1926 the Italian government revoked his citizenship and pressured Brazilian officials to arrest Frola for subversive activity and trumped-up murder charges—the pretext of choice by fascist officials who hoped to have their opponents extradited.[52]

Upon his arrival in Argentina on May 20, 1930, Frola went right to work, beginning a whirlwind speaking tour.: first in Buenos Aires at various venues in which he commemorated Garibaldi and Matteotti and lectured on the origins of fascism; then on to Rosario de Santa Fe, where he was heard delivering a speech on "Why We Are Antifascists"; later to Bahia Blanca, where he spoke on "Democracy and Fascism"; and then in Junin on "Italy in Chains" and in Chacabuco on "The Return of the Middle Ages." By August he was back in Buenos Aires, speaking among other places in the city's Italian neighborhood of La Boca on "Fascism and the Working Class." In addition to speech making, Frola gave interviews to all of the major Italian and Argentine left-wing periodicals in the country and established contacts with Argentina's Socialist Party. In August he met with the two most prominent socialist congressmen in the Argentine government, Adolfo Dickmann and Angel Giménez. General Uriburu's right-wing coup d'état in September shifted Frola's activities more squarely to fighting fascism within the Italian community, and he was soon reported to be organizing the antifascists' celebration of XX Settembre, liberal Italy's patriotic holiday honoring the conquest of Rome in 1870.[53] During these months Frola corresponded with Arturo Labriola and arranged his visit to Latin America; he also planned a series of lectures by another former socialist deputy, Francesco Ciccotti, who settled in Buenos Aires in 1931. Most importantly, he organized the Concentrazione Anti-fascista in 1930, which included delegates from the Italian Republican Party, the Italian Socialist Party, the Argentine Socialist Party, the Italian Human Rights League, and the Italian Antifascist Union. Through the Concentrazione, Frola attempted to unify the antifascist movement in Argentina, which although numerically large was still fractured along party lines.[54]

In December 1930, Frola began his most important Argentine endeavor, launching the first Italian antifascist daily in Buenos Aires. He gave the paper the name *Il Risorgimento*, explaining,

> We choose this name and place it under the aegis of Mazzini, Garibaldi, and Matteotti. The first an apostle of liberty, the second the architect, the third the consecration, with his supreme sacrifice and eternal valor. . . . Risorgimento because it is Italian and so must be antifascist. For liberty against violence, for justice against arbitrariness, democracy against dictatorship, republic against the monarchy, freedom of conscience against theocracy.[55]

Though himself an atheist and internationalist, Frola adeptly played the fascists at their own game by employing patriotic and religious imagery to undermine fascism's rhetorical grip over Italian national identity. Admitting as much, he explained, "We are not patriots according to the way in which the term is used today. But we are not against the *patria* as the fascists who call us 'anti-Italians' would have you believe."[56]

A close analysis of how Italian identity was defined within the pages of *Il Risorgimento* and its use of imagery reveals much about the *fuorusciti* concept of the *patria* and its political use of identity. Frola also defined Italy broadly: "Italy is a force, a reality of labor and spirit." More than a territory, it was a set of ideas, a spiritual creation, the work of great Italian minds:

> Italy is the law of Beccaria, Romagnosi, Carrara; the thoughts of Bruno, Ardigó, and Croce; the science of Galileo, Volta, Pacinotti; the art of Michelangelo, Leonardo, Rossini; the poetry of Dante, Foscolo, and Carducci; the politics of Machiavelli, Gioberti, Cavour; the vision of Mazzini, the heroism of Garibaldi, the martyrdom of the students of 1821, and the conscious sacrifice of Giacomo Matteotti.[57]

For Frola, Italy was also the labor of its millions of anonymous farmers, workers, miners, and artisans, "who worked to build the edifice of a new society in which poverty, illiteracy, prejudice were abolished." In short, "Italy signifies thought, liberty, justice, and labor."[58] All of these "Italian" national qualities are in fact universal ones. Frola, along with his fellow exiles, are in fact using the rhetoric of nationalism to promote a universalist agenda. It is, in short, an Italian national project for the betterment of all mankind.

According to Frola, fascism, in contrast, "is darkness, violence, arbitrariness, and parasitism." It is an "anti-Italy" where the truncheon has replaced thought and where the rule of law is hijacked by rapacious criminals who use the state as an instrument of repression, turning Italy into "a horrible prison" and "throwing the Italian people into the darkness of ignorance, misery, and slavery."[59] Fascist Italy, labeled by Frola as the anti-*patria*, was referred to in the articles as "Mussolandia," and Mussolini and his followers as members of the "Dynasty of Predappio," both obvious attempts at separating Mussolini and his regime from Italy and the Italian people.

Lest the message not be clear in the text, the newspaper's political cartoons hammered home the point that the fascists were nothing more than villainous thugs who hijacked and exploited the Italian nation. One such cartoon showed a group of Blackshirts sticking up "Italia," personified by a beautiful woman; another shows a grotesque female personification of "Mussolandia" with its foot over an enchained Italia, with the text reading, "Mussolandia has enslaved Italy, has beaten her down by treachery, and now has her on the ground with a foot on her chest, ready to suffocate her."[60] Yet another depicted a group of Blackshirts with pistols and knives in hand triumphantly parading Italia down the street in chains, while the front page of another issue showed "fascist" pigs greedily feeding on the Italian peninsula, turning it into a trough with the headline, "The Fascist Concept of the *Patria*."[61]

The brand of Italian identity advanced by Frola's *Il Risorgimento* was both anticlerical and antimonarchic, but neither antireligious nor antipatriotic. Frola accused both the king and the pope of enabling Mussolini's rise to power and in so doing betraying both their country and their God. It was an argument similar to the one made by Gaetano Salvemini, the famed *fuoruscito* who was delivering his Harvard lecture series on the origins of Italian fascism around the same time. *Il Risorgimento* depicted King Victor Emmanuel III, called "The Useless Citizen," as kneeling and giving the fascist salute to an enthroned Mussolini in one issue, while Pope Pius XI, "The Other Accomplice," is shown embracing a black-shirted fascist beneath a shocked Jesus Christ looking on. To drive home the message, another image showed clergymen and fascists dancing around Christ on the cross, and a December issue boldly declared, "The Fascists Killed Christmas." Most graphic of all, another cartoon depicted a brutish Mussolini murdering Italia, with the pope and king behind him.[62]

"Enemies of Italian Liberty and of the Argentine Nation," ran the heading of a daily column that listed members of Fasci all'Estero in Argentina. According to Frola, the fascists were not just the enemies of Italy but also a threat to Argentina and its democratic ideals: "Our battle is a battle for democracy, and here we are close to one another. Our goal is to strengthen the bonds between Italians and Argentines in a common program of work, peace, and progress."[63] Playing off Argentine notions of identity, Frola warned that fascist Italy's representatives were two-faced: despite their friendly overtures, they were attempting to export their fascist terror to South America. One cartoon depicted the fascist abroad as a handsome suitor bearing flowers, masking his true persona as a bloodthirsty brute, while another showed a ship named "Mussolandia" steaming toward Argentina with a cargo of spies, thieves, and murderers. To play off the vanity of Argentines, Frola also claimed that Argentina was a nation too civilized to allow Italo Balbo's squadron to make a stop over there on his trans-Atlantic flight. Other articles quoted or perhaps fabricated disparaging remarks made by Margherita Sarfatti, then Mussolini's mistress, about Argentina and democracy. In a full-page article, Frola declared in no uncertain terms that "the fascists are Argentina's enemies. They are enemies in theory and in practice. In theory: because fascism is dictatorship and violence while Argentina is democracy and liberty. In practice: because fascism is imperialistic and thinks that they can send their adventurers into this land to do as they like."[64] With its identity defined by its faith in liberty and democracy, Frola concluded, "Argentina is on balance antifascist."[65]

Frola's definition of Argentine identity, like his definition of Italian identity, was based on a set of values and beliefs rather than defined by blood or cultural heritage. It was an ideational concept of national identity that would have been familiar to New World audiences. Just as the fascists had advanced a concept of Italian-ness that required Italians to believe in their ideological tenets in order to be Italian, Frola, like other antifascists around the world, countered with an alternative vision of Italian identity that was anchored in a belief in liberty and democracy.

The last surviving copies of *Il Risorgimento* contain affixed to them the address label of one Luigi Fabbri, Casilla Correo 141, R. O. del U., Montevideo. Fabbri was none other than the most influential anarchist *fuoruscito* living in South America. While fellow anarchist Severino di Giovanni stole the headlines of the day with his 1928 bombing of the Italian Embassy in Buenos Aires and his 1930 capture and execution, in the long run it was the writings and tireless efforts of Luigi Fabbri and his daughter Luce that rallied the anarchists of Latin America around the antifascist cause. Fabbri had been a longtime associate of the famed anarchist intellectual Errico Malatesta. He spent his first period in exile in Paris from 1926 to 1929, where he contributed articles to many different anarchist publications and emerged as a leading anarchist voice in the antifascist movement. He relocated with his daughter to South America in 1930. With their home base in Montevideo, the father and daughter pair moved freely back and forth across the river and, according to Italian police files, "were as active in Argentina as they were in Montevideo."[66] On March 16, 1930, Fabbri started his own anarchist antifascist journal in Buenos Aires, *Studi Sociali*, which placed Italian antifascism in the context of anarchism's international struggle. In a clear attempt to influence Argentine as well as Italian public opinion and reach out to the working classes in Latin America, Fabbri translated works on Italian anarchism by Malatesta into Spanish and wrote a Spanish-language biography and interpretive essay on Malatesta. Fabbri was also a regular contributor to the local anarchist biweekly *La Protesta*, for which he wrote an Italian-language page.[67]

Fabbri, unlike Frola, stuck to his internationalist roots, most often writing about fascism in universal rather than national terms: "Anarchism holds high the principle of liberty in the face of fascism, which exalts the principle of authority. As its irreconcilable antithesis, the anarchists are its most hostile, intransigent, and permanent enemies."[68] Liberty for Fabbri was not conjured as a symbol of the Italian nation but instead used as the defining idea of the international anarchist cause. Fascism was likewise not just an Italian phenomenon but an international system that threatened to envelop the entire world. It was seen by Fabbri as one of the worst manifestations of the forces of reaction and the state's abuse of power.[69] According to Fabbri, the situation was indeed bleak, with the complicity of capitalist plutocrats and the Church, the fascist movement was posed to destroy democracy: "If the revolution does not come soon to stop the current reactionary offensive against liberty and against the proletariat, then fascism, in its worst form, will win, and an era of fear and barbarity will rule over all of mankind."[70]

Favoring internationalist over nationalist rhetoric, Fabbri in his works described Mazzini not as an Italian patriot but rather as a hero to humanity, "whose great love was for the people and for the downtrodden." Similarly, Fabbri often referred to the Risorgimento and its heroes not in their Italian context but in the context of 1848 and the European-wide revolutions for the liberty of all peoples oppressed by the mechanisms of the state.[71] Even though Fabbri did not associate his brand of antifascism with Italian identity, he was quick to deny the fascists their claims over it. In one of his very first antifascist tracts, he declared that "fascism, with its violence, has done little to improve the declining fortunes of the *patria*, nor can it be said that fascism has revived or validated any patriotic ideals."[72] In fact, according to Fabbri, "fascism is much further away than international socialism from the Italian spirit, from its long tradition of idealism and humanism." Thanks to the fascists' brutal and vicious crimes, "in the name of the *patria* they have vilified Italy abroad, while internally making its name synonymous with high-handedness, the abuse of power, and servitude."[73] That even a lifelong devotee of anarchism was moved to challenge fascism's grip over Italy's national image speaks to the importance of the theme of Italian identity in the debates over fascism.[74]

Just as Buffarini's treatment of Garibaldi was suggestive of how fascist sympathizers defined their identity, the ways antifascist *fuorusciti* articulated the values of the Risorgimento and its iconic figures are also illustrative of their particular way of envisioning Italian identity. Taken together, the *fuorusciti* examined here all characterized the Risorgimento and its heroes in universal rather than national terms. The Risorgimento was a movement for liberty and justice, and Garibaldi and Mazzini in their fight for freedom and democracy belonged as much to humanity in general as to Italy in particular. This treatment of the Risorgimento placed Italian identity in a much broader international context than either that of fascists or their sympathizers in Argentina. It also would differ from the notions of identity formulated by antifascist members of the local Italian community.

The *fuorusciti* in fact occupied an ambiguous position in Argentina, especially within the Italian community. On the one hand, Argentina had become for them a safe haven if not a new home. Many brought their families with them and raised their children in their new land and took an interest in the community. As Frola movingly explained, "Many of us have found a second *patria* here, with Argentine wives and children. Many have identified ourselves with this people who have opened their borders to men from all over the world."[75] On the other hand, unlike the majority of Italian immigrants and their children who had left Italy for socioeconomic reasons years and even decades before the fascist seizure of power, these *fuorusciti* were recent political exiles whose overriding priority was the liberation of their homeland from fascist tyranny. Therefore, while certainly not in the same category as the fascist propagandists sent by the regime to indoctrinate the Italian community, these antifascists were not always able to understand or relate to the often conflicted notions of identity within the immigrant community. In other words, although the *fuorusciti* and Italian immigrant antifascists shared much in common, they were not one and the same.

ITALIAN IDENTITY AMONG COMMUNITY ANTIFASCISTS

The local antifascist movement was also strong in Argentina, thanks in large part to the involvement of a number of prominent members of the community and the support of long-standing community institutions. Identified by the fascist regime as Freemasons, demo-liberals, and republicans, many though not all of these antifascist leaders were far away politically from the socialist and anarchist *fuorusciti* discussed above. They identified most with the Italy of the liberal era, along with the democratic values of the Risorgimento. They gathered support for their cause among the mass of Italian immigrants and their children whose families had arrived in Argentina at the end of the previous century. Traditional values and old regional loyalties rather than social justice were the rallying cries for most.

These antifascists worked through a more politically moderate circle of long-standing community associations that turned antifascist. All of these associations were formed in the nineteenth century and relied upon their strong Risorgimento-era traditions to respond to the fascist regime's manipulation of Italian identity. Among the oldest, the Società Italia Unita had been founded fifty years prior to the fascist seizure of power in Italy. Designed as a mutual-aid society, the Società Italia Unita founded Italian elementary schools that rivaled those run by the fascist Direzione Italiani all'Estero. Many regional associations, the Circolo Venezia Giulia first among them, also closed ranks in the face of fascist propaganda and rallied their members around the antifascist banner. Other organizations like the Società Italiana di M. S. Belgrano, with the majority of its members Argentines of Italian descent, resisted the fascists' attempted co-optation of Italian identity, while choosing to avoid the politically charged "antifascist" label.[76]

The Nuova Società Dante Alighieri was one of the only community associations formed expressly to combat fascism. When the original Dante Alighieri Society became co-opted by the fascist regime in 1934, many of its members in Argentina left to form their own "new" Dante Alighieri, which would become in a few short years the central rallying point for prominent antifascists within the community. Its founding charter declared, "The Dante Alighieri has as its mission the promotion of the Italian language and Italian culture; it does not have a political agenda. . . . The Nuova Dante believes that Italy is something much more than any government that may temporarily exert its control over our peninsula, and Italian culture is much more important than any political party."[77] When the society was accused of being traitors to the Italian cause and saboteurs of Italian identity, Luigi Delfino, the first president of the Nuova Dante, responded by insisting that their opposition to Mussolini's vision of an imperialistic and violent Italy did not make them traitors, since the Nuova Dante promoted Italy's true identity, an identity based on civil virtue and humanism.[78] Delfino was a highly regarded surgeon and upstanding member of the community who immigrated to Argentina in 1906 and was an implacable foe of the fascists. Unlike many of the *fuorusciti*, no hint of prior subversive activity could be found on Delfino. Italian police investigated him after he was made the president of the antifascist association. Much to their dismay, they found no evidence of his involvement in any "subversive party." When questioned by police, members of his hometown of Zuccarello in Liguria reported that Delfino "was a person worthy of respect, who had always harbored patriotic sentiments." He was also remembered as "an active and intelligent person" who, without financial means, had managed to gain his degrees in medicine and surgery by earning a prestigious scholarship. He had also served with distinction in the Italian military with the rank of medical lieutenant, certainly not the figure of a "subversive anti-Italian" as the regime would have wanted people to believe.[79] He was instead exactly the type of man that the Italian consulate had a hard time discrediting. With Delfino at the helm, the Nuova Dante competed against and often undermined the activities of the official society.

When, in February 1936, an automobile accident led to Delfino's untimely death, the society's work was taken over by another well-respected member of the community, Torcuato di Tella.[80]

Di Tella, a wealthy industrialist from one of the most prominent Italo-Argentine families, was the most important antifascist leader to emerge from within the community. The primary shareholder and president of the Sociedad Industrial Americana Maquinarias, Di Tella used his resources and influence to promote the antifascist cause. He corresponded often with the cream of the international antifascist movement: Francesco Saverio Nitti, the former liberal prime minister; Filippo Turati, the founder of the Italian Socialist Party; Carlo Sforza, the aristocratic head of the Mazzini Society in New York; and Gaetano Salvemini, the maverick journalist and antifascist intellectual. In addition to his new role as the president of the Nuova Dante, Di Tella also established and subsidized one of the main wartime antifascist newspapers in Argentina.[81] It was in fact through the Italian-language press, funded by individuals like Di Tella, that many of these local antifascists articulated their own sense of Italian national identity, an identity entangled with the national identity of their new Argentine home.

The *fuoruscito* Francesco Frola had few kind words for the Italian community's local antifascist newspapers and their brand of antifascism. He wrote that *La Patria degli Italiani*, the long-established mouthpiece of the Italian community, "supports antifascism but not our antifascism. It is the traditional newspaper of the community: it is old and wears slippers. It can no longer keep pace. We understand it but we cannot identify with it."[82] These flippant lines, perhaps merely a device to justify the need for his own newspaper, do nevertheless indicate a certain level of frustration and lack of sympathy on the part of some of the *fuorusciti* toward antifascists within the community. It is not unlike the way in which Italian fascists had expressed frustration with their own sympathizers in the community. Both instances highlight the different sense of Italian national identity on the part of immigrants in an Argentine environment.

La Patria degli Italiani, as the oldest and most widely circulated Italian-language daily, expressed a distinct brand of antifascism that articulated many of the values shared by nonfascist members of the community. Self-described as "more than a just an organ of information, [this newspaper] is a symbol, a flag, perhaps among the last in the struggle to defend the rights of free Italians, their liberal traditions, and Italian-ness."[83] Founded in 1876, *La Patria* was steeped in nineteenth-century Italian liberalism. By the time the fascist regime came to power, *La Patria* was a well-established community institution. It had long served as a pillar of support to the community, a mouthpiece to voice its concerns, and a link to the distant *patria* of its readership. Each issue covered the major news stories from Italy as well as the events and happenings within the Italian communities in Argentina. Its pages also celebrated both Argentine and Italian patriots. Christopher Columbus, Manuel Belgrano, and Giuseppe Garibaldi figured prominently within its pages, each described as a key Italian contributor to the Argentine nation-state. Its expressed mission was to instill in its readers a patriotic love for Italy, their distant homeland, while at the same time to assist their integration into the fabric of their new Argentine homeland.[84]

Identifying itself as a product of the Risorgimento and its liberal and democratic ideals, the editorship asserted that *La Patria* was "the only Italian newspaper made for all Italians. It is the longstanding newspaper of the emigrants. It inspires a patriotism that is not monopolized by parties or governments, but motivated by feeling and practicality rather than presumptuous and empty chatter." Although claiming to remain above political squabbling, "it has never betrayed and will never betray its liberalism, which has always been its flag, the flag of Italy itself."[85] Liberalism was in fact for the editorship of *La Patria* the cornerstone of Italy's identity as a nation. Crediting the liberal regime with all of Italy's greatest accomplishments, the paper declared, "The history of Italy is nothing if not the history of liberalism."[86]

"We want to provide our compatriots with a free and truly independent newspaper, which is not associated with any sect or faction," insisted one editorial in 1929, while another clarified its stance even further: "'Neither slave nor rebel': this is the motto of every Italian who lives abroad to work and does not play politics."[87] Strictly speaking, *La Patria* never defined itself as antifascist, because, as the editorship explained, "Antifascism is a negation, while liberalism and democracy are affirmations and have their own existence. *La Patria* can only exist as a newspaper based on permanent, rather than contingent, principles, and those principles are liberal and democratic."[88] By refusing to submit to the fascist regime's pressure and holding true to its liberal and democratic principles, *La Patria*'s defiant stand did place the paper squarely in the antifascist camp. Its editorship's refusal to explicitly associate itself with the antifascist cause, however, exasperated many other antifascists, Frola first among them.

The way in which the First World War was remembered further highlights the community's attachment to democratic values. *La Patria degli Italiani* along with other community newspapers commemorated the anniversary of the end of the First World War by offering its own patriotic interpretation of the war and its symbolic importance. It also honored Italy's fallen martyrs and celebrated Italy's victory over its enemies. Yet, rather than recounting the war as the regenerative birth of the new fascist Italy consecrated by the blood its martyrs, the war instead represented a sacrifice in the name of peace and democracy. As one article movingly declared, "The war and the victory for those who fought and died was a sacrificial offering of peace, liberty, labor to all future generations from two generations who were tired of hatred and could no longer tolerate the abuse of power."[89] Far from ushering in a new era of violent national expansion, victory in the war was instead an end of an age of violence and the triumph of liberal democracy over the forces of oppression.

It was during its last days, while in the midst of its confrontation with the Italian embassy and *Il Mattino d'Italia*, that *La Patria* countered fascism's propaganda with its own definition of patriotism and its own conceptualization of an Italian identity abroad. Challenging the regime's claim that a true Italian abroad must become a fascist, *La Patria* insisted that politics held no place in an emigrant's sense of identity. According to the paper, emigrants left Italy in search of work and a better life for their families, not to participate in political movements. This emigrant identity, unlike that of the fascist propaganda, was not contingent upon any ideology: "his is not a hollow nationalism. . . . The emigrant feels that he cannot be anything other than an Italian, and if he is not an Italian than he is nothing."[90] Fascism, with its strong-arm tactics, perverted this almost innate sense of national identity into something else entirely. "Patriotism, which had been a spontaneous expression, has become extraneously imposed. An individual is no longer measured by the merits of his actions and accomplishments, but by the weakness of his spine and by his ability to genuflect."[91] No doubt frustrating antifascist *fuorusciti*, this innate sense of Italian identity also did not hinge on espousing the antifascist principles of justice and liberty.

"*La Patria*, the flag of the emigrants, has suffered and will suffer with them to the last breath"; with the end in sight, *La Patria* made common cause with its immigrant readership.[92] As its confrontation with the fascists reached its climax late in 1931, *La Patria* styled itself as a center of resistance and a champion of the Italian community in the face of fascist aggression. "We share the pain and protests of our compatriots. We have become the organ of the indignant and the displaced who, in spite of their bitterness, continue to maintain the patriotic faith in the hope of a return to the traditions and the unity of purpose for Italy and for Argentina."[93] If their struggle was the community's struggle, than their enemies were likewise enemies of the community:

> The enemies of the *La Patria* are false friends of the community, launching their depraved intentions against Italians, against Italian institutions, and against newspapers. The ambassador, the consuls, and the authorities' lackeys are trying to destroy *La Patria*, and at the same time destroy all the Italian institutions around it.[94]

La Patria's stand against fascism was by extension a defense of the community and the community's own shared values, which for *La Patria* signified a liberal and patriotic version of Italian identity based on traditions and mutual Italian Argentine cooperation, an Italian identity far away from that of the fascists.

For the editors of *La Patria degli Italiani*, "the *patria*" signified more than just their Italian homeland—the *patria was* the community: a community of Italian emigrants in Argentina, a community with a shared set of beliefs, values, and traditions. In many ways, it was this identity, the product of over fifty years of Italian life in Argentina rather than any abstract notions of "Italy," that the newspaper fought so fervently to defend. As one of the paper's last editorials declared,

> Now more than ever we have the feeling that this defense is being enthusiastically supported, now more than ever we have felt the anxiety of our compatriots who do not want to fall victim to adventurers, and who need a free voice, which beyond freely expressing the community's sentiments will also prevent them from becoming the easy prey to extremist ideas.[95]

Defiant to the end, *La Patria*, after its offices shut down, became a martyr in the community's defense of its identity from fascist intrusions.

After *La Patria* ceased publication in 1931, *L'Italia del Popolo* emerged as the most widely circulated Italian-language daily in the community. The paper had been founded in 1917 by Folco Testena but was taken over by Vittorio Mosca in the 1920s. Born in Turin in 1896, Mosca came from a family of journalists. His father had been the editor of *La Stampa*, and his brother, Alfredo, collaborated with him on *L'Italia del Popolo*. Unlike *La Patria*, which resisted the antifascist label, *L'Italia del Popolo* under Mosca's direction embraced it, boldly declaring, "You cannot be a good Italian, if you are not an antifascist."[96] Based on radical republican and socialist principles, *L'Italia del Popolo* declared itself against the fascist regime as early as 1922.[97]

Throughout the fascist period right up to the war years, *L'Italia del Popolo* responded directly to the fascist regime's propaganda initiatives and tactics in the republic. In commenting on Parini's call for a more active and aggressive promotion of Italian identity in Argentina, *L'Italia del Popolo* warned that "all these new initiatives with the *fasci* stamped on them will not garner any sympathy from the Italians here, nor from the Argentines," going on to declare, "If the fascists truly loved Italian-ness, they would slow down and stop their new initiatives; instead, they are taking their cues from Parini and adding fuel to the fire, worsening what is already a delicate situation."[98] *L'Italia del Popolo* was also well aware of the threat posed by fascism's control over the Scuole Italiane all'Estero, frequently warning its readers of the "poisonous imperialistic propaganda" being inculcated in the fascist-run schools, while actively promoting the antifascist Italian schools like Italia Unita and Edmundo de Amicis, which preserved a "true sense of Italian-ness, based on Italy's noble democratic traditions."[99]

L'Italia del Popolo, above all else, challenged the fascist regime's attempted monopoly over Italian identity; as one article declared, "fascism wants to impose its identity on our nationality through force, and brutal violence. As men, as citizens, and as Italians, we must rebel."[100] Scoffing at Parini's exalted title of director of Italians abroad, Mosca responded, "Our supreme pride has always been to have never had directors near or far away. . . . In a free country, we behave like a free people and do not tolerate directors and *condottieri*."[101] Responding to Parini's assertion that "the fascist membership card must become the symbol of Italian identity," *L'Italia del Popolo* declared that this was "fascism's fundamental error here and elsewhere. The membership card is the symbol of a party, and the word *party* derives from the word *part* because it is just that, a part and not all of a people."[102] Attacking the fascist tactic of labeling their political opponents abroad "anti-Italians," the paper retorted, "Just because we do not follow their orders, the fascists call us 'renouncers, scoundrels, traitors of the *patria*.' It does not matter to them that we defend the interests of Italian workers, and the Italian language, and literature and Italian history. . . . We are considered anti-Italians because, like all the peoples of the Americas, we love liberty."[103] Fascism's claims over identity prompted *L'Italia del Popolo* to provide its own definition of what constituted an Italian living in Argentina.

A 1931 article posed the questions, "Who is a good Italian? What does it mean to be a good Italian?" The article went on to respond that it was not enough simply to be born Italian or to speak Italian, asserting that someone is only a good Italian if he is "conscious of his Italian-ness, if his internal and external life is inspired by the Italian tradition . . . whose glory derives from its search for liberty."[104] The article explained that, "throughout the ages, the Italian people have searched for and have wanted liberty, and have always hated tyranny." Citing famous Italians of different periods from Dante and Machiavelli, to Galileo and Giordano Bruno, to Mazzini and Garibaldi, the editorial went on to insist that Italians have always fought for the cause of liberty and rebelled against ignorance and oppression. When Italian identity was seen as synonymous with liberty, fascism could only be seen as incompatible with Italian identity since "fascism is in every way the negation of liberty." Therefore, "fascism is not Italy, it is the anti-Italy, and as it has been said, whoever wants to be a good Italian must be antifascist."[105]

"Italy without liberty would no longer be Italy; liberty without Italy would no longer be liberty": so ran a headline quoting Risorgimento-era British poet Algernon Charles Swinburne.[106] In addition to liberty, *L'Italia del Popolo* linked Italian identity with the values of the Risorgimento: "Our job is to be Italian, which means remaining faithful to the Garibaldian and Mazzinian traditions of our Risorgimento." [107] In contrast, "among the many crimes committed by the fascists, certainly not least among them was to have renounced the traditions of the Risorgimento, the traditions of XX Settembre." [108] Here again the fascist regime failed to live up to their Italian identity by abandoning the values that defined it. For *L'Italia del Popolo*, without these values, "Today what many Italians living abroad think is their *patria* no longer exists. It has become an encampment of adventurers, usurpers, and murderers. Our *patria* is one of liberty and justice. In Italy it has disappeared, disappeared for all those who want to live their lives honestly and from their own labor."[109] More than a geographical space or even a shared language and culture, *L'Italia del Popolo*, like the other antifascist newspapers, advanced an ideational national identity based on a set of values and beliefs, those values being above all else liberty and justice.

With an identity based on the principles of liberty and justice, the conceptualization of Italian identity espoused by *L'Italia del Popolo* had more in common with the Argentine nation than the fascist state in Italy. "Free Italians identify perfectly with the Argentine nation and would be ready tomorrow if necessary to spill their blood for the republic's liberty and independence," one article declared, while another explained, "Italy and America are linked in our hearts by tight bonds. Our national revolution was so similar to the revolutions that established the American nations."[110] Not to confuse Italy with the fascist state, another declared, "The federal republic of Argentina is the antithesis of the fascist state; it rejects violence and the suspension of individual liberty."[111] By using a shared set of values as the basis for establishing a national identity, antifascists were able to identify themselves more closely with the Argentine state without sacrificing their sense of Italian-ness.

Italian emigrant's links to Argentina went much deeper than just a shared set of beliefs. "The Italians who work here and who made their homes here identify completely with the host nation to the extent that they no longer feel like they are foreigners."[112] In fact, according to *L'Italia del Popolo*, Argentina was their "second *patria*," and Italians living in the republic had a duty to contribute to its wealth and prosperity, in addition to supporting their Italian homeland.[113] In stark contrast to the fascist program, this meant toning down "excessive Italian nationalist" rhetoric in the interest of creating a stronger sense of unity with the wider Argentine population.[114] This close identification with Argentina is also a significant departure from *fuorusciti* writings, such as those of Frola and Fabbri, which spoke of identity in the abstract, detached from the Italian Argentine community's own sense of itself in relation to the Argentine nation.

Article after article in *L'Italia del Popolo* separated Italian immigrants from the fascist activists within Argentina. Unlike the Italian immigrants who had become an integral part of Argentine society, "the fascists are 'foreigners' here and act like foreigners."[115] Accordingly, Argentines "cannot confuse the fascists with the Italians who have come here to build roads, make cities grow, populate the countryside, and give children to the Argentine *patria*. The fascists have done none of this. They only spread trouble and hatred, by introducing a savage system of political struggle."[116] *L'Italia del Popolo*'s understanding of emigration and emigrant identity was fundamentally different from that of the fascist propaganda. Its emigrants were honest and hardworking laborers in search of a better life and anxious to prove their loyalty to their new nations, not battalions of militant pioneers spreading Italy abroad. It was also unlike the image of the Italian abroad described by the *fuorusciti*. The emigrants according to *L'Italia del Popolo* were more anxious to make their new homes in Argentina rather than fight Italian political battles abroad.

During the late 1930s *L'Italia del Popolo* also framed its opposition to Mussolini's aggressive foreign policies in terms of Italian identity. When Mussolini invaded Ethiopia, its headline declared, "The Enemies of Italy Are Not the Africans, but the Fascists."[117] Similarly, Mussolini's alliance with Hitler was "deeply anti-Italian, unpatriotic, and antinational."[118] In the name of Italian patriotism, the paper also urged all free Italians to support the Spanish republic in order to "demonstrate that our people is worthy of liberty."[119] At the start of the Second World War, a new antifascist newspaper, *Italia Libre*, would overshadow *L'Italia del Popolo*. It would build off of many of the same tropes of Italian identity as well as elaborate on its own brand of Italian identity in Argentina.

"Mussolini has said: 'In Argentina there are 1,797,000 Italians. . . . Those 1,797,000 say back: leave us alone!" So began the circular announcing the inauguration of a new antifascist newspaper in Argentina.[120] Funded by Torcuato di Tella and edited by Nicolas Cilla, *Italia Libre* was the main antifascist periodical during the war years. Unlike the more radical *L'Italia del Popolo*, it cultivated a traditional liberal version of Italian identity that nevertheless espoused a similar faith in individual liberty and democracy. In a departure from the other Italian antifascist newspapers, the majority of this paper was written in Spanish, targeting especially second- and third-generation Italians living in Argentina. Much like the others, however, one of its expressed goals was to counter fascism's pretensions over Italian identity by offering an antifascist alternative. It also similarly favored the incorporation of Italians into Argentina's political life.[121] To this end, articles on Argentina's constitution and the life and times of Domingo F. Sarmiento appeared side by side with those on Garibaldi and Mazzini.

Its opening circular expressed alarm at the fascist regime's aggressive attempt to win over the Italians in Argentina. Its editorial staff condemned the regime's exploitation of Italy's good name, its efforts to indoctrinate the youth, and its expressed goal of preventing immigrant assimilation in Argentine society. Responding directly to the fascist propaganda, *Italia Libre* declared, "The great majority of the Italians [here] are already participating in Argentina's national life; their children are Argentines; they have already contributed to this nation's progress with their labor and as model citizens. Their savings are HERE; their aspirations are HERE; their daily problems are Argentine problems."[122] Thus, while Italians in Argentina continued to nurture affection for their homeland, they were now living in Argentina, and their first duties and responsibilities were to their new home rather than to the distant *patria* of their families.

As was also true of *L'Italia del Popolo*, the Risorgimento and Mussolini's betrayal of its ideals were a theme of choice, highlighted throughout. A particularly telling cartoon depicts a stern Garibaldi striking down the fascist emblem in front of a cowering Mussolini. In Garibaldi's hand is a banner with Italy's royal emblem and the phrase "Italian Unity," with Mazzini's and Cavour's names on the banner's staff.[123] *Italia Libre* also spoke of a "second Risorgimento," not the "Risorgimento" brought on by Mussolini in the fascist literature, but instead the coming Risorgimento that would liberate Italy from its fascist captors. "One must not confuse the government with Italy: fascism is an enemy camped on the soil of the *patria*."[124] Just like the other antifascist newspapers before it, *Italia Libre* sought to wrest Italian national identity from fascism's grip by insisting that true Italian patriots could not be anything but antifascist. As one article explains, "If the Italian people truly had the freedom to express their opinion, they would be the first to support Britain and France," while another called on all Italians to fight against Italy's enemies, clarifying that, "The enemy of the *patria* is not in Paris or London: the only true enemy of Italy is in Rome!"[125]

Hector Cozzolino, in an *Italia Libre* article entitled "Italianidad," directly responded to the assertion in fascist propaganda that to be an antifascist signified being an anti-Italian. According to Cozzolino, it was the fascists who had betrayed their Italian identity. "Italian-ness is a feeling inspired by the common good of the Italian *patria*, and respect for its traditions and civic development . . . but is this the Italian-ness of the Dopolavoro and of the cowardly profascist publications? No, it is a strange Italian-ness that dictates and imposes the will of an irresponsible minority."[126] Defending the Italian identity of his fellow Italo-Argentines, Cozzolino went on to declare, "The free Italians who live with dignity in this great and generous country . . . will never reject their Italian-ness, even far away from their venerated *patria*; they will make any sacrifice for the resurgence of a free and bountiful Italy."[127] Thus, according to Cozzolino, Italian identity was alive and well within Argentina. The very fact that so many members of the community did not support fascism was in and of itself an assertion of that identity.

In one of his *Italia Libre* editorials, Nicolas Cilla argued that the fascist regime and its propaganda blitz in Argentina had the opposite of its intended effect. According to Cilla, many Italians in Argentina only began to lose their sense of communion with the *patria* after the advent of fascism. Inverting the fascist claims that they had renewed Italian identity abroad, Cilla argued that Italians in Argentina prior to fascism had always remained loyal to Italy. "It was natural that the Italians living in America, even if they were influenced by the customs of their new countries, maintained an affectionate memory of their distant *patria* and remained interested in its economic and civil progress." All this, however, changed after 1922: "Fascism's propaganda, its parades and ceremonies, left little impression on the Italians of America. . . . As the [fascist] movement progressed, the Italian immigrants of America felt more and more morally separated from an Italy that they no longer understood."[128] The Italy these immigrants knew and loved had been the Italy of the Risorgimento, which valued individual freedom. After the rise of fascism, Italian immigrants shared more in common ideologically with Argentina, a nation with a liberal political system and constitutional guarantees "based more or less on the same principles of the Risorgimento." In terms of values and beliefs, Argentina for the Italian immigrant had become more "Italian" than the regime in power in Italy. As a result, Cilla concluded, "the Italians of America in general, and particularly in Argentina, felt less solidarity with their country of origin and identified more with their adopted countries."[129] In another article, Cilla spoke of the fascist regime's "militant penetration" into Argentina, which while gaining a few fanatical recruits, "demonstrated how unpopular the regime has become to the vast majority Italians who have assimilated to and respect the ideals of the New World and its democratic system of government."[130] In other words, by being good Italians, immigrants found it easy to assimilate into an Argentine nation that valued the same ideals.

This way of viewing Italian national identity departs significantly from both the fascist and the antifascist narratives, which had simply written their values into their patriotic myths of the nation. Italian immigrants instead wrote their own version of Italy's national narrative, a narrative that seamlessly incorporated Argentina's national iconography, populating their pantheon of Italian heroes with Argentine patriots. The result was a hybrid Italian identity unique to the community.

Italian identity in the pages of most of the community's antifascist periodicals centered on the democratic values and beliefs that derived from the French Revolution and were the cornerstones of the republics in the Americas. Interestingly, the fascists, by insisting in their propaganda that to be a good Italian meant to be a good fascist, had played into the antifascists' hands by enabling them to separate their own definition of an Italian identity from simple links of culture and blood. These antifascist periodicals, unlike those of the *fuorusciti*, also did much more than simply advance an ideational sense of identity. They called Argentina their new home and were well aware that they had carved out new lives in the South American republic and now shared a common destiny with other Argentines. In short, assimilation into Argentina's society, rather than the liberation of Italy, was their main priority, a fact that both the fascists abroad and the *fuorusciti* exiles never fully appreciated.

Members of the Italian community accentuated the Italian stamp on the Argentine nation from the very origins of the New World to the founding of the nation. In speaking of Columbus's gift to humanity and western civilization, *La Patria degli Italiani*, for example, emphasized the fraternal bond Columbus Day had created among Italians and Argentines. "Italians are in solidarity with Argentines and Spaniards in honoring Columbus, who entrusted his genius to Spanish caravels and shared his pain, suffering, and glory with the sailors of that generous nation."[131] Similarly, in the pages of the Italian community press, May 25, 1810, the date of Argentina's independence, was spoken of in the same breath as September 20, 1870, and the Italian Risorgimento: both benchmarks in the triumph of liberal democracy.[132]

Following this logic, Manual Belgrano, the son of an Italian merchant and one of Argentina's founding fathers, also deserved a place among Italy's patriotic leaders since Argentina's independence was interpreted as an inspirational precursor to Italy's Risorgimento. In their fight for freedom and liberty, the founding fathers of Argentina embodied those values that also served as the foundation of Italy's unification.[133] In 1927 a statue of Manuel Belgrano sent to Italy by the immigrant community in Argentina was erected in Genoa, an event that underscored the significance of Belgrano to the community's own Italian national narrative. The Italian acceptance of the statue to Belgrano was for the community more than just an act of friendship but rather a physical acknowledgment of their community's presence in Italy's national narrative. In celebrating the event, an article in *La Patria degli Italiani* declared, "In Belgrano one sees a symbol of the energy, sobriety, and modesty of the millions of Italians who crossed over to the River Plate full of hope. . . . Today it is enough to just write down the name of one son of Italians, MANUEL BELGRANO: Italian thought and Italian action in Argentina, full of enthusiasm and without vanity, he provided the foundation of Argentina's civil virtue"[134]

A look at how the images of Garibaldi and the Risorgimento are employed in these community newspapers is also suggestive of the underlying differences between local and international antifascist movements. These newspapers, like those of the *fuorusciti*, linked Garibaldi with the ideals of liberty and justice. However, they additionally associated him specifically with Italian unity and the values of the liberal Italy. They identified him with the Italy of their past, the Italy that they had left to seek out a new life in Argentina. To these writers, Garibaldi embodied the particular values and aspirations of the Italian community in Argentina. "Garibaldi Is Ours!" ran the headline of an article in *Italia del Popolo*, which challenged directly the fascist regime's co-optation of the Italian patriot.[135] Giuseppe Garibaldi, who fought for freedom and justice both in the hills of Italy and on the Pampas of Argentina, was another patriotic hero in the community's Italian national narrative. He also encapsulated in his personage the two nations' shared values and common purpose. To these writers, Garibaldi was not only the great leader of Italy's unification. An immigrant in Argentina like them, he also played an important role in bringing democracy and civilization to Argentina as well as Italy. In discussing Italian contributions to Argentina, a *La Patria degli Italiani* article linked both Mazzini and Garibaldi to the foundation of Argentina, explaining that "in two beautiful squares in Buenos Aires we find statues in honor of Mazzini and Garibaldi, the thought and action of Italian independence and also the thought and action of Argentine liberty."[136] Unlike the more universal image of the *fuorusciti*, the Risorgimento and its heroes were intimately associated with the collective identity of the community.

CONCLUSION

Historian Craig Calhoun in a recent study on national identity explains the central importance of understanding "the contemporary conditions that make [nationalism] effective in people's lives and that affect both their attempts to orient themselves in the world and their actions."[137] It was in large part the fascist regime's inability to appreciate the political and social realities of the Italian community in Argentina that explains the lack of understanding between the Italian community and the regime, and also explains why antifascist *fuorusciti* had difficulty relating to members of the local antifascist movement. The fascists as well as the antifascist *fuorusciti* had formulated their concepts of a national identity abroad based on their own needs, without taking into account the particular conditions that affected the lives of Italians in Argentina. What they failed to comprehend was that the priorities and concerns of the community were not the same as those of the regime or the international antifascist movement.

Whether supporting or opposing the fascist regime, members of the Italian community used the propaganda to serve their own ends, at once challenging fascism's claims over Italian identity while at the same time using its propaganda as a way to help them assimilate into the Argentine nation. In many, though not all, cases, the Italian community, including those sympathetic to fascism, moved in the opposite direction from what the regime had intended. Members of the Italian community in Argentina demonstrated an ideational sense of a national identity that countered that of the fascists. These ideals, even among the supporters of fascism, were liberty, democracy, and a commitment to the values of the Risorgimento, ideals that had more in common with those of their new nation in opposition to those of the fascist political ideology. This debate, therefore, underscores the important influence that New World national models played in informing how Italian immigrants viewed their Old World national identity. That the fascist regime had no way of silencing their opponents or controlling the way their messages were received and debated also demonstrates the weaknesses and limitations inherent in promoting a national identity outside of the nation-state.

In the end, the writings of these individuals suggest that the Italian community in Argentina rejected fascist Italy's definition of an Italian identity abroad. With deep roots in Argentina and a shared set of beliefs, the Italians in Argentina demonstrated that they had become more than just "Italians living abroad." After over fifty years of immigration, they had carved out their own niche in Argentine society and created their own sense of an Italian national identity outside of the *patria*, an identity they fiercely defended in the face of the fascist propaganda blitz.

NOTES

1. See, for example, Judith Casali de Babot and María Victoria Grillo, *Fascismo y antifascismo en Europa y Argentina en el siglo XX* (San Miguel de Tucumán: Instituto de Investigaciones Historicas, Universidad Nacional de Tucumán, 2002); Federica Bertagna, *La stampa italiana in Argentina* (Rome: Donzelli Editore, 2009); Pantaleone Sergi, "Fascismo e antifascismo nella stampa italiana in Argentina: Cosí fu spenta 'la Patria degli Italiani,'" *Altreitalie* 42 (2007): 4–44; Ronald C. Newton, "*Ducini, Prominenti, Antifascisti*: Italian Fascism and the Italo-Argentine Collectivity, 1922–1945," *Americas* 51, no. 1 (1994): 41–66; M. L. Leiva, "Il movimiento antifascista italiano in Argentina (1922–1945)," in *Gli Italiani fuori d'Italia: Gli emigranti italiani nei movimienti operai dei paesi d'adozione, 1880–1940*, ed. Bruno Bezza, 553–82 (Milan: Franco Angelli Editori, 1983); Pietro Rinaldo Fanesi, "El anti-fascismo italiano en Argentina (1922–1945)," *Estudios Migratorios Latinoamericanos* 4, no. 12 (1989): 319–352; Clara Aldrighi, *Antifascismo italiano en Montevideo: El dialogo politico entre Luigi Fabbri y Carlo Rosselli* (Montevideo: Universidad de la Republica, 1996); Clara Aldrighi, "Luigi Fabbri en Uruguay, 1929–1935," *Estudios Migratorios Latinoamericanos* 12, no. 37 (1997): 389–422; Camilla Cattarulla, "Cosa direste a Mussolini se aveste occasione di parlargli? Un inchiesta de 'Il Mattino d'Italia,'" in *Fascisti in Sud America*, ed. Eugenia Scarzanella, 175–203 (Florence: Le Lettere, 2005). Of these works, María Victoria Grillo's and Camilla Catarulla's analyses of immigrant responses to fascism most closely resemble my approach to

the question of identity. Grillo recognizes the various factors that influence Italian immigrant identity, including class consciousness as well as politics, and Catarulla's study of a sampling of individual responses to a fascist survey conducted by *Il Mattino d'Italia* takes into account the role of immigrant experiences in Argentina and their influence on immigrant interpretations of fascism.

2. Fernando Devoto, *Historia de los Italianos en la Argentina* (Buenos Aires: Editorial Biblios, 2006), 372–373.

3. Eric Hobsbawm, *Nations and Nationalism since 1780: Programme, Myth, and Reality* (Cambridge: Cambridge University Press, 1993), 130.

4. In this chapter I am purposefully excluding Vittorio Valdani and *Il Mattino d'Italia*, which I discussed instead in chapter 3 in the context of the regime's activities in Argentina. My reading of the documentary evidence leads me to believe that the newspaper and its views did not represent an independent or representative voice within the community but were instead filtered and controlled by the fascist state and its agents. For a different interpretation see Scarzanella, *Fascisti in Sud America*, which uses *Il Mattino d'Italia* as the focus of their study of fascism and responses to it within the community in Argentina. For an alternative discussion of Vittorio Valdani as well as Arsenio Guido Buffarini, see Ronald C. Newton, "Ducini, Prominenti, Antifascist: Italian Fascism and the Italo-Argentine Community." Newton especially highlights the role of Buffarini in the community. My study agrees with this assessment.

5. Buffarini, Arsenio Guido, *Tutta un'esistenza di italianità: Arsenio Guido Buffarini e las sua opera: Un trentennio vissuto combattendo per la gloria dell'Italia e per la fraternitá Italo-Argentina* (Buenos Aires, 1931), 466.

6. Ibid.

7. Pignatti to Parini, August 22, 1930, Le Carte del Gabinetto del Ministro e della Segretaria Generale dal 1923 al 1943, file 819, Archivio Storico del Ministero degli Affari Esteri (hereafter cites in notes as ASMAE).

8. Ministry of Foreign Affirs, "Pro-Memoria per il Ministro," November 12, 1930, Inventario della Serie Affari Politici (1919–1930), file 808, ASMAE.

9. Buffarini, *Tutta un'esistenza di italianità*.

10. "Impressioni di Viaggiatori sul Fascismo," *La Nación*, 1926, in Buffarini, *Tutta un'esistenza di italianità*, 498–99.

11. Buffarini, "I rapporti fra la Federazione Generale delle Societá Italiane e il governo fascista," May 15, 1926, in Buffarini, *Tutta un'esistenza di italianità*, 447.

12. Buffarini, *Tutta un'esistenza di italianità*, 702.

13. "Confraternidad Italo-Argentina," *La Razón*, October 1925, in Buffarini, *Tutta un'esistenza di italianità*, 400.

14. Buffarini, *Tutta un'esistenza di italianità*, 703.

15. Ibid. These themes are found throughout Buffarini's work.

16. Dionisio Petriella and Sara Sosa Miatello, *Diccionario Biográfico Italo-Argentino* (Buenos Aires: Asociación Dante Alighieri de Buenos Aires, 1976).

17. Folco Testena, "A viso aperto," *Il Giornale d'Italia*, December 9, 1931.

18. Folco Testena, "Difendere e Difondere nel popolo la lingua e il pensiero d'Italia," *Il Giornale d'Italia*, December 14, 1931.

19. Folco Testena, "Necessità d'espandere la cultura italiana superiore," *Il Giornale d'Italia*, December 24, 1931.

20. Ibid.

21. Folco Testena, "Fascismo e Democrazia," *Il Giornale d'Italia*, December 25, 1931.

22. Ibid.

23. Ibid.

24. Folco Testena, "Gli italiani e la politica argentina," *Il Giornale d'Italia*, December 26, 1931.

25. Ibid.
26. Ibid.
27. Ibid.
28. Ibid.
29. Ibid.

30. *Mattino d'Italia*, December 18, 1931; for Testena's response, see "Legittima difesa," *Il Giornale d'Italia*, December 19, 1931.

31. Goffredo Marchetti, *Risposte di buon senso alle principali obbiezioni che si fanno all'estero contro il fascismo* (La Plata: Mandolin and Bonaventura, 1940).

32. Ibid., 18.
33. Ibid., 22.
34. Ibid., 15.
35. Ibid.
36. Ibid., 37.
37. Ibid.
38. Ibid, 25.

39. Italian Embassy in Buenos Aires to Ministero della Cultura Popolare, March 4, 1940, 4, Ministero della Cultura Popolare (hereafter cited in notes as Minculpop) Direzioni Servizi della Propaganda, file 10, Archivio Centrale dello Stato (hereafter cites in notes as ACS).

40. Buffarini, *Tutta un'esistenza di italianità*, 191.
41. Ibid., 354–55.
42. Ibid., 340–41.

43. The best general work on the *fuorusciti* is Charles Delzell's classic study *Mussolini's Enemies: The Italian Anti-fascist Resistance* (Princeton, NJ: Princeton University Press, 1961). See also Alfonso Bartolini, *Storia della resistenza italiana all'estero* (Padova: Rebellato, 1965), and, for Argentina, Fanesi, "El anti-fascismo italiano en Argentina."

44. For example, see Clara Aldrighi, *Anti-fascismo italiano en Montevideo* and "Luigi Fabbri en Uruguay."

45. This chapter focuses on the theme of antifascism narrowly in the context of Italian national identity abroad. For a more general examination of native Argentine antifascism and its collaboration with Italian antifascists, see Andrés Bisso, *El antifascismo argentino: Selección documental y estudio preliminar* (Buenos Aires: Editorial Buenos Libros, 2007).

46. Francesco Frola, "La Pugnalata nella schiena," *Il Risorgimento*, December 29, 1930. The nearly complete collection of *Il Risorgimento* is available on microfilm housed in the University of Texas at Austin Latin American Collection, reels 8A, 29 and 30.

47. For the purposes my discussion here, I focus on the work and writings of those *fuorusciti* who either spent most of their time in Argentina or whose propaganda had an important influence on the region. For another discussion of the prominent Italian antifascists in Argentina examined here, see Fanesi, "El antifascismo italiano en Argentina."

48. "Gasperini, Domenico," Casellario Politico Centrale (hereafter cited in notes as CPC), file 4956, 2300, ACS.

49. Philip V. Cannistraro and Brian R. Sullivan, *Il Duce's Other Woman: The Untold True Story of Margherita Sarfatti, Benito Mussolini's Jewish Mistress, and How She Helped Him Come to Power* (New York: William Morrow, 1993), 55–56.

50. "Gasperini, Domenico," CPC, file 4956, 2300, ACS.
51. Ibid.

52. "Nemici palesi e occulti boicottano 'Risorgimento,'" *Il Risorgimento*, December 5, 1930.

53. Information on Frola's activities comes from his Italian police file, CPC, file 2188, ACS, and his own memoirs, *Recuerdos de un anti-fascista, 1925–1938* (N.p.: Editorial Mexico Nuevo, 1939), 145–52.

54. Consolato Italiano Bahia Blanca, "Dispaccio n. 2081/72 Avv. Francesco Frola—Antifascista," CPC, file 2188, ACS.

55. Frola, *Requerdos de un anti-fascista*, 149.
56. "Il concetto di patria ed i fascisti," *Il Risorgimento*, December 17, 1930.
57. "Italia ed anti-Italia," *Il Risorgimento*, December 1, 1930.
58. Ibid.
59. Ibid.
60. "La collettività italiana: Prima e dopo il fascismo," *Il Risorgimento*, December 12, 1930.
61. "Il concetto di patria ed i fascisti," *Il Risorgimento*, December 17, 1930.

62. All of the cartoons discussed above can be found in the December 1930 and January 1931 issues of *Il Risorgimento*.
63. *Il Risorgimento*, December 1, 1930.
64. Ibid.
65. Ibid.
66. "Fabbri, Luigi," CPC, file 1906, ACS.
67. Ibid.
68. Luigi Fabbri, "La lotta anarchista contro il fascismo," *La Lotta Umana*, February 23, 1928, included in the collection of Fabbri's writings compiled by Gaetano Manfredonia in *La lutte humaine: Luigi Fabbri, le mouvement anarchiste italien et la lutte contre le fascisme* (Paris: Editions du Monde Libertaire, 1994) 347–352.
69. Luigi Fabbri, "La impotencia de la democracia capitalista," *La Revista Blanca*, June 1, 1931, in Manfredonia, *La lutte humaine*, 317–18.
70. Ibid.
71. Luigi Fabbri, "Las dictadoras contro la libertad de los pueblos," *La Protesta*, May 2 and May 18, 1927, in Manfredonia, *La lutte humaine*, 279.
72. Fabbri, *La contro-rivoluzione preventiva (riflessioni sul fascismo)* (Bologna: Licinio Capellu, 1922), 66.
73. Ibid
74. Luigi Fabbri passed way in June 1934, but his work would be continued by his daughter Luce. Luce took over as the editor of *Studi Sociali* and wrote her own history of the fascist regime in Spanish titled *Camisas negras* (Buenos Aires: Ediciones Nervio, 1935). Beyond a history of the fascist seizure of power in Italy, Luce Fabbri's book detailed the mechanisms of fascist state control along with the ways Mussolini silenced and intimidated the opposition, while using his control over the schools, the radio waves, and the press to indoctrinate the masses. Like her father before her, Luce framed work in universal terms, Fabbri described a world swaying between two opposite spiritual and moral systems: one of liberty and one of dictatorship, with fascist Italy serving as the model for the latter.
75. *Il Risorgimento*, December 1, 1930.
76. Italian Embassy in Buenos Aires to Foreign Ministry, May 4, 1937, Minculpop Direzione Serviz della Propaganda, file 7, ACS.
77. Letter of Torquato di Tela, April 23, 1937, Inventario degli Archivi Microfilmati delle Associazioni Italiane in Argentina, role 89, ASMAE.
78. Letter of Delfino, Buenos Aires, 1935, Inventario degli Archivi Microfilmati delle Associazioni Italiane in Argentina, role 89, ASMAE.
79. "Delfino, Luigi," CPC, file 1675, ACS.
80. Ibid.
81. Regia Ambassciata d'Italia Buenos Aires, "Torquato di Tella ingeniere ed anti-fascista," CPC, file 1822, ASC; see also Ronald C. Newton, "*Ducini, Prominenti, Antifascisti*," 64.
82. "Accordo compatto e tenace," *Il Risorgimento*, December 1, 1930.
83. "Ai lettori," *La Patria degli Italiani*, September 3, 1931.
84. These observations are drawn from issues of *La Patria degli Italiani* during the last decade of its existence: 1921–1931.
85. "A tutti gli Italiani," *La Patria degli Italiani*, September 4, 1931.
86. "Per fissare le posizione," *La Patria degli Italiani*, December 30, 1929. The theme of liberalism is also identified and discussed as a central component to the paper's antifascism in Sergi, "Fascismo e antifascismo nella stampa italiana."
87. "Ai connazionali," *La Patria degli Italiani*, November 4, 1929; "Per fissare le posizione," *La Patria degli Italiani*, December 30, 1929.
88. "Né fascisti né antifascisti," *La Patria degli Italiani*, November 28, 1929.
89. "XI Anniversario della Vittoria," *La Patria degli Italiani*, November 4, 1929.
90. "Per fissare le posizione," *La Patria degli Italiani*, December 30, 1929.
91. "La bandiera," *La Patria degli Italiani*, August 15, 1931.
92. Ibid.
93. Ibid.
94. "Dissolvimento e rinnovazione," *La Patria degli Italiani*, September 12, 1931.

95. "Mai come ora . . . ," *La Patria degli Italiani*, September 24, 1931.
96. "Non può essere buon italiano chi non é antifascista," *L'Italia del Popolo*, December 10, 1931.
97. I focus here narrowly on articles that relate to Italian identity. For a more in-depth analysis of *L'Italia del Popolo*'s overall antifascist agenda, see Bertagna, *La stampa italiana in Argentina*.
98. "Parliamo Italiano, ma . . . parliamo con franchezza," *L'Italia del Popolo*, January 21, 1932.
99. Engenio Alfa, "Le scuole Italiane ed il loro sviluppo," *L'Italia del Popolo*, March 14, 1935.
100. "Commentando il discorso di Piero Parini," *L'Italia del Popolo*, December 26, 1931.
101. "L'abisso fra la vecchia immigrazione italiana e l'imperialismo della nuova," *L'Italia del Popolo*, April 27, 1938.
102. Ibid.
103. Ibid.
104. "Non può essere buon italiano chi non é antifascista," *L'Italia del Popolo*, December 10, 1931.
105. Ibid.
106. "'L'Italia senza libertà non sarebbe piú l'Italia; e la libertà senza l'Italia non sarebbe piú la libertà!'" *L'Italia del Popolo*, September 22, 1936.
107. "Il XX settembre é ancora programma degli italiani . . ." *L'Italia del Popolo*, September 20, 1938.
108. Ibid.
109. "Gli italiani all'estero, la patria, il fascismo e la Guerra d'Africa," *L'Italia del Popolo*, February 4, 1936.
110. "Organizzazione militare fascista italiana in Buenos Aires," *L'Italia del Popolo*, April 5, 1938; "L'abisso fra la vecchia immigrazione italiana e l'imperialismo della nuova," *L'Italia del Popolo*, April 27, 1938.
111. Orsini di Saint-Just, "La fratellanza italo-argentina nelle sue ragioni storiche e morali," *L'Italia del Popolo*, April 10, 1933.
112. "Argentinofobia fascista," *L'Italia del Popolo*, January 30, 1930.
113. "Difendere la produzione argentina," *L'Italia del Popolo*, January 12, 1932.
114. Ibid.
115. "Organizzazione militare fascista italiana in Buenos Aires," *L'Italia del Popolo*, April 5, 1938.
116. "Gli italiani non hanno niente da temere dai decreti contro i partiti totalitari stranieri," *L'Italia del Popolo*, May 15, 1939.
117. Ettore Brazini, "Abbasso la Guerra, imperialista! Viva l'Italia libera!," *L'Italia del Popolo*, January 17, 1935.
118. "Il XX settembre é ancora programma degli italiani . . ." *L'Italia del Popolo*, September 20, 1938.
119. Mario Nicoletti, "I volontari italiani dimostrano che il nostro popolo e degno della libertà," *L'Italia del Popolo*, November 8, 1936.
120. "La crcular-programa de nuestro periódico," dated August 1, 1940, reproduced in *Italia Libre*, August 21, 1940. *Italia Libre* is available on microfilm in the Latin American periodical collection at the University of Texas at Austin.
121. Ibid.
122. Ibid.
123. Ibid.
124. "El llamado del 10 de Julio," *Italia Libre*, August 21, 1940.
125. Ibid.
126. Hector Cozzolino, "Italianidad," *Italia Libre*, March 1, 1941.
127. Ibid.
128. Nicolas Cilla, "Nuestra tarea: Preparar espiritualmente a los Italianos el sugundo y definitivo 'Risorgimento,'" *Italia Libre*, January 25, 1941.
129. Ibid.

130. "Italia y America Latina," *Italia Libre*, September 20, 1940.

131. *La Patria degli Italiani*, October 12, 1929.

132. This connection between Argentina's and Italy's national past is most explicit in the pages of *Italia Libre*, although *L'Italia del Popolo* and *La Patria degli Italiani* both ran articles honoring Argentina's national celebrations and identified Manuel Belgrano as one of their own. See, for example, "9 luglio 1816-9 luglio 1929," *La Patria degli Italiani*, July 9, 1929; "Davanti alla storia," *L'Italia del Popolo*, February 21, 1932.

133. "1810 Maggio XXV 1932: La fede degli uomini liberi per la grandezza Argentina," *L'Italia del Popolo*, May 25, 1932.

134. "Nel 12 Ottobre, Giorno di Colombo, Italia Esalta il Generale Belgrano," *La Patria degli Italiani*, October 12, 1927.

135. "Strappiamo al fascismo le grandi figure della democrazia: Garibaldi è nostro," *L'Italia del Popolo*, May 5, 1932.

136. *La Patria degli Italiani*, October 12, 1927.

137. Craig Calhoun, "Nationalism Matters," in *Nationalism in the New World*, ed. Don H. Doyle and Marco Antonio Pamplona (Athens: University of Georgia Press, 2006), 32.

Chapter Six

Italian Identity and Argentina's National Debate

On June 5, 1940, as Nazi Germany's armies marched through Western Europe, Argentine Congressman Agustín Rodríguez Araya stated what many of his countrymen were undoubtedly aware of: "We have arrived at a point in our political and social evolution in which external factors and influences are forcing us make an effort to recover the essential attributes of Argentine identity."[1] Even before the onset of the Second World War, both the Italian fascist regime and Nazi Germany had long been infiltrating the republic with its national propaganda. As the Argentine congressman alluded to in his remarks before the Chamber of Deputies: foreign political ideologies and propaganda efforts in Argentina were inspiring Argentines of different political persuasions to reaffirm their own national project.

What Rodríguez Araya left unstated was that more than external factors were at play in Argentina during the 1930s. Fascist Italy arrived in Argentina during one of the most tumultuous periods in the nation's history: the so-called *década infame*, a key moment in the creation of Argentina's modern political identity, in which nothing less than its democracy hung in the balance. For the first time in its history, Argentine nationalists began to challenge the national narrative by directly attacking the democratic foundation of Argentina's national project. Whether as a model to be emulated or as a cautionary example to be avoided, Argentines on both the right and left referred to Italian fascism in formulating their own visions of the Argentine nation. Just as the Argentine context of the debate influenced how Italian national identity was reimagined in Argentina, the Italian national debate similarly influenced Argentina's own debate over its national narrative.

The dynamics of identity formation in Argentina as well as in other New World nations are in many ways distinct from the models proposed by Benedict Anderson, Anthony D. Smith, and Eric Hobsbawn in that they did not rely primarily on the creation of a set of cultural, ethnic, or historical attributes to imagine a collective identity. As the authors in Don H. Doyle and Marco Antonio Pamplona's edited volume *Nationalism in the New World* demonstrate, these nationalisms instead relied on a unifying set of values and beliefs from which to construct a more inclusive and multiethnic national identity based on shared ideas.[2] Fascist Italy's antidemocratic, ethnic-based identity, which called on its emigrants to resist assimilation, tore at the very fabric of Argentina's ideational national identity.

What transpired in Argentina highlights one of the problems inherent to promoting a national project in another sovereign nation. The national agenda promoted by the Italian regime could not but alienate the wider Argentine population. Even those sympathetic to the regime and its political ideology would be hard-pressed to support its intrusive foreign nationalization agenda. In the end, Argentina's ideational democratic national discourse was able to withstand, at least for the moment, the attacks on its national project, both from at home as well as abroad.

THE ARGENTINE NATION: BETWEEN DEMOCRACY AND DICTATORSHIP

Throughout Argentina's history as a nation, democracy was as much a collective fiction as a political reality. As one of the new American republics that gained its independence in the wake of the French Revolution, it was a nation defined by its democratic identity. Due to its vast expanses, problematic relationship with Spain's cultural heritage, and lack of a rich Creole or indigenous cultural heritage from which to construct a cultural identity, Argentine intellectuals since independence based their conceptualization of the nation on a set of democratic principles: that of a people united and defined by their shared commitment to a republican civil society based on individual rights and freedom. This conceptualization of the nation, however, would be tested over the course of Argentina's history as a nation.

After independence, Argentina underwent a period of civil war and dictatorship plagued by conflicts between the Unitarians, who favored a stronger centralized government and the interests of the urban commercial elite, and the Federalists, who fought for greater provincial autonomy and favored the rural interests of the cattle ranchers. Federalist caudillos, rural strongmen with their own militias, dominated the period, relying on a web of patronage and clientelism to maintain power. In 1829 the most successful of these caudillo chieftains, Juan Manuel de Rosas, took control of Buenos Aires and ruled by decree as his opponents fled into exile. In 1852 these political exiles, known as *La Generación de 1837*, defeated Rosas and returned to build a new Argentine nation.[3]

Once in power, the new political elite, led by Bartolomé Mitre, Domingo Faustino Sarmiento, and Juan Bautista Alberdi, strengthened the power of the state, stabilized the economy, and strove to create a new, stronger Argentine nation based on the principles of liberalism and progress. They cultivated an Argentine identity based on a civil society inspired by the United States. They looked to Europe culturally and strove to create a cosmopolitan Creole (native Argentine) identity, which was distinct from Spain, but also in contrast to the perceived barbarity of the countryside. The two pillars of their nationalization project were public education in order to create a patriotic civil society and European immigration, which it was thought would create a new Argentine population that could tame the wilderness.[4]

The recent work of Jorge Myers and Jean H. Delaney illustrate how Argentine intellectuals negotiated their own New World identity in the nineteenth and early twentieth centuries. Both authors highlight the role played by Argentina's founding ideals of democracy and individual liberty, arguing that most national discourses defined Argentina as a nation of the future, and rather than creating a constellation of cultural myths and historic narratives to unify the people, they strove to create an inclusive collective identity based on a shared set of values. Both authors, however, also trace the emergence of a more ethnic-based national discourse that was attached to the core of Argentina's ideational national identity. Myers identifies the rise of a cultural nationalism in the writings of mid-nineteenth-century elites who defined the national discourse in terms of civilization (liberal, cosmopolitan, and European) in contrast to the countryside (savage, wild, and barbarous). Delaney highlights the rise of ethnic as well as cultural definitions of the nation that emerged out of the writings of Ricardo Rojas, who wrote on the mystical pull of the Argentine soil and idealized the rural life of the Pampas.[5]

During the late nineteenth century, Argentina saw unprecedented economic growth based on the export of cattle and wheat. Politically, Argentina was ruled by a small oligarchic elite with very limited popular participation. Immigration, urbanization, and industrialization during the turn of the century, however, led to the rise of mass party politics and election reforms spearheaded by the charismatic Radical Party leader Hipólito Yrigoyen. From 1912 to 1930, Argentina enjoyed its first taste of free mass elections and popular participation in government. Its democratic experiment was short lived. Political instability, labor unrest, and ultimately the economic crash of 1929 hit Argentina especially hard, discrediting the Radical Party and opening the way for a military coup on September 6, 1930, led by General José F. Uriburu.[6]

The new government was the result of a temporary alliance between conservatives and nationalists. The conservatives favored preserving Argentina's political institutions and democratic traditions as well as the social status quo, but they hoped to rule Argentina in the manner of the traditional oligarchic elite. In contrast, the nationalists wanted to radically change the structure of society by creating a personalist dictatorship and establishing an all-powerful authoritarian corporatist state. Uriburu was himself a nationalist, and in his year in power he attempted to implement this agenda. An open admirer of the Duce, Uriburu used the structure of Mussolini's Italy as his model and even created his own *squadristi*-inspired paramilitary organization: the Legión Cívica Argentina. The conservatives, alarmed by his extremist policies, forced Uriburu to call new presidential elections in 1931, which they then fixed to ensure that their candidate, Agustín P. Justo, would win. Justo as well as his successor, Roberto M. Ortiz, ruled over what has become known as the *década infame*, which lasted until another military coup in 1943. Once president, Justo relied on a coalition of conservative parties to consolidate his hold over power and was careful to restore the façade of democracy to the Argentine political process, avoiding openly repressive measures. He allowed the existence of opposition parties, both on the right and on the left, and allowed them seats in Congress, while at the same time ensuring through rigged elections that they remained outside of halls of presidential power. This period was one of intense national debate and civil unrest as Socialist and Radical Party members pressed for a return to true democracy, while right-wing nationalists took to the streets promoting fascist-style authoritarian solutions.[7] With Argentina's political destiny swaying between democracy and dictatorship, Italian fascist propaganda had a direct and immediate relevance to the discussions of the day. Underlying this political debate is a national one: the question of how to define Argentina's identity as a nation. What follows is an exploration of how Argentines on both the left and the right politically used the Italian propaganda to project their own conceptualizations of the Argentine national project and why the government ultimately condemned the Italian national project as a threat to Argentina's identity as a nation.

ARGENTINE NATIONALISTS LOOK TO ITALIAN FASCISM

Argentine nationalism as it developed in the early twentieth century was primarily a right-wing political movement. Its leaders were disaffected members of the Argentine elite who rejected the liberal and positivist ideologies that predominated in their day and were instead drawn to idealist philosophy and Catholic spiritualism. Nationalist intellectuals such as Leopoldo Lujones and Manuel Gálvez exalted Argentina's Spanish Creole cultural heritage and favored the moral purity of rural life over the decadent culture of cosmopolitan Buenos Aires. They resented Britain's historical dominance over the economy but were far more troubled by the menacing anarchist and radical tendencies of the immigrant working classes. They attacked immigrants for their materialistic self-interests, loose morals, and lack of culture, saving their most vehement diatribes for the Jews, who they accused of conspiring at all times to destroy the Argentine nation and enslave its people.[8] The nationalists associated Argentine national identity with idyllic representations of the Gaucho and the Pampas: Juan Manuel de Rosas, the caudillo who ruled Argentina with an iron fist in the early nineteenth century, became a symbol of Argentine cultural independence, and a mischievous fictional gaucho created by José Hernandez named Martín Fierro became an iconic national figure.

Historians of Argentine nationalism have identified the 1920s and 1930s as the height of right-wing intellectual discourses, which stemmed from the earlier writings of Rojas and the intellectuals described by Delaney. Unlike Rojas, these nationalists directly challenged the ideational model of Argentina's national identity by creating a xenophobic ethnic-cultural identity that highlighted Argentina's Spanish and Catholic roots and advanced an exclusionary model of identity. This movement also openly criticized Argentina's democratic institutions and ideals, suggesting in their place authoritarian solutions and rocking the foundation of Argentina's identity as a nation.[9]

Uriburu's aforementioned dictatorship was the key moment in the development of the Argentine Right. Many of the disparate nationalist groups came together to support Uriburu's attempt to create a fascist-style government before he was forced to resign in 1931. Uriburu would die a few months later in Paris, but his movement, along with other nationalist factions, continued to flourish throughout the 1930s. These "patriotic" leagues competed with each other for national attention, staging rallies and marches and battling their radical and socialist foes on the streets and in the press.[10]

After the death of Uriburu, there was no single individual or party who could unify these disparate nationalist groups. Many flocked around personalities and newspapers, but no one emerged as a leader and no one newspaper or party dominated the nationalist discourse. While many of the earlier nationalist thinkers retreated from public life or shied away from the more extremist turn the movement was taking, Manuel Gálvez remained at the center of nationalist thought. A novelist and biographer who began his career at the turn of the century, Gálvez wrote articles and tracts that had a great influence on the movement, while a fellow nationalist, Martínez Zuviría, turned heads with his virulently anti-Semitic tomes. Senator Matías Sánchez-Sorondo, the Argentine minister of the interior under Uriburu, along with his son Marcelo also emerged as prominent figures in the nationalist camp, the father as a senator and later the president of the Argentine Commission on Culture, and the son as a Spanish Civil War correspondent for *La Nación*, a mainstream daily newspaper.[11] As for the press, *La Fronda*, the long-standing conservative-nationalist voice in the community, continued on, while a new wave of nationalist papers emerged, the first of which was the short-lived *La Nueva República*, soon followed by *Crisol*, a Catholic-nationalist newspaper edited by Enrique Oses, and *La Bandera Argentina*, edited by Juan E. Carulla, former head of Uriburu's Legión Cívica.

Inspired by the apparent success of Mussolini's fascist state in Italy, the nationalists' rhetoric became increasingly antidemocratic and authoritarian as many soaked up the Italian regime's propaganda. Right-wing nationalists were especially influenced by fascist Italy's political program, looking toward fascist Italy as a model and fascism more generally as a possible solution to Argentina's sociopolitical problems, which included foreign economic dominance of the economy, severe economic depression, and a corrupt conservative government. They did much more than simply reproduce Italian propaganda, however. Federico Finchelstein's recent work on Italian fascist propaganda and Argentine nationalism demonstrates quite effectively the ways in which the nationalists adapted the fascist political program to suit their own ideological beliefs. According to Finchelstein, the nationalists selectively incorporated certain elements of the fascist program while rejecting others, a process that ultimately crystallized into a uniquely Argentine brand of fascism. Like Italian fascism, Argentine nationalism rejected rational Enlightenment ideas, made violence integral to its ideological program, and created a cultlike following around its leaders. In a departure from its Italian counterpart, however, Argentina's fascism was more clerical in character, rejecting Italy's totalitarian model while exhibiting a shrill anti-Semitism.[12]

Nationalist newspapers throughout the 1930s reported regularly on Mussolini's accomplishments in Italy, relying on information provided by the Italian embassy and the Roma Press news service. The articles that made use of the Roma Press focused especially on fascist accomplishments, such as the famed battle of the births and the battle for the grain, as well as the success of the corporatist state.[13] *La Fronda* reproduced photos and propaganda materials requested from the Ministry of Popular Culture, while other nationalist newspapers reprinted full-length speeches and articles by Mussolini that had been published in the Italian daily *L'Italia del Popolo*, everything from Mussolini's condemnation of socialism to excerpts from his *Enciclopedia Italiana* definition of fascism.[14] A *La Bandera Argentina* headline proclaimed, "Mussolini's political and social doctrines continue to excite the world."[15] *La Bandera Argentina*, in fact, made the fullest use of the Italian propaganda, devoting a regular column to Roma Press pieces. Titled "Summary of Fascism's International Activities," the section included news information as well as full-length propaganda articles that celebrated fascist Italy and provided the regime's perspective on international affairs. The majority of these articles recounted the success of corporatism, the political genius of Mussolini, and the tremendous architectural and cultural accomplishments of the regime.

Nationalist politicians also expressed their admiration for Italian fascism, first among them Senator Matías Sánchez-Sorondo. A champion for the Italian regime against its opponents within Argentina, he opposed the League of Nations' sanctions against Italy after Mussolini's invasion of Ethiopia. Sánchez-Sorondo also looked to introduce programs in Argentina that emulated the Italian fascist state. During a 1937 visit to Rome, he expressed his desire to "see how one applies fascist principles in all areas, including jurisprudence," and declared that he "was captivated by Mussolini's personality and was anxious to meet with him personally."[16] Upon his return to Buenos Aires, Sánchez-Sorondo, according to the Italian embassy, "expressed his complete satisfaction with his trip to Italy and openly admired the extraordinary accomplishments [of the regime] in all fields, adding that, 'my meetings with the Duce were unforgettable.'"[17]

Following the rise of fascist movements throughout Europe, articles in the nationalist press also discussed its universal application. "The Fascist Revolution will conquer the entire world," declared one issue of *La Bandera Argentina*, while another proclaimed that "fascism is marching across all of the world's roads; it will not be long before it takes control of the seats of government in all nations with solid cultural and historical traditions."[18] An article in *Crisol* honoring Mussolini's March on Rome announced that "today's celebration is not only important for Italians and the children of Italians, but also of special interest and significance for all of mankind."[19] Describing the accomplishments of Mussolini's regime, the article went on to declare that "the powerful achievements of fascism within the state are so numerous it is almost impossible to list them all, but most of them are known throughout the world due to their transcendent and fundamental importance."[20] Another regular column in *La Bandera Argentina* titled "Fascism on the March" detailed the international spread of the fascist movement worldwide, from Spain and Romania to Great Britain and Japan. Identifying with fascism, its success abroad was used as a way of legitimating the paper's own fascist-style platform.[21] For Argentina's nationalists, what began as an Italian phenomenon now reached across the ocean, garnering universal recognition.

The Italian regime's attack on liberal democracy was one of the most significant ways in which Italian fascism influenced Argentine nationalism. In 1932 Manuel Gálvez wrote on the very subject in an article titled "Fascism in Argentina." After recounting a nationalist meeting in which Juan E. Carulla spoke of Italian fascist doctrine as the solution to the world's problems, he explained:

> The most interesting [part of the evening] was not the words or views of Carulla but the fact that for the first time these views were expressed in front of an exclusively Argentine audience, which enthusiastically applauded him. It is a significant event that demonstrates how fascism is becoming known and admired by us more and more each day.[22]

For Gálvez, it was a sign that Argentines, with Mussolini's Italy in mind, began to question their own nation's faith in democracy, for "Mussolini was the first statesman to condemn democratic liberalism. Since then peoples have begun to open their eyes and see clearly. Everyone realized that equality was a lie and parliamentarianism a gigantic farce. Slowly the truths that this great statesman proclaimed are penetrating our environment."[23] Even though Argentina was far from a perfect democracy, other than Uriburu, few had ever openly challenged democracy as the ideological foundation of the nation. All this seemed to be changing: "In the past 'democracy' had been a sacred idea, now Argentines are aware that democracy is fractured throughout the world."[24] Gálvez's remarks suggest that the nationalist movement was using the case of fascist Italy to attack directly the core founding principles of Argentina's national project.

"Is Fascism necessary in our country? I believe it is." These were the words of Gálvez two years later in his tract *Este pueblo necesita . . .*, one of the most open appeals by any nationalist for a fascist regime in Argentina.[25] According to Gálvez, Argentines needed all of the fascist "values" being extolled in the Italian regime's propaganda: a culture of youth, patriotism, a "heroic sense of life," austerity, a new political order, discipline, hierarchy, authority, and idealism. For Gálvez, Argentina's decadent and corrupt democracy could not save the nation from what he described as its "spiritual impoverishment" and "materialistic sense of life." No, only "a fascist regime or something like it could produce results." Fascism was "not only social, political, and economic, but also spiritual and moral." It was a transcendental solution to modern society's problems.[26] For all of his talk of fascism's creative social and spiritual qualities, Gálvez was most attracted to its authoritarian and reactionary qualities. "What we are missing is an iron fist like that of Mussolini, Hitler, or Dollfuss, which will not only save the country from destructive and barbarous communism but will also save it for the Christian family and morality."[27] In the end, what mattered most was the upholding of the traditional establishment in the face of a perceived communist threat.

Sharing Gálvez's critique of liberal democracy, an article in *La Bandera Argentina* declared that "we believe along with Benito Mussolini that out of an entire political parliament 50 percent are stupid and 40 percent are scoundrels," while another proclaimed that, like the Duce, "we do not put off today's solutions for tomorrow, nor do we waste time with useless parliamentary debate."[28] Quoting freely from Mussolini's speeches, nationalists warned their radical and socialist opponents in Congress, who they labeled "demagogues," to take notice. Unlike in Italy, however, all this remained talk; the nationalists were quick to criticize but slow to act. There was no Argentine Mussolini, and no one dared to openly attack the conservative regime headed by President Justo. Nevertheless, it is significant that the Argentine nationalists admired Mussolini's antidemocratic authoritarian model. This is in stark contrast to many fascist sympathizers within the Italian community who had tried so hard to reconcile the two ideological systems.[29]

Different nationalist writers emphasized different aspects of the Italian fascist program. For Carulla's *La Bandera Argentina*, the essence of fascist doctrine lay in its corporatist structure. In the pages of *La Bandera Argentina*, corporatism was nothing less than "a new political civilization that consists essentially in the living bond between the individual and the state."[30] It was the system that promised to solve all of Argentina's socioeconomic woes caused by economic depression and British and American influence.[31] Of all of the nationalists, the writers of *La Bandera Argentina* were the most attracted to this "revolutionary" aspect of the fascist system, following in the path of their late hero General Uriburu, who had attempted to establish a corporatist system during his dictatorship.

Other nationalist voices remained socially conservative and shied away from any hint of revolutionary change. For example, Enrique Oses's *Crisol*, while not rejecting corporatism, interpreted fascism as above all else a reactionary nationalist movement, an instrument to save the world from the red menace. As Oses explained, "Fascism is in essence a nationalist sentiment. It is therefore against socialism, freemasonry, and abject capitalist and democratic regimes."[32] It was synonymous with order and authority, and its true value rested precisely on its antiliberalism and anticommunism.[33] But if Oses embraced fascism as a form of authoritarian nationalism, he rejected outright its totalitarian thesis, calling it "simply monstrous" that the "the state is everything" and criticizing Mussolini's infringement on Catholicism by attempting to "create a religion of the state."[34]

If nationalism drew these Argentines to the fascist cause, it would also be nationalism that would keep them apart. Nationalist papers in fact distinguished their movements from the Italian regime. *La Fronda*, for example, explained, "It might well be said that *La Fronda* is not fascist but nationalist, that is to say before and above all an Argentine newspaper in the defense of Argentine interests."[35] Outspokenly xenophobic and nativist, the Argentine nationalists could not but find the Italian regime's national project abroad objectionable.

Although Argentine nationalists admired Mussolini's political doctrine and its potentially universal applications, they were less than thrilled with his nationalization project in Argentina. As early as the 1920s, Argentine nationalists were already wary of the fascist regime's overtures toward Italian immigrant communities, as well as its militaristic portrayal of Italian immigrants abroad. A 1924 work by a nationalist novelist, Carlos Néstor Maciel, titled *La italianización de la Argentina* articulated many of these concerns. He argued that the Italian exhortation to preserve "Italian identity abroad" was irrefutable evidence that "Italian immigrants do not come to become Argentines, to incorporate themselves into our nationality.... They instead organize within their own associations controlled by fanatics of *italianidad*."[36] Alarmed by Mussolini's interpretation of emigration as expansion, Maciel characterized the Italian government's initiatives as "imperialism through immigration," declaring that, "the activities of the Italian government toward its emigrants reveal its poorly veiled tendency toward a transoceanic imperialism, based on Italian colonies without the flag.... This work, based on supposed cultural and racial antecedents, is aimed at intensifying who knows what unconfessable action by those [immigrants] destined for our country."[37] This xenophobic current in Argentine nationalism, together with the Italian regime's actual nationalization project at work within their country, would ultimately prevent the Italian fascists from having any hope of a substantial alliance.

Maciel's views toward immigrants, Italian or otherwise, were shared by many members of the nationalist press. An article in *La Fronda* titled "Welcome to Work" made its stance on immigration unmistakably clear: "We want 'gringos' on the docks, in the factory, in the field, and in the shops. But we do not want them in the Casa Rosada, nor in the Congress, nor in the courts, nor in the university, nor in the school. They are welcome to work but not to govern."[38] *La Bandera Argentina* articles echoed these sentiments, demanding, "By what right do foreign communities ask to participate in the political and administrative life of our country?"[39] To this nationalist, immigrants "should only live among us on the condition that they make themselves Argentine and renounce their original nationality, language, and sense of independence from our nation."[40] Such conditions were the exact antithesis of the fascist regime's mission to preserve an Italian national identity abroad.

The nationalists found nothing at all appealing in the Italian regime's efforts to preserve the Italian language and national identity in their nation, since "nothing keeps a foreigner more foreign in our country than his inability or unwillingness to learn our language." They were disgusted by the fact that foreign governments actually controlled and operated schools in Argentina that inculcated foreign patriotism, and they disapproved of the foreign-language press, whose "very existence and circulation is proof of that our transoceanic guests . . . wish to maintain their racial and sentimental independence, and to preserve their customs and their language."[41] A 1932 *La Bandera Argentina* article directly challenged the Italian regime's national program abroad. Its author commented on an unnamed foreign-language newspaper that had posed the question whether or not their compatriots should participate in Argentine political life. This paper could have easily been any of the Italian-language dailies, which were all debating Parini's comments on this issue at the time. The author of the piece called their discussion "absurd," explaining that foreign participation in politics "could only be done when the foreign communities give up their identity as "colonies" and when their level of culture guarantees their social security."[42] As it was, "Argentina has been a land of dangerous experimentation, allowing foreign communities to implant themselves here without making sure that they adapt and assimilate into our nationality."[43] These sentiments, which the Italian embassy labeled as not only antiforeign but also anti-Italian, demonstrate that the regime's nationalist agenda abroad could never be reconciled with Argentina's own nationalist agenda.[44]

The conservative and elitist nature of many of these movements disappointed the Italian embassy as much as their xenophobic brand of nationalism hindered its efforts. A 1937 report by the Italian embassy in Buenos Aires on the activities of profascist groups in Argentina concluded "none of them has succeeded in finding the right path."[45] Ambassador Guariglia explained, "It is most difficult for them to understand Mussolini's maxim to 'live dangerously.' When they encounter their first difficulty, exactly the moment when it would be necessary to show energy and strength, they instead give up." Of another group of nationalists he complained that "many of its leadership include the names of Argentina's high society, and this is perhaps its major defect: too many 'señoritos,' as they call them here."[46] Guariglia similarly thought little of the ideological content of the Legión Cívica Argentina, which while claiming to be profascist "has only a poorly defined program." In describing the movement's official newspaper, Guariglia expressed his frustration:

> Its biweekly newspaper titled *Combat* is a truly pitiful thing. One does not even understand what they really want to "combat"; what is instead clear is that they want to preserve and defend the interests of the conservative capitalist bourgeoisie. Far from revolutionary, the members of the legion are reactionaries, and their movement is at its core generically conservative and nationalist.

With all the trappings of fascism: uniforms, salutes, insignia, and the like, Guariglia lamented that these movements, while attracted to fascism, did not share enough of its ideological content or the will to act on its ideas. In the end, Italian officials were disillusioned by the right-wing movements that had seemed to show much promise.

By the time the Italian embassy filed its report, Argentine nationalists were also losing interest in the Italian regime. Nazi Germany stole the spotlight, as the nationalist papers shifted their news services to German agencies and articles admiring Hitler's Germany began to get front-page attention. The Argentine nationalists were especially united with the Nazis in their hatred of Jews, an important feature of Argentine nationalism that the Italian propaganda was never able to take advantage of. Enrique Oses would become the editor of *El Pampero*, a nationalist daily funded by the German embassy. In the end, the Nazi conception of Aryan supremacy, biological racism, and paganistic rituals disturbed many members of the nationalist camp, who remained Catholic-conservative traditionalists. The ideology that fit these nationalists best was that of Franco's Spain. During the Spanish Civil War, Franco's *hispanidad* campaign was quick to gain supporters within Argentina. *Hispanidad* aimed at promoting traditional Spanish customs and ideals with the goal of creating greater political and cultural unity among the Hispanic nations of the world.[47] Less interested in reforming actual links to Spain, Argentine nationalists incorporated this *franquista* ideology into their own political platform, stressing its Catholic and antiliberal elements along with the need to defend Argentina's traditional Hispanic political culture in the face of foreign intrusions.[48] Thus, while many nationalists had flirted with Italian fascism and German Nazism, they were most comfortable with Franco's movement. Beyond the cultural identification most nationalists made with Spain, Franco's Catholic and conservative rhetoric was far more reassuring to them compared to the more extreme and modernist ideologies of the two fascist regimes.

In the end, it had been Italy's nationalist project of spreading Italian influence abroad more than anything else that doomed the fascist Italian regime's potential to collaborate with these nationalist movements. However appealing the fascist political program may have been, it could not be reconciled with the threat that its nationalist program posed to native Argentines' own nationalist agenda.

THE OPPONENTS OF FASCISM SPEAK OUT

"Fascism is advancing. This is a reality that we cannot close our eyes to," warned a 1933 issue of *La Vanguardia*, the official organ of the Argentine Socialist Party. The nationalists were not the only ones watching the fascist regimes in Europe. If Italian fascism was an inspiration to nationalists, it was a cautionary tale to their left-wing anarchist, communist, and especially socialist opponents. Far from a model to be emulated, the Italian fascist regime was instead a dark reminder of what could happen one day in Argentina should the nationalists get their way. Just as the nationalists had done, these left-wing activists applied Italian fascism to the Argentine context, but they depicted the regime's ideology as a threat to its democratic identity as a nation rather than as a solution to its problems.[49]

The nationalist forces unleashed in Argentina after Uriburu's dictatorship alarmed its opponents on the left, many of whom saw in this movement an attack on Argentina's democratic traditions. Left-wing activists in Argentina linked the Italian regime's fascist propaganda with its nationalist admirers, using the example of the Italian fascist state and later Nazi Germany to warn their followers of the dangers posed by both homegrown and foreign fascisms. An antifascist writing in the anarchist daily *La Protesta* explained this connection best: "I refer here especially to Italian fascism. But in what follows it could be said *país a donde vas, fascismo que encuentras*—since each country has in its bosom a politically degenerative phenomenon that more or less resembles fascism. Uriburu was painful proof of this for the Republic of Argentina."[50] These sentiments were echoed in a communist-run periodical, *Contra-Fascismo*, which cautioned its readers that "fascism cannot be reduced to just those satellites of Mussolini and Hitler. Fascism is a vast phenomenon . . . it is everyone."[51] Alluding to nationalist groups in Argentina, another issue explained that "it is not necessary for the reaction to wear a colored shirt or to punctuate its speeches with Alalà! in order for it to carry out a concrete and systematic fascistization plan."[52]

Fascism in the left-wing press was nothing but the worst form of a reactionary dictatorship. "The suppression of liberty and the defense of a regime established through the use of all the available resources of the military, police, and judicial apparatus," according to *La Protesta*, and "a primitive movement that attempts to perpetuate, through an absolutist regime, the privileges of the oligarchic and elite classes," whose "danger does not reside in the strength of its ideas but in the material support that the powerful classes of the country have given it," according to *La Vanguardia*.[53] A cartoon in *La Batalla*, the communist newspaper of Rosario, illustrates this connection by personifying "reaction" as the grim reaper "clearing the way for fascism."[54] Its caption reads, "Slashing away day after day more precious democratic and popular liberties, reaction is clearing an open path toward fascist barbarity."[55] *La Batalla* went on to call on Argentines to unite and stop "reaction" from reaching its ultimate goal of destroying democracy in Argentina and establishing a fascist regime in its place.

Argentine socialists were especially unconvinced by Italian fascism's modernist pretensions and far from impressed by its supposed transcendental solution to the world's economic and political problems. As *La Vanguardia* explained, "No one is fooled: its enough to scratch the surface of fascism a little to see under its false varnish of modernity the same stagnant policies of oppression that have characterized the tyrannies of the past."[56] In the end, what mattered most was the results of the fascist system and not its ideological subtleties, as another newspaper explained: "We all know that fascism, whatever its political or social ideology may be, if it even has one, is a system of force that attempts to sweep away rights, converting the dominated masses into a herd of sheep. In this way Italian fascism, and that of Germany and all the others that imitate it, are all the same."[57] It was exactly this system of oppression and dictatorship that mobilized left-wing radicals to the antifascist banner.

In a stirring speech on October 14, 1933, commemorating the death of a former comrade at the hands of a nationalist gunman, socialist Deputy Buyan declared, "We must not forget what happened in Italy and Germany. In these countries the success of fascism has meant the abolition of all liberties and all rights."[58] Left-wing papers reminded their readers after every violent nationalist act that this was how fascism had taken hold in Italy. Linking the nationalist agitation in their country with the *squadrismo* violence of the 1920s, a *La Vanguardia* article explained that "fascism implanted itself in Italy through blood and fire, its opponents, among them Matteotti, were cowardly murdered with impunity, local socialist headquarters were looted and burned. This regime, imposed through violence and terror, was sustained by the fascist militias created for that purpose."[59] Argentines must therefore, in the words of *La Protesta*, "prepare themselves for the fight at the first signs of fascist barbarity" perpetrated by "the praetorians of Argentine fascism."[60] For as another article cautioned, if Argentines did not take action soon, "fascism will plunge our people into a miserable despotic oppression—as it has done in Italy and is doing it now in Germany."[61]

The front page of a 1933 issue of *La Vanguardia* announced a "Rally Sunday Against Fascism."[62] The purpose of the rally was "to stir public opinion, to mobilize the people of the capital, to awaken the consciences of all Argentines, and to enlist them in the fight without quarter of the democratic forces against the fascist, liberticidal, and antinational reaction, which threatens to return the country to barbarity and violence."[63] As these lines suggest, the fight against the nationalists was more than a just political debate. At stake were two competing visions of the Argentine nation. Just as it had for the nationalists, Italy would figure prominently in this debate.

One of the featured speakers at the rally, socialist Deputy Miguel B. Navello, compared the current political situation in Argentina to the Italian case. He asserted that the nationalists in Argentina were emulating their Italian counterparts, "who for them are a source of inspiration." According to Navello, as the Italian fascists had done before them, the nationalists were a small minority who were attempting to deceive the people into believing that democracy in their nation was fractured and in need of being supplanted by a new system. It was a strategy that "we have already seen through the barbarous experiments of Mussolini and Hitler."[64] Navello, therefore, urged his listeners to defend their democracy and popular sovereignty by opposing fascism and dictatorship.[65]

Socialist Deputy Nicolás Repetto and Senator Alfredo L. Palacios were two of the event's other keynote speakers. They were the most influential Argentine socialist leaders to take up the antifascist cause. Born in Buenos Aires in 1871, Repetto was the son of Italian immigrants who attended an Italian primary school run by the Unione e Benevolenza mutual-aid society. A surgeon as well as a politician, Repetto emerged as one of the most important Socialist Party leaders in Argentina. He served eight terms representing the federal capital in the Argentine Chamber of Deputies from 1913 to 1943 and was the editor-in-chief of *La Vanguardia* during the 1930s. Palacios was another leading member of the Socialist Party in Argentina. Born in 1880 in Buenos Aires, he was law professor and president of the University of La Plata. He was the first socialist deputy elected in Argentina in 1904 and was a member of the Senate throughout the 1930s, during which time he championed social causes, including prison and education reform, as well as rights for women and children. Both Repetto and Palacios spearheaded the Argentine antifascist movement throughout the 1930s, collaborating with the Italian antifascist press and speaking out against fascism before the Argentine Congress.

Repetto often made reference to Mussolini's seizure of power in order to explain the dangers of Argentine nationalism. According to Repetto, Mussolini and later Hitler deceived their peoples into believing that they could change society. "They validated themselves by calling for deep economic and social transformations, but implanted instead cruel dictatorships that are on balance bourgeois."[66] Focusing on the Italian case, Repetto had more than a superficial knowledge of the fascist movement. He cited at length the first fascist manifesto of Piazza San Sepolcro in 1919 to explain how Mussolini "used an extremely leftist program of social revolution to work a thousand miracles and implant a rigid dictatorship controlled exclusively by himself."[67] Aware that many of his nationalist adversaries were especially influenced by Mussolini's corporatist program, Repetto went to great lengths to demonstrate that the so-called corporatist state was nothing more than an illusion. He explained: "The council of corporations is in practice only a farce. In Italy and in Germany the legislative assembly is just a gross fiction. The only authority that exists there is that of the dictator above all else."[68] For Repetto, it was all show, one more example of how Mussolini had deceived his people and the world. "In actuality, what goes on in the council of corporations is nothing more than a vulgar proceeding more or less out of protocol. It is a farce like everything else related to this decorative fascist organization." Turning back to the Argentine case, Repetto went on to declare, "And this is what some deluded individuals dream of implanting in Argentina."[69]

Repetto made common cause with the Italian antifascist movement, advising members of the Italian community to fight against fascism not only in Italy but also in Argentina: "Italian workers in residence here share with us the work of moving this new nation forward, and collaborating with us in the urgent and serious task of defending the liberties and democratic institutions of our country."[70] He described the founding of the antifascist paper *Italia Libre* as "a work of propaganda supporting liberty, democratic institutions, and the preservation of human culture, [values] that are so dear to the Italian people, who began the Renaissance, and made important contributions in the development of the arts and sciences."[71]

Palacios also spoke out against the Italian fascist dictatorship, separating it from his conceptualization of an Italian national identity. He declared, "I want to make it clear that I am not raising my voice against Italy.... Argentines hate dictatorship, but we love Italy."[72] Palacios depicted Argentines and Italians as kindred peoples, sharing a common Latin heritage as well as a love for liberty. These shared ideals were for Palacios embodied by Garibaldi, who "fought for the liberty of his people, wearing the legendary poncho of the Argentine gaucho, noble and chivalrous like himself." Just as members of the Italian community in Argentina attached their own symbolism to the iconic figure of Garibaldi, Palacios attached a distinctly American quality to the Risorgimento hero. For according to Palacios, "it is true what has been said that the Garibaldian legend is full of America. It was American lead in the shots of the Thousand in the Homeric campaign of the Sicilies."[73] Throughout Argentina's young history, Palacios declared, "Argentines have admired Italian heroism in its times of liberty and tragedy. Italy's pain during the last war pierced our hearts as if it was our pain."[74] All this, however, changed after the fascist government in Italy betrayed its nation's values and principles and embarked on a path of destruction and conquest. "But now, Italians, my dear senators, who used to defend the sacred soil of their *patria* ... are sending forth conquering armies to destroy and dominate distant and harmless peoples.... We are therefore protesting, as Argentines, against the right of conquest."[75] According to Palacios, opposing the fascist dictatorship reaffirmed Argentina's own tenuous sense of identity based on the principles of liberty and democracy. For Palacios, Argentina would cease to be Argentina were it to reject its faith in democracy, just as Italian identity is no longer the same after the fascists rejected Italy's liberal democratic traditions. For both Repetto and Palacios, fascist tyranny was destroying the Italian nation and threatening to destroy Argentina. Free Argentines and Italians, therefore, had to join together to fight the fascist menace at home and abroad.

This call for solidarity in the fight against fascism was echoed by others in the radical press. A 1932 article in *La Protesta* called on all antifascists to act: "we must find a way to express in concrete international acts our solidarity against fascism . . . especially in these American nations, nations of immigrants where it is not hard to find together with refugees from fascist nations, also the hate-filled champions of fascism . . . agents abroad sent by the fascist governments of their nations."[76] Most articles in the radical press used the example of fascist Italy to speak of the danger of Argentine nationalism. This writer, however, alerted his readers to the actual work of the Italian regime within Argentina, highlighting in particular Italy's national agenda. Aware of the dangers posed by the programs the Italian regime was enacting, he warned that "Italian fascists are intent on infiltrating and implanting their specifically fascist and sectarian Fasci di Combattimento, along with their very own party schools, recreational and after-work programs, and sports organizations, which are nothing more than military training camps."[77] He went on to call for "more solidarity, solidarity in the struggle against Italian fascist maneuvers abroad and not just solidarity in the form of assistance and the red cross. Do not leave this work to the small antifascist groups of their respective countries. Transform their small isolated activism into an international activism."[78]

La Vanguardia echoed this antifascist's concern over fascist Italy's nationalization project in Argentina. A 1934 front-page article warned of Italian fascism's "dangerous infiltration" into the nation. "There is no locality of importance in the interior that does not have a local 'Fascio Italiano,' controlled by a 'fiduciario' who is usually an Italian consul or vice consul. These 'fascios' are actually foreign propaganda agencies."[79] The article went on to list all of the Italian regime's nationalization activities on Argentine soil, from its schools and cultural institutes to the Dopolavoro and Balilla, concluding that these fascist programs "are contrary to our nation's institutions because they are operated openly by foreign diplomats and are indoctrinating Argentine children with a love for the *patria* of their parents over their own and a love for traditions that are not our own."[80] *La Vanguardia* implored the government to take action, attacking its "inexcusable tolerance" for the fascist propaganda arriving on its shores.

During the 1930s, a number of antifascist organizations and fronts did in fact acknowledge the danger posed by the foreign fascist propaganda and answered the call for greater solidarity. There were, for example, the Frente Único Popular Argentino Antifascista y Antiguerrero, La Defensa Popular por las Víctimas de la Reacción, and El Comité de Ayuda Antifascista. For the most part, these groups attracted members from left-wing political parties, published only sporadically, and were unable to create widespread public awareness of what they perceived to be the fascist threat.[81] The organ of one of these associations lamented that the Argentine general public "appears to have been lulled to sleep in a suicidal false sense of security. They assume that fascism is too exotic a plant for South America and that they are far away from its danger."[82] It would take a lot more than a few strong words from the radical left-wing press to mobilize the public against the fascist threat and force Argentine authorities to act. It was not until the end of the 1930s when the wider Argentine public finally became aware of the fascist threat and would stir its government to action.

PUBLIC ATTENTION TURNS TO THE ITALIAN NATIONAL PROJECT

Throughout much of the 1920s and 1930s, serious debate over the Italian fascist regime and its national agenda in Argentina remained confined to extreme right- and left-wing activists. Front-page coverage of the Italian regime in mainstream newspapers focused on its international policies with but an occasional mention of a fascist program, commemoration, or dignitary's visit. Whether these pieces depicted the regime in a favorable or unfavorable light, they tended to view it as relatively benign and kept their commentary brief.[83] Very little mention was made of the Italian regime's actions within Argentina. Often these activities were simply reported on as social events within the Italian community, without much discussion. This would begin to change in 1937.

On the evening of July 15, 1937, Luigi Federzoni, president of the Italian Senate and member of the fascist Grand Council, concluded his tour of the South American republic as the guest of honor at a banquet held in La Plata. It was the last stop on what had been up to that point a successful tour that included visits to Brazil and Uruguay. Around 2,500 people attended the event hosted by the newly formed association, Amigos de Italia, whose members were Argentine elites sympathetic to fascist Italy. Special guests included Dr. Fresco, the governor of the province of Buenos Aires, and Dr. Amoedo the vice governor, among other dignitaries and national politicians. It was supposed to be a warm and celebratory send-off but turned into something else entirely. Newspaper accounts of Federzoni's speech varied greatly, but what is clear is that two of his comments in particular did not sit well with his Argentine audience. One newspaper observed that "from its very beginning the tone of Mr. Federzoni's speech was unusually aggressive, turning scandalous after he referred to Italians who obtained Argentine citizenship."[84] According to most reports, Federzoni told his audience that Italians who had become naturalized citizens "should not be loved at all, since no one can expect anything from those who renounce their nationality."[85] At this point the guests began to grow restless as Federzoni went on to discuss

Mussolini's Italy, lamenting the fact that Argentines did not seem to appreciate fascism's great accomplishments. He declared, "Argentina, they say, is Calle Florida, and walking down that street I did not see one Italian book," and then added something to the effect that "Argentines do not have the sophistication to appreciate the greatness of Italian culture."[86] At this point Vice Governor Amoedo, "visibly disturbed by the aggressive words he heard against our country," left with his wife, followed shortly thereafter by Governor Fresco, who departed before giving his own scheduled remarks.[87]

"Federzoni Attacked Argentine Culture," "An Insulting Farewell," and "Federzoni Spoke Disparagingly of Our Country" ran the following day's headlines.[88] *La Tribuna Libre* questioned if Federzoni thought he was in Ethiopia given his disrespectful tone: "in alphabetical order we may be listed under 'A' like Abyssinia, but to the international community we are considered a great country on the South American continent." The article went on to ask if Federzoni actually believed that "he would find everyone here wearing black shirts and speaking Italian," adding that instead, "before leaving the illustrious visitor has just learned that the Republic of Argentina is thoroughly democratic and Argentine citizens are as Argentine as Italians are Italian."[89] *Crítica* reported that "Federzoni violated the most basic rules of discretion and of hospitality . . . his speech crossed the line," adding that "the grandiloquent Italian senator's outrageous act was typical of fascist functionaries." Witnesses and members of the press corps were especially disturbed by Federzoni's comments about naturalized Argentines. Still a young nation with all of its citizens the children or descendants of immigrants, Argentina's identity as a nation depended upon assimilation and naturalization. Perhaps without even realizing it, Federzoni had directly challenged the very basis of Argentina's own national project.

If Argentines were bothered by his allusion to their immigrant citizens, they were absolutely appalled by his slight of Argentine culture. As *Crítica* scoffed:

> The picturesque senator claimed that we do not know the peninsula's culture. When he said: "on Calle Florida I did not see one Italian book," certainly the orator did not mean Francesco Nitti, nor Mazzini, nor Benedetto Croce, the great liberal mind. He must have been referring the impoverished fascist literature that in the last fifteen years has not produced anything worth mentioning and to those little writers who shamelessly pile on praise for the "duce" and for fascist "culture."

Not everyone in the press attacked the fascist dignitary. *La Nación* chose to await an explanation from Federzoni before condemning his remarks, adding that "Our correspondent only perceived his comments to be pleasant . . . and at no point [did he] speak injurious words against the Argentine Republic."[90] *El Argentino* went even further, categorically denying that Federzoni spoke poorly of Argentina's culture. It interviewed witnesses from the event to support its claim. One of these witnesses did however admit, "The one thing that he did say that could have been misunderstood was that Argentina in terms of its culture should make fascism and the New Italy more well known. And he complained that there were not any great bookstores that popularized fascist ideas, while there were an abundance of such stores for leftist doctrines."[91] Even from this sympathetic witness, it is clear that Federzoni's was at least somewhat critical of Argentina's cultural milieu. Given the flurry of accounts throughout the press, it is difficult to determine the veracity of any one account of what transpired that July night, but it is undeniable that the incident attracted a great deal of public attention.

Perhaps it was the English-language daily the *Buenos Aires Herald* that hit on the fundamental problem with the speech, commenting that "Federzoni appeared to have forgotten that he was speaking before Argentines, even if fascist Argentines."[92] The truth is that Federzoni's comments were no different from those uttered by Parini and other Italian officials, both within Italy as well as in Argentina in front of the Italian community. Members of the regime spoke long and often about the need for Italians to preserve their national identity abroad and resist assimilation—well in line with Federzoni's attack on naturalized Italo-Argentines. Furthermore, Federzoni's evaluation of Argentine culture bore more than a casual resemblance to the articles Franco Ciarlantini had been writing on the subject since 1927. The only difference was, as the *Herald* pointed out, Federzoni forgot that he was speaking to an Argentine rather than Italian audience. Argentina had since the days of Sarmiento relied on assimilation to solidify its own unity as a nation. For obvious reasons, Argentines *wanted* their immigrants to "renounce" their foreign nationalities, a fact lost on Federzoni, who failed to look beyond Italy's own interests in speaking to a foreign audience. Federzoni should have also known to steer clear of any possible slight of Argentine culture. What would have been an inopportune remark anywhere else was absolutely scandalous in front of an Argentine audience always anxious to demonstrate its cultural sophistication.

In his report on the fallout from Federzoni's speech, the Italian ambassador in Buenos Aires reassured the Foreign Ministry that there was nothing wrong with Federzoni's remarks and they should not have been perceived as insulting. This is in fact a telling sign of what was fundamentally wrong with fascist Italy's nationalization strategy in the republic. For years Italian agents had been demanding that their immigrants remain loyal to Italy, preserve their culture and language, and devote themselves to the Duce in complete disregard for the effect such tactics would have on Argentine sensibilities. It was only a matter of time before Argentines would become aware of the regime's programs in Argentina and the threat they posed to their own identity as a nation. The Federzoni fiasco was a step in that direction, turning the public's eyes toward Italian fascist activities. It was an indication of what was to come.

The following year this increased public awareness in Argentina of fascist Italy's national activities in their nation turned into panic when the press discovered that Italy's Axis partner was also operating within the republic. In April 1938, German associations in Buenos Aires held a plebiscite to voice their support for Hitler's annexation of Austria.[93] Not legally recognized, the plebiscite was nothing more than a symbolic gesture of support for Hitler orchestrated by the German embassy. This public display by the German community in support of Nazism, however, shocked many Argentines, who had been unaware of foreign propaganda efforts in their nation. With tensions running high, more disturbing news came later in the month when an Argentine education inspector uncovered subversive Nazi propaganda in the German schools in La Plata. Rumors in the press spread quickly of Nazi-fascist plots, vast underground spy networks, and conspiracies to overthrow the government.[94] Every meeting within the German community was looked on with suspicion. The newspaper accounts gave the impression that all German immigrants within Argentina were Nazi agents sent by the Reich. The most outrageous story of Nazi subversion broke in June 1939, when Argentine newspapers exposed a supposed Nazi plot to annex Patagonia to Germany. According to the rumor, the Nazis had long coveted Patagonia's wealth in minerals and livestock. Berlin secretly coordinated emigration into the region, sending settlers and tourists there to survey the land and lay the groundwork for its "nazification."[95] Using these lurid tales in the press as evidence, the Argentine police investigated, finding that while many of the press accounts were grossly exaggerated there was indeed an alarming amount of Nazi propaganda and German associations in the country.[96]

The attention Nazi propaganda had attracted made the public more aware of fascist Italy's own national ambitions in the republic. Argentines quickly realized that the Italian regime was also trying to spread a foreign national project in their country. While lacking the caché of the Nazi propaganda, the Argentine press found Italian fascism to be equally subversive. For example, one local paper alerted its readers to the "Dangerous fascist invasion of Paraná." It described the work of Italian consular officials and members of the Italian community who were organizing a local Fasci, creating fascist schools, youth programs, after-work centers.[97] The article questioned, "Why is it necessary for these groups that are so different from our democratic principles to form themselves in Paraná." It went on to ask,

> Would Mr. Benito Mussolini let Argentine democratic organizations form within the Italian Empire? We frankly do not think so. And in this we agree with Mussolini's way of thinking. Every government acts in their territorial

jurisdiction as lord and master. With that being said, we think that it is bad, very bad, that fascism is establishing itself here, and what is more this meddling tramples over our sovereignty.[98]

This challenge to Argentina's sovereignty as a nation was a theme echoed by members of the Argentine government, who would identify Italian fascism, along with German Nazism, as foreign doctrines contrary to the Argentine nation.

THE ARGENTINE GOVERNMENT TAKES ACTION

In 1938, taking advantage of the opportunity created by the public outcry against the Nazi threat, socialist Deputy Enrique Dickmann and radical Deputy Raúl Damonte Taborda launched a highly publicized campaign in the Chamber of Deputies to suppress Nazi-fascist propaganda within Argentina. Dickmann, a Russian-born Jew, had long been an outspoken opponent of the Nazis and had followed carefully their rise to power in Germany. He repeatedly warned the Chamber of Deputies of "the infiltration of foreign ideologies" into Argentine politics and society. According to Dickmann, these Nazi-fascist activities "are not recent or sporadic; they are not isolated or localized: they are linked together by a serious and extraordinary premeditated plan."[99]

Damonte Taborda, the leading antifascist within the Radical Party, shared Dickmann's concerns. "Organized foreign groups have for the first time in Argentina's history dared to come to our *patria* to attack our liberty, our democracy, and our very own sovereignty."[100] Damante Taborda called for action in the face of this "foreign imperialism," declaring that "we must demonstrate to the powerful nations of the world that we constitute a sovereign nationality that knows how to confront danger with resolve, speed, and energy."[101] According to Damonte Taborda, Nazism and fascism were foreign systems of thought that had no place in an Argentine nation founded on liberal democratic principles. In fact, their brand of totalitarian authoritarianism was something different entirely from anything found within Argentina's national past, not even Manuel de Rosas, the famed caudillo strongman who ruled Argentina as a brutal dictator, could be compared with these "anti-Argentine vermin," for as Damonte Taborda declared, "The representatives of this foreign imperialism are not acting in the spirit of the gaucho tyrant Rosas, who was popularly chosen and animated by nationalist sentiments."[102] Even Argentina's most tyrannical dictators were careful not to openly attack the democratic foundations of Argentine identity. In Argentina, democracy in practice could be suspended or "safeguarded" by a dictatorial regime but never rejected outright; it was simply too much a part of Argentina's national fabric. This argument against the Nazi-fascist propaganda made explicit the importance of Argentina's collective set of democratic values and principles, which served as the cornerstones of its ideational national identity. Promoting a project that challenged those ideals was, therefore, tantamount to challenging the very basis of Argentina's identity as a nation. For both Dickmann and Damante Taborda, the totalitarian regimes endangered Argentina in theory as well as in practice: in theory, by espousing totalitarian ideologies contrary to Argentina's democratic principles, and in practice, by attempting to spread those ideologies onto Argentine soil.

Damonte Taborda, along with Dickmann, equated fascist Italy's activities in Argentina with those of Nazi Germany, characterizing both as dangerous violations of Argentina's national sovereignty.[103] Much of the Nazi German propaganda campaign, as described by Dickmann and Damonte Taborda, was in fact strikingly similar to the Italian model. Beginning in 1934, the Nazis coordinated their activities abroad with their ministry of propaganda and made similar use of the German diplomatic corps to organize their efforts within Argentina. Just like the Italians had before them, they established their own news services, radio broadcasts, and community newspaper to propagandize the regime. The Nazis also took advantage of the local network of German organizations, co-opting existing ones for the regime and establishing new Nazi associations. They similarly took control over German schools supervised by the embassy, which conducted classes in German, celebrated German holidays, made use of German history and geography texts, and instructed students to be loyal and devoted to the Führer.[104] It was, in short, a program of study similar to the curriculum of the Italian schools. In fact, most of the Nazi propaganda sent to Argentina, with the important exceptions of Aryan racial theories and anti-Semitism, was a carbon copy of the Italian national program.

In spite of the similarity between the two totalitarian regime's initiatives, neither Dickmann nor Damonte Taborda was as alarmed by fascist Italy's efforts as they were by Nazi Germany's. Dickmann declared, "I consider German National Socialism more dangerous because of its organizational ability, its methodology, intelligence, vigor, tenacity, and objectives," explaining that

> the Italian fascist effort is almost innocuous for two reasons: the Italian immigrant in this country is in general an individualist and a liberal; and it is difficult to control him, he is undisciplined like all Latins. Moreover, the children of Italians who are born in Argentina are Argentines 100 percent without reservation. These considerations sterilize in large part the work of Italian fascism in our country."[105]

Dickmann supported his observations with statistics. He highlighted the fact that even though both the Nazis and Italian fascists recruited the same number of people into their respective organizations, because of their community's smaller size, the Nazi membership within the German community was proportionally much larger. According to Dickmann, Italian community leaders' independent stances, liberal backgrounds, and desire to assimilate into Argentine culture conspired against fascist Italy's efforts. In making his case, Dickmann fell back on well-established stereotypes: the Germans were typically efficient, organized, and in lockstep with directives from Berlin, while the Italians were typically Latin in their inefficiency and contempt for authority.

The Italian ambassador relayed Dickmann's comments to the Foreign Ministry in Rome and the Italian ambassador in Berlin.[106] One wonders what went through their minds as they read the translation of his speeches. Dickmann's dismissive evaluation of over ten years of work must have been a tough pill to swallow. It would seem as though the Nazis had overshadowed the Italian fascists, beating them at their own game as they had done in so many other policy areas. And yet Italian officials no doubt took some pleasure in the fact that the Italian propaganda had managed to slip under the radar and infiltrate Argentina without attracting the same amount of fear as that of the Nazis. This fact suggests that perhaps the Italian fascists had done something right. They were able to implement a national program similar to the Nazi's over a longer period of time, influencing in some form or another members of the Italian community as well as Argentine nationalists, without alarming the general public or the government. In fact, the Italian propaganda initiative would be cut short not because of its own failures but because of its association with Nazi Germany.

Before long, Italian propaganda and especially its school program came under investigation, as the Argentine Congress debated the passage of new legislation restricting the activities of foreign associations, regulating foreign instruction in schools, and establishing a commission to investigate propaganda that was deemed a threat to Argentina's national sovereignty.

The Italian schools, which somehow despite their many years of disseminating the fascist Italian national project had managed to escape scrutiny, were the first to be labeled, along with those of the Nazis, as threats to Argentine sovereignty.[107] In 1938 the Argentine government restricted the activities of these schools. Prohibiting foreign anthems, salutes, and commemorations, it instructed all schools to instead sing the Argentine national anthem at the start of the day, required that Argentine national holidays be observed, and stated that only pictures of Argentine patriots and national symbols could adorn classroom walls. It further required that all lessons with the exception of foreign-language classes be conducted in Spanish by teachers who were Argentine citizens certified by the Argentine Board of Education. History and geography classes were to emphasize the people and history of Argentina, rather than foreign subjects. Most importantly, foreign schools were forbidden to teach "political and racial ideologies contrary to the principles of the Constitution and laws of the country" and were obligated to instead "formulate a program of lectures on the Preamble and the Rights and Guarantees of the National Constitution."[108] On December 21, 1939, the Argentine Department of Education took further measures. It banned the use of foreign-published textbooks and required all classes, even those teaching foreign languages, to adopt "texts that are written exclusively for Argentine children." The language readings were prohibited from including "themes related to current events in foreign countries." In their place, readings were to include the Argentine National Anthem, and Constitution, events in Argentine history, Argentine legends and traditions, as well as "moral lectures, readings, and anecdotes, which cultivate the great spiritual values that sustain our democracy."[109] The new rules in effect made the schools, as the Italian ambassador quipped, "Argentine public schools funded by the Italian Government." Every effort was therefore made to resist or delay implementing these new changes, as Argentine school inspectors soon found out.[110]

The fascist-run school in Mendoza was one of the first to be targeted by the Argentine government in their crackdown on foreign schools, for as the Italian consul in Mendoza explained, "they look upon us with disfavor because we promote a political agenda that is extremely fascist, and because we have too many portraits of the king and the Duce on display."[111] An Argentine inspector to the schools in La Plata also expressed concern over the schools' Italian national agenda, explaining that "we grant foreigners the right to teach their citizens in their mother tongue, but we cannot allow them to propagate their political and national ideologies. Even the children of foreigners born in their own *patria*, but today residents of this country, must educate themselves in an Argentine manner."[112] Two years later another Argentine inspector to La Plata was alarmed by the fact that "the children are educated under the fascist system, and they are not taught anything about Argentina's programs." To make matters worse, "The principal in the Italian school is a fascist sent directly by the Italian government to spread partisan propaganda."[113]

Argentine inspectors soon turned their eyes to the fascist Italian schools run by the Pro-Schola and the Dante Alighieri. They determined that "these schools do not comply with the new government guidelines."[114] With only passing references in the curriculum to "the history of Argentina and civic instruction," inspectors found most lessons filled instead with the history of Italy, Imperial Rome, and the fascist state. "In all of the geography lessons they have directly substituted ours for foreign instruction. For example, fourth graders are only taught the 'physical and political geography of Italy' . . . while Argentine instruction is excluded."[115] Inspectors were also shocked by the apparent lack of commitment to the instruction of the Spanish language and outraged by the fact that the Italian textbooks did not make any reference at all to Argentina and its civic traditions, instead claiming Italy as the true *patria* of its students. Not surprisingly, the inspectors concluded that too little effort had been made to inspire Argentine national identity and patriotism: "In terms of sentiments of nationality and love of the *patria*, I do not believe that they dedicate preferential attention to Argentine patriotism.... I do not observe in the students a noble and profound love for their true [Argentine] *patria*." [116] Labeling these schools "completely anti-Argentine in their agenda and activities," the government revoked the certification of many of the schools' degrees, although they allowed them to continue to function until the early years of the war, when they would come under the scrutiny of the Congressional Commission on Anti-Argentine Activities. [117]

The Argentine government was also alarmed by the presence of foreign associations that operated under the direct supervision of foreign governments. Many of the Italian associations, such as the Società Dante Alighieri, the Fasci all'Estero, and the Ballila and Dopolavoro, fell under this category. On May 15, 1939, the Argentine government passed a law restricting the activities of these associations. The law banned the use of emblems, anthems, uniforms, or symbols pertaining to foreign political parties. It required that all of the associations' regulations and statutes be written in Spanish and sent to government authorities, and most importantly, it prohibited them from organizing any event that involved their members in foreign political propaganda. [118] Even though the associations themselves were not shut down, they could no longer spread the fascist Italian national message with legal impunity, cutting off one of the Italian regime's major propaganda arms.

Since 1938 Damonte Taborda and Dickmann had been calling for the formation of a special commission to investigate and suppress all Nazi and fascist activities within the nation. They would have to wait nearly three years for the commission to take action. In 1941 world events forced the reluctant hand of the Argentine conservatives in power at the time. The Argentine government under the administrations of Roberto M. Ortiz and Ramón S. Castillo had been on notoriously friendly terms with the Axis powers. This position became more difficult to uphold after the outbreak of World War II, which arrived quite literally on South American shores in December 1939. During that month, the German pocket battleship the *Graf Spee* slugged it out with three British cruisers off the South American coastline, retreating into the mouth of the River Plate, where the ship was scuttled in full view of onlookers in Montevideo and its crew interned in Argentina. Even before they entered the war, the U.S. State Department officials were mindful of Nazi-fascist fifth columnists and saboteurs operating in their own backyard and applied political and economic pressure on all of the nations of Latin America to root out these cells. The 1941 bombing of Pearl Harbor followed by the United States entry into the war would later put even more pressure on the Argentine government to act. Although Argentina remained adamantly neutral until the very end of the war, the government did agree to implement the investigatory commission. In the end, the immediacy of the world war and United States pressure moved the government to act on Damonte Taborda's and Dickmann's persistent recommendations.

In 1941 the Argentine government opened up its Congressional Investigatory Commission on Anti-Argentine Activities. The evidence collected by the commission now fills thirty-five boxes in Argentina's congressional archive. The investigators collected newspapers and printed propaganda, received and filed private denouncements, and recorded the testimony of witnesses. They also gathered fiscal records and membership rosters from the various foreign associations within their country. The vast majority of this evidence focused on the Nazi regime's operations. There was also, however, a substantial number of reports on Italian fascism. Investigators compiled the names and addresses of Italians enrolled in the Fascist Party abroad and of the regime's financial backers. Among the many collaborators listed, Arsenio Guido Buffarini's name appeared often. He was described as a "militant fascist" who "enjoys great sympathy within the Italian community, even among nonfascists, due to his open personality," but who had lost most of his influence "the day he turned into a fascist propagandist."[119] Vittorio Valdani also figured prominently, identified as the most important financial supporter of the regime within the community, as well as one of the regime's most faithful subordinates, who, unlike Buffarini, was "hated by a great majority of the community, including fascists."[120]

Argentine investigators also closely examined the Italian-language press, providing extensive clippings and summaries of Italian fascist periodicals, including *Il Mattino d'Italia* and *Il Giornale d'Italia*, as well as *La Rivista Mensile della Federazione Italiana*. Investigators labeled *Il Mattino d'Italia* "the principle organ of fascist propaganda in Argentina," directed by Michele Intaglietta, "an ultra-fascist *squadrista*" sent from Rome and directly answerable to the fascist regime.[121] Some of the propaganda works sent by the regime also found their way into the files of the commission, as did Stefani and Roma Press news wires. Everything from Parini's instructions to Italians living abroad to works celebrating the great accomplishments of the Duce and accounts of Italy's heroic efforts in the Second World War.[122]

The investigation also followed closely the activities of the fascist and profascist Italian organizations in Argentina, highlighting their direct contact with Rome in violation of Argentine law. Of the Pro-Schola, investigators wrote, "The president is the militant fascist Giuseppe Fiocchi, who runs Italian fascist schools" and "is controlled by the embassy." The report also called the Società Dante Alighieri "a fascist institution with its central office in Italy, with twenty branches in all of Argentina's major cities. Italian

Schools and the Italo-Argentine Studies Institute depend on it. It is controlled by the government in Rome."[123] Over a dozen other associations were listed categorized as "in the orbit of fascism," having "fascist tendencies," or "including many fascist sympathizers in its ranks."[124] In sum, Argentine officials had finally recognized the highly subversive nature of the Italian fascist activities that had been developing for over a decade without censure.

Despite the substantial amount of evidence on Italian fascist activities collected by the commission, four out of the five published *informes* reporting on its findings focused exclusively on Nazi activities. The textbooks of the Italian schools abroad were in fact the only pieces of evidence discussed substantially within the reports. These texts figured prominently in *Informe no. 4*, which reproduced illustrations from the Italian fascist first and second grade primers. Citing passages and illustrations from the fascist texts that exhorted loyalty to the Duce, the king, and the ideals of fascist Italy as damming evidence, the commission concluded that, while the Italian schools were less militant than the parallel Nazi programs, both "shared the same political goal of orienting and educating children in totalitarianism."[125] Given this political agenda "contrary to the Constitution and laws of the country," along with the promotion of a foreign national project in expressed violation of Argentine law, these schools were condemned as "anti-Argentine organizations," and it was recommended that their activities be suspended.[126] It is particularly telling that in their condemnation of the schools that they conflated national identity with political ideology. The schools were deemed "anti-Argentine" because of their totalitarian program, which is antithetical to Argentina's ideational conceptualization of its national identity and therefore by definition foreign and un-Argentine.

Schools were one of the most basic tools of nation building. It was in the classroom where governments shaped young minds by inculcating patriotic loyalty to the *patria* and infusing them with a sense of a national identity. The Italian fascists had understood all this, making the schools the centerpiece of their nationalization efforts. Nor was it a point lost on the Argentine inspectors, who took time away from their fixation with the Nazi propaganda to warn their compatriots of the Italian fascist threat to Argentina's national identity through its schools abroad. That out of all of the evidence they collected the investigators chose to only report on the activities of the Italian schools abroad demonstrates the importance they placed on primary education. In targeting Italian Argentine children, the Italian regime was competing directly with the Argentine government for the hearts and minds of its youth. The regime had blatantly interfered with Argentina's own national project. It was an affront to its national sovereignty that the government no longer tolerated.

CONCLUSION

By attempting to promote an Italian national project abroad while at the same time spreading a fascist ideological program, the Italian fascist regime failed at both. In the end, the nationalist agenda of spreading an Italian identity abroad undermined its universalist agenda by alienating otherwise receptive Argentine nationalist movements. At the same time, the universalist mission to promote the totalitarian political system abroad alarmed Argentines the most, enabling left-wing radicals to use it to discredit their nationalist adversaries by associating them with a foreign political ideology that attacked the values upon which Argentina's democratic national narrative was founded. Ultimately, both its nationalist and universalist agendas ran afoul of the Argentine government once public attention turned to the propaganda activities of foreign nations. The government could not allow totalitarian ideologies to threaten Argentine democracy, nor could it permit foreign regimes to advance their national projects within its sovereign territory.

The debates inspired in Argentina by the foreign propaganda arriving on its shores do more than simply attest to the ultimate failure of fascist propaganda. They also provide a clear articulation of how Argentines strove to define their identity as nation. Just as Italian fascist writers were grappling with the question of an emigrant identity outside of the nation, Argentine writers were questioning their own identity as a nation of immigrants. At the very same moment that Italy attempted to promote its national programs in Argentina, Argentines were anxiously reaffirming their own national identity in the face of internal and external threats. Argentina's ideational national identity based on the principles of liberty and democracy proved to be quite durable as it won out over foreign ideological threats. It also managed to hold on to its democratic national narrative in spite of periods of domestic turmoil, corruption, and political repression over the course of the 1930s.

In the end, the Argentine government interpreted fascist Italy's nationalization project targeting its Italian immigrants along with Italian fascism's attack on its democratic ideals as direct challenges to their own national discourses and their own state's nationalization project. It was a confrontation that the Italian fascists could not win. With the mechanisms of the state firmly in the hands of the Argentine government, it was only a matter of time before it would suppress the fascist regime's insidious nationalization activities inside its borders. Powerless to stop them, the Italian embassy could only watch as Argentine officials uncovered and dismantled the propaganda machine the regime worked so hard to implement.

Of course, the Italian embassy had other things to worry about. By the time the Commission on Anti-Argentine Activities concluded its work, Italian fascism's days were already numbered. The champions of the antifascist cause in the Argentine Congress would, however, have little time to celebrate. In 1943 another military coup dissolved Congress, and by 1946 all of the politicians who fought so hard to defend Argentine democracy in the face of the fascist menace, from Repetto and Palacios to Dickmann and Damonte Taborda, found themselves either in prison or in exile after Juan Domingo Perón, an admirer of Mussolini, came to power.

Over the next forty years, Argentine politics would continue to sway between democracy and dictatorship. Argentina weathered the tumultuous *década infame*, and the government of the time rejected outright the foreign national propaganda arriving on its shores, reaffirming its faith in the democratic ideal. During the same period, however, Argentine nationalists, influenced by the Italian fascist propaganda, had developed a new style of right-wing national identity that laid the ideological foundation for the authoritarian regimes to come, casting a dark shadow over Argentina's political landscape to this day.

NOTES

1. Agustín Rodríguez Araya, Speech before the Argentine Chamber of Deputies, June 5, Cámara de Diputados, *Diario de sesiones de la Cámara de Diputados* (Buenos Aires: Imprenta del Congreso Nacional, 1940).
2. Don H. Doyle and Marco Antonio Pamplona, eds., *Nationalism in the New World* (Athens: University of Georgia Press, 2006).
3. David Rock, *Argentina, 1516–1987* (Berkeley: University of California Press, 1987), 102–17.
4. Jorge Myers, "Language, History, and Politics in Argentine Identity, 1840–1880," in Doyle and Pamplona, *Nationalism in the New World*, 121.
5. Jean H. Delaney, "Imagining *El Ser Argentino*: Cultural Nationalism and Romantic Concepts of Nationhood in Early Twentieth Century Argentina," *Journal of Latin American Studies* 34 (2002): 625–58; Jorge Myers, "Language, History, and Politics in Argentine Identity."
6. Rock, *Argentina*, 199–213.
7. Ibid., 214–20.
8. The focus of this chapter is Argentine responses to Italy's national project. For more information of Argentine nationalist thought, see Federico Finchelstein, *Transatlantic Fascism: Ideology, Violence, and the Sacred in Argentina and Italy, 1919–1945* (Durham, NC: Duke University Press, 2010). It is an excellent exploration of the influence of fascist Italy's propaganda on the emerging political ideology of the Argentine Right. See also David Rock, *Authoritarian Argentina: The Nationalist Movement, Its His tory and Its Impact* (Berkeley: University of California Press, 1993); Sandra McGee Deutsch and Ronald H. Dolkart, eds., *The Argentine Right: Its History and Intellectual Origins, 1910 to the Present* (Wilmington, DE: SR Books, 1993).
9. See, for example, the aforementioned works by Finchelstein, Rock, and Deustch and Dolkart, as well as Sandra McGee Deutsch, *Las Derechas: The Extreme Right in Argentina, Chile and Brazil, 1890–1939* (Stanford, CA: Stanford University Press, 1999).
10. Rock, *Authoritarian Argentina*, 87–124; Deutsch and Dolkart, *Argentine Right*, 65–98.
11. Rock, *Authoritarian Argentina*, 87–124; Deutsch and Dolkart, *Argentine Right*, 65–98.
12. See Finchelstein, *Transatlantic Fascism*.

13. See, for example, Carlos M. Quinodoz, "Natalidad en crisis: El ejemplo de Italia," *Crisol*, June 25, 1939, and Emilio Rosso, "El corporativismo y sus criticos," *Crisol*, August 27, 1937.

14. *La Fronda*, October 28, 1934 in Ministero della Cultura Populare Direzione Servizi della Propaganda, file 4, Archivio Centrale dello Stato.

15. See, for example, transcribed speeches by Mussolini before the Italian senate in *La Bandera Argentina*, February 18, 1934, and Mussolini on the decadence of Bolshevism in *Crisol*, July 11, 1937; "Las doctrinas políticas y sociales del Duce continúan apasionando al mundo," *La Bandera Argentina*, August 5, 1932.

16. "La visita in Italia del Dr. Sanchez Sorondo," *La Nación*, April, 12, 1937.

17. Italian Embassy in Buenos Aires to Ministry of Foreign Affairs, October 8, 1937, Inventario della Serie Politici (1931–1945), Argentina file 18, Archivio Storico del Ministero degli Affari Esteri (hereafter cited in notes as ASMAE).

18. "El Fascismo Marcha," *La Bandera Argentina*, February 10, 1934.

19. "A 15 año de la marcha sobre Roma," *Crisol*, October 28, 1937.

20. Ibid.

21. See *La Bandera Argentina* issues from January to March 1934.

22. Manuel Gálvez, "El fascismo en la Argentina," *Il Mattino d'Italia*, reprinted *La Bandera Argentina*, August 31, 1932.

23. Ibid.

24. Ibid.

25. Manuel Gálvez, *Este pueblo necesita . . .* (Buenos Aires: Libreria de A. Garcia Santos, 1934), 129.

26. Ibid., 132.

27. Ibid., 132–33.

28. "Que es nuestro nacionalismo," *La Bandera Argentina*, August 4, 1932; "Una leccion de democrcia nueva ha dictado al mundo Benito Mussolini," *La Bandera Argentina*, August 11, 1932.

29. See discussion in chapter 5.

30. "Estado fascista y estado liberal," *La Bandera Argentina*, October 15, 1932.

31. "A lo que podríamos llegar en material del régimen corporativo," *La Bandera Argentina*, August 12, 1932.

32. Enrique Oses, "El fascismo según Mussolini," *Crisol*, June 12, 1932.

33. Ibid.

34. Ibid. Seven years later, Oses reconciled totalitarianism with Catholic doctrine by resurrecting the concept of divine right of rule: "The totalitarian political thesis . . . institutes an authority that cannot have any true or real foundation if it is not [emanating] from God," and "the totalitarian thesis walks by His side in obedience with the goals and destinies that He has assigned for a man's life." And what of the contradictions between the two that he himself pointed to in the past? Apparently these "supposed" contradictions were "nothing more than one of the most miserable and despicable lies disseminated around the world by Judaic propagandists to create demonic and malevolent confusion." When all else fails, the nationalists could always fall back on the Jews, their scapegoats of choice to save them from ideological inconsistency. "La autoridad, la iglesia, el totalitarismo," *Crisol*, March, 4, 1939.

35. *La Fronda*, February 17, 1932, as quoted in Deutsch and Dolkart, *Argentine Right*, 79.

36. Carlos Néstor Maciel, *La italianización de la Argentina: Tras huella de nuestros antepasados* (Buenos Aires: J. Menedez y Hijo, 1924), 119–20.

37. Maciel, *La italianización de la Argentina*, 197.

38. "Bienvenidos para trabajar," *La Fronda*, November 21, 1938.

39. "Los extranjeros en la vida politica y administrativa del país," *La Bandera Argentina*, August 12, 1932.

40. Ibid.

41. Ibid.

42. "Actualidad de las ideas de Sarmiento sobre los extranjeros," *La Bandera Argentina*, August 14, 1932.

43. "Los extranjeros en la vida politica y administrativa del país," *La Bandera Argentina*, August 12, 1932.

44. The Italian embassy cited the aforementioned *La Fronda* article, "Bienvendios para trabajar," as an example of anti-Italian sentiment. Inventario della Serie Politici (1931–1945), Argentina file 20, ASMAE.

45. Guariglia to Ciano, August 4, 1937, Inventario della Serie Politici (1931–1945), Argentina file 20, ASMAE.

46. Ibid.

47. William B. Bristol, "Hispanidad in South America, 1936–1948" (PhD diss., University of Pennsylvania, 1947), 1.

48. Finchelstein's analysis of *hispanidad* in the final chapter of *Transatlantic Fascism* provides a transnational perspective on the movement by highlighting the role of Argentine intellectuals in their formulation of the concept.

49. The most recent and thorough discussion of Argentina's overall antifascist movement is Andrés Bisso, *El antifascismo argentino: Selección documental y estudio preliminar* (Buenos Aires: Editorial Buenos Libros, 2007).

50. El Antifascista, "Solidaridad contra el fascismo," *La Protesta*, March 30, 1932.

51. "Fascismo y fenomeno fascista universal," *Contra-Fascismo*, April 25, 1936. These rare periodicals are available on microfilm in the University of Texas Austin Latin American periodicals collection.

52. *Contra-Fascismo*, August–September 1936.

53. *La Protesta*, February 4, 1932; *La Vanguardia*, September 21, 1933.

54. *La Batalla*, August 31, 1935.

55. Ibid.

56. *La Vanguardia*, September 24, 1933.

57. *El Despertar*, reprinted in *La Vanguardia*, October 19, 1933.

58. "Manifestaciones de Buyan," *La Vanguardia*, October 15, 1933.

59. "El agente del Duce," *La Vanguardia*, October 15, 1933.

60. *La Protesta*, April 20, 1932.

61. "El mitín del Domingo contra fascismo," *La Vanguardia*, September 21, 1933.

62. "El mítin de hoy," *La Vanguardia*, September 24, 1933.

63. "El mítin del Domingo contra fascismo," *La Vanguardia*, September 21, 1933.

64. "Discorso del Deputado Miguel B. Navello," *La Vanguardia*, September 25, 1933.

65. Ibid.

66. Nicolás Repetto, *La Vanguardia*, October 7, 1933.

67. Ibid.

68. "La farsa del regimen corporativo," *La Vanguardia*, October 7, 1933.

69. Ibid.

70. Ibid.

71. Nicolás Repetto, *Italia Libre*, August 21, 1940.

72. Alfredo L. Palacios, Speech before the Argentine Senate, May 1936, published in the *Diario de sesiones*; reprinted in *L'Italia del Popolo*, May 16, 1936. A revised and updated version of the speech was published in *Italia Libre*, January 4, 1941.

73. Ibid.

74. Ibid.

75. Ibid.

76. El Antifascista, "Solidaridad contra el fascismo," *La Protesta*, March 30, 1932.

77. Ibid.

78. Ibid.

79. "Infiltración peligrosa," *La Vanguardia*, January 9, 1934.

80. Ibid.

81. This information is based on the fragmented publications of the aforementioned groups, collected and microfilmed by the University of Texas at Austin, Publicaciones de Organizaciónes Antifascistas (1930–1945), roll 6.

82. Aristibulo Echegaray, "La Lucha Antifascista y Nuestro Comité," *Contra-Fascismo*, August–September 1936.

83. In general, the right-of-center mainstream newspapers such as *La Nación* and *La Razón* looked favorably upon the regime, with *La Prensa*, a mainstream conservative daily, the exception, while the left-of-center papers, *Crítica, Noticias Graficas*, and *La Tribuna Libre*, often criticized Mussolini and his international policies. For a detailed evaluation of the Argentine press by the Italian ambassador discussing their political leanings and disposition toward fascism, see "Rapporto-Stampa n. 28," Ministero della Cultura Popolare Reports (1922–1944), file 18, Archivio Centrale dello Stato.

84. *El Orden*, July 16, 1937.

85. "Federzoni Agravio a nuestro pais anoche," *La Voz del Interior*, July 16, 1937. Newspaper clippings and notes from the Italian Embassy in Buenos Aires on Federzoni's visit are in Inventario della Serie Politici (1931–1945) Argentina, file 15, ASMAE.

86. "En terminos despectivos para nuestro país, habló anoche el Dr. Federzoni," *El Dia de la Plata*, July 16, 1937.

87. *El Orden*, July 16, 1937.

88. *El Dia de la Plata, Crítica, Buenos Aires Herald*, July 16, 1937.

89. "Desde el Balcón," *La Tribuna Libre*, July 17, 1937.

90. *La Nación*, July 17, 1937.

91. *El Argentino*, July 17, 1937.

92. *Buenos Aires Herald*, July 17, 1937.

93. Ambassador of Buenos Aires to Foreign Ministry, "Allarmi per propaganda straniera in Argentina," April 16, 1938, Inventario della Serie Politici (1931–1945), Argentina file 20, ASMAE.

94. See, for examples, articles in the Argentine dailies *La Razón, La Prensa*, and especially *Noticias Graficas* during the months of April and May 1938.

95. "Como trabajo el nazismo para anexar la patagonia al Reich," *Crítica*, June 2, 1939. It was later proven that this so-called Patagonia Plot was a hoax. For more information on Nazi espionage activities and press reactions, see Ronald C. Newton's detailed study, *The "Nazi Menace" in Argentina, 1931–1947* (Stanford, CA: Stanford University Press, 1992).

96. For the full investigation of Nazi espionage, see the Secretos y Reservados collection in the Archivo General de la Nación Intermedio.

97. "Peligrosa invasion Fascista en Paraná," *Libre Palabra*, October 16, 1938.

98. Ibid.

99. Dickmann's speeches to the Chamber of Deputies are found in the official minutes of the chamber, *Diario de sesiones*, for those dates and were also compiled in the single volume: *La infiltracion Nazi-Fascista en la Argentina* (Buenos Aires: Ediciones Sociales Argentinas, 1939), 7–8.

100. Raúl Damonte Taborda, Speech before the Chamber of Deputies, *Diario de Sesiones*, June 15, 1939.

101. Ibid., June 5, 1940.

102. Ibid.

103. Dickmann, *La infiltracion Nazi-Fascista*, 11–12.

104. Ibid.

105. Ibid.

106. Italian Ambassador in Buenos Aires to Foreign Ministry, May 30, 1938, Inventario della Serie Affari Politici (1931–1945), Argentina file 20, ASMAE.

107. Italian Ambassador in Buenos Aires to Ministry of Foreign Affairs, August 8, 1938, Inventario della Serie Affari Politici (1931–1945), Argentina file 20, ASMAE.

108. Consejo Nacional de Educacion (Argentina), disposición exp. 17815/M/937, September 28, 1938, Inventario della Serie Affari Politici (1931–1945), Argentina file 20, ASMAE.

109. Consejo Naciónal de Educación (Argentina), "Resolución," December 21, 1939, Comisión Investigadora de Actividades Anti-Argentinas, box 23.3-23.6, Archivo del Congreso de la Nacíon (hereafter cited in notes as ACN).

110. Italian Ambassador in Buenos Aires to Minister of Foreign Affairs, June 24, 1938, Inventario della Serie Affari Politici (1931–1945), Argentina file 21, ASMAE.

111. Romizi, Consul in Mendoza to DIES, January 29, 1937, DGRC Archivio Scuole (1936–1945), file 57, ASMAE.

112. G. Baroni, Consul in La Plata, April 21, 1938, DGRC Archivio Scuole (1936–1945), file 58, ASMAE.

113. "La Plata, lugares de reunion de elementos fascista," Comisión Investigadora de Actividades Anti-Argentinas, box 1.3-1.4, ACN.

114. Benito F. Vaccarezza, Argentine Inspector General of Private Schools, *Inspeccion general de escuelas particulares da cuenta de los programas de enseñanza del idioma italiano que se imparten en las escuelas dependientes de la asociación italiana Pro-Schola*, July, 7, 1939, "Expediente 15461-I 139," Fondo del Ministerio de Educación, 1939: 28, AGNI.

115. Ibid.

116. Ibid.

117. Consejo Naciónal de Educación (Argentina), "Desaprovando programas y libros de escuela particular," December 13, 1939, Fondo del Ministerio de Educacíon, 1939: 28, AGNI.

118. Decree May 15, 1939, in *Diario de sesiones*, June 9, 1939.

119. "Fascismo Italiano," Comisión Investigadora de Actividades Anti-Argentinas, box 22.3-23.2, ACN.

120. Ibid.

121. Ibid.

122. Ibid.

123. Ibid.

124. Ibid.

125. Comisión Investigadora de Actividades Anti-Argentinas, *Informe no. 4*, Buenos Aires, September 30, 1941.

126. Ibid.

Conclusion

This book began by posing the question of how a national project works outside of the nation-state, how discourses on national identity change when transplanted onto another nation's soil. Mussolini's experiences in Argentina offer some suggestive answers to this question by illustrating both the possibilities as well as the limitations of promoting a national project abroad.

Over the course of the 1920s, the Italian regime developed the concept of an extraterritorial Italian national identity. It was lauded by members of the regime as a "fascist solution" to the emigration problem that the liberal regime had failed to resolve. Rhetoric notwithstanding, much of this agenda continued liberal-era policies and relied on preexisting state institutions. Furthermore, by the 1930s fascism's strategy abroad proved to be more nationalist than fascist as the project of promoting Italian identity undermined fascism's revolutionary international agenda. The fascist regime's national project abroad did, however, represent a departure from the past in a number of significant ways. Unlike earlier conceptualizations of Italian national identity, the fascist regime moved beyond traditional ethnic-cultural models of Italian identity by insisting that one must also be a fascist in order to be a true Italian. The fascist Italian identity abroad was as ideational as it was ethnocultural since it claimed that in addition to being ethnically Italian, one can only become an Italian abroad by embodying the values and beliefs of the fascist regime.

To promote this new national identity, the fascist regime attempted to indoctrinate the children of Italian emigrants through its system of schools in Argentina as well as through other state-controlled organizations. Mussolini no doubt assumed that the state-sponsored national project abroad would be able to operate in much the same way as it had at home. He could not have realized how different his national project would look once it arrived on foreign shores, nor could he have imagined the responses it provoked.

Italian fascists had assumed that by promoting an Italian national identity in Argentina they would be able to garner support for their regime and its political agenda. In this endeavor, they failed abjectly. But contrary to their assumptions, they did not fail because the Italian emigrants in Argentina had abandoned their cultural heritage by assimilating into Argentine society. They failed instead because the majority of Italians abroad rejected the regime's appropriation of Italy's national identity. The antifascists within Argentina reaffirmed their sense of Italian national identity by opposing fascism, while those members of the community sympathetic to the fascist regime articulated their own understanding of Italian national identity, which often contradicted the regime's model.

Once the regime introduced its national project in Argentina, it had no control over the discourse. Italians as well as Argentines were free to interpret the propaganda in any way they saw fit, operating within the relatively free Italian public sphere in Argentina. It was, ironically enough, a free Italian public sphere that regime helped create by arguing in its propaganda that Italians living abroad were just as integral to the Italian nation as Italians living in Italy. Unlike a national project within the borders of the nation-state, Italian fascists lost whatever hegemonic control over the discourse they may have had when their national message crossed the ocean. They could not fall back on the apparatus of the state to indoctrinate their compatriots abroad. Supporting the Italian fascist regime and adopting its brand of Italian national identity was a voluntary act, and despite the regime's efforts, Italian national identity meant very different things to different people. Even those who rejected outright the regime's efforts did in the process articulate their own sense of an Italian national identity with its own set of myths and pantheon of national heroes. These different conceptualizations of the nation were no less valid than that of the Italian regime and equally important to our understanding of how national identities are constructed. Native Argentines, confronted with a foreign nationalist project and political ideology within their country, were also prompted to rethink and rearticulate their own sense of national identity. In short, though it failed in its political objectives, the regime's propaganda did succeed in provoking no small amount of debate and discussion over the question of national identity within Argentina.

The Italian fascists had in fact failed to appreciate the Argentine context in formulating their project. Argentina was a nation of immigrants united by an ideational sense of national identity founded on a faith in democracy. By trying to convince Italian immigrants living in Argentina to remain loyal to Italy, with a national identity separate from the rest of society, they were pulling at the very fabric of Argentina's national model. They also had fantastically underestimated the natural pull toward assimilation felt by many Italian immigrants. Even those sympathetic to the regime were preoccupied with integrating themselves into Argentine society. With all of their material interests and livelihoods as well as the lives of their children now dependent on the fortunes of their new nation, they could not but have identified with Argentina, even if they chose to also maintain their identities as Italians. Furthermore, while the regime's universalist message may have been appealing to Argentine nationalists, the Italian fascists' national project in Argentina most definitely was not. Ultimately, the Italian regime's only thinly disguised promotion of a national identity within another sovereign state was doomed to failure as soon as the Argentine government recognized the threat it posed to its own national project.

The example of Il Duce's national project in Argentina demonstrates the complex ways national identities are formed. Whatever control the regime had over the national discourse at home was lost once abroad. Not only did the state have no way of influencing how the national project was received and interpreted abroad, it also had to contend with competing concepts of Italian national identity as well as rival national projects from the host nations. National identities are much more elastic and fluid than they at first appear, and as this project demonstrates, the act of imagining the nation is not the exclusive patrimony of nation-states or political parties. Instead, these identities are negotiated, contested, and reimagined from below by members of the community who are actively engaged in the discourse. Even those Italians in Argentina who had left the nation many years earlier continued to feel the pull toward their homeland and were in dialogue with the Italian state in shaping their own national identity as Italian immigrants in Argentina. The intricate way the Italian community integrated itself into Argentina's national life, while at the same time maintaining and reestablishing connections with the Italian nation of its origin, is but one striking example of the how identities are constantly redefined and negotiated across time and across borders.

The case of Il Duce's national project in Argentina is not unique or exceptional. It is instead a representative example of an increasingly common modern phenomenon. Today many nations with large emigrant populations are similarly redefining their national projects to incorporate into them their emigrants abroad, and emigrants are in turn transforming those national discourses within their new nations. Italy's experiences in Argentina are an especially relevant model for the nations of Latin America today. Many of these nations' migration patterns mirror the Italian historical emigration experience. Latin American emigrants today are leading even more transnational lives than the Italian emigrants of the past. As more and more Latin Americans immigrate to the United States and Europe, attain dual citizenship, send remittances back to their home country, and establish business and familial links across borders, Latin American governments are now faced with the same question of a national identity abroad faced by the Italian regime.[1] This is especially true in nations with large numbers of emigrants who have made significant financial contributions to the home country's economy, not to mention the cultural impact they have had through the transfer of consumer goods and return travel. The political role these citizens could play through voting abroad is potentially even more impactful than the Italian case has already proven to be.[2]

Proportionally as well as financially, the number of citizens abroad in some nations is even more significant than that of the Italian case, making their impact that much more important. Emigrants from nations like Mexico, Colombia, and the Dominican Republic now play an important role in shaping the national agendas of their home countries, making them a valuable component of these nation's new national projects. This is especially true for a small nation like El Salvador. In El Salvador over 25 percent of the population has emigrated, and remittances from relatives living in the United States is actually the leading source of export earnings and over 16 percent of the nation's gross domestic product.[3] Just as the Italian regimes had done in the past, the government of El Salvador has created state agencies to preserve and foster its national identity within its community abroad. The Salvadoran Dirección General de Atención a las Comunidades en el Exterior bears a striking resemblance in its functions to Italy's Direzione Generale degli Italiani all'Estero by providing its emigrants with legal and social counseling and information services. El Salvador's Foreign Ministry is also advocating for the rights of its citizens abroad as well as creating a new national concept of the nation to reintegrate these communities into its national project in much the same way Italian governments did in the past.[4]

The Philippines represent another fascinating comparison to the Italian case. Similar to El Salvador, the Philippine government takes an active interest in its citizens abroad. Since the 1970s it has in fact not only promoted emigration but actually brokered overseas labor arrangements, providing institutional training, support, and research for its migrant workers.[5] Robyn Rodriguez in her recent *Migrants for Export: How the Philippine State Brokers Labor with the World* argues that this labor export apparatus has redefined notions of national identity in the Philippines. According to Rodriguez, these migrants, far from being considered less worthy of citizenship, are actually exalted as national heroes and are expected to fulfill their obligations as Philippine citizens by sending home remittances to support the national economy and by returning home at the end of their labor contracts. For this process to work, maintaining linkages with the home country and instilling patriotism and national identity abroad is essential.[6]

The Philippine and Salvadoran cases are but two of many modern manifestations of the same discourse on national identity abroad illustrated by the Italian case. In both instances, we see attempts by the nation-state to create an extraterritorial state-sponsored national identity. As Salvadoran emigrants and Philippine migrants become more and more involved politically, it will be interesting to see how this debate over the national identity question and the changes in that discourse it engenders plays out, making Italy an especially relevant point of reference.

Italy's national debate in Argentina during the 1920s and 1930s is but one of many transnational examples that challenge us to adjust our own preconceptions about national identity formation and develop new paradigms for understanding our place in the world today. Just as in the case of the Italian community in Argentina, we see emigrant communities around the world actively engaging in national discourses with their nations of origin, fascinating everyday expressions of the power of a people to create their own national destinies from below in dialogue with the state models imposed from above. It is a phenomenon that demonstrates the continued relevance of national projects to the state as well as the power of the people both at home and abroad to make and remake the national narrative.

NOTES

1. Cristina Escobar, "Extraterritorial Political Rights and Dual Citizenship in Latin America," *Latin American Research Review* 42, no. 3 (2007): 43–75.
2. Escobar's article provides an excellent comparative analysis of voting and extraterritorial citizenship in Latin American today.
3. Sarah Gammage, "Exporting People and Recruiting Remittances: A Developmental Strategy for El Salvador?" *Latin American Perspectives* 33, no. 6 (2006): 75.
4. Ibid., 89–92.
5. Robyn Magalit Rodriguez, *Migrants for Export: How the Philippine State Brokers Labor to the World* (Minneapolis: University of Minnesota Press, 2010).
6. Ibid., 92.

Bibliography

ARCHIVAL COLLECTIONS

Italy

Archivio Centrale dello Stato (ACS)

- Carte Cornelio di Marzio
- Casellario Politico Centrale
- Ministero della Cultura Popolare Direzione Generale Propaganda
- Ministero della Cultura Popolare Direzione Servizi della Propaganda
- Ministero della Cultura Popolare, Gabinetto.
- Ministero della Cultura Popolare Reports (1922–1944).
- NUPIE (Nuclei di propaganda in Italia e all'estero, 1932–1945)
- Partito Nazionale Fascista, Servizi Vari
- Segretaria Particolare del Duce.

Archivio Storico del Ministero degli Affari Esteri (ASMAE)

- Archivio Scuole (1923–1928)
- Archivio Scuole (1929–1935)
- DGRC Archivio Scuole (1936–1945)
- Inventario degli Archivi Microfilmati delle Associazioni Italiane in Argentina
- Inventario del Fondo "Commissione Centrale Arbitrale per L'Emigrazione" (1915–1929)

- Inventario della Serie Affari Politici (1919–1930)
- Inventario della Serie Affari Politici (1931–1945)
- Le Carte del Gabinetto del Ministro e della Segretaria Generale dal 1923 al 1943
- Ministero Cultura Popolare (1920–1944)

Archivio Storico della Camera dei Deputati (ASCD)

- Fondo Giovanni Giuriati

Argentina

Archivo General de la Nación Intermedio (AGNI)

- Fondo del Ministerio de Educación
- Secretos y Reservados

Archivo del Congreso de la Nacíon (ACN)

- Comisión Investigadora de Actividades Anti-Argentinas

Centro de Estudios Migratorios Latino Americanos (CEMLA)

Biblioteca Nacional de la Republica Argentina

- Hemeroteca
- Periódicos antiguos

United States of America

University of Texas at Austin

- Latin American Periodicals Collection

PERIODICAL SOURCES

Italy

- Augustea
- Il Bollettino dell'Emigrazione
- Gerarchia

- Il Legionario
- Le Pagine delle Dante
- Il Popolo d'Italia

Argentina

- El Argentino
- La Bandera Argentina
- Buenos Aires Herald
- Crisol
- *Crítica*
- El Dia de la Plata
- La Fronda
- Il Giornale d'Italia
- L'Italia del Popolo
- Italia Libre
- Il Mattino d'Italia
- La Nación
- Noticias Graficas
- El Orden
- El Pampero
- La Patria degli Italiani
- La Prensa
- La Protesta
- La Razón
- Il Risorgimento
- La Tribuna Libre
- La Vanguardia

PRIMARY SOURCES

Arena, Celestino. *Italiani per il mondo: Politica nazionale dell'emigrazione*. Milan: Alpes, 1927.
Bagagli, Clementina, ed. *Letture classe prima: Scuole italiane all'estero*. Rome: Librería dello Stato, 1933.
———. *Letture classe seconda: Scuole italiane all'estero*. Rome: Librería dello Stato, 1932.
Bontempelli, Massimo. *Noi, gli Aria: Interpretazioni sudamericane*. Edited by Sebastiano Martelli. Palermo: Sellerio, 1994.
Borsella, Giovanni. *L'emigrante italiano e l'Argentina*. Milan: Fratelli Treves, 1925.
Buffarini, Arsenio Guido. *Tutta un'esistenza di italianità: Arsenio Guido Buffarini e la sua opera: Un trentennio vissuto combattendo per la gloria dell'Italia e per la fraternitá Italo-Argentina*. Buenos Aires, 1931.
Cámara de Diputados. *Diario de sesiones de la Cámara de Diputados*. Buenos Aires: Imprenta del Congreso Nacional, 1933–1943.
Camera dei Deputati, *Atti del Parlamento italiano, Discussioni*. Vol. 7. Rome, 1927.

Cantalupo, Roberto. *Racconti poltica dell'altra pace*. Milan: Istituto per gli Studi di Politica Internazionale, 1940.
Ciarlantini, Franco. *Viaggio in Argentina*. Milan: Edizioni Alpes, 1929.
Comisión Investigadora de Actividades Antiargentinas. *Despacho e informe*. Buenos Aires, 1942.
———. *Informe no. 4*. Buenos Aires, September 30, 1941.
Commissariato Generale dell'Emigrazione. *Manuale di geografia economica di legislazione sociale e di notizie utile per gli Italiani all'estero*. Rome: Commissariato Generale dell'Emigrazione, 1926.
Conference Internationale de l'Emigration et de l'Immigration, Rome, May 15–31, 1924. "Acte finale." Rome: Commissariat General Italien de L'Emigration, 1924.
———. "Travaux de la conference." Rome: Commissariat General Italien de L'Emigration, 1924.
Cordova, Antonino. *Gli aspetti presenti e futuri dell'emigrazione*. Turin: Lattes, 1923.
de Glauco, Scilla, ed. *La Nuova Italia*, New York: Nikolas Press, 1939.
Dickmann, Enrique. *La infiltracion Nazi-Fascista en la Argentina*. Buenos Aires: Ediciones Sociales Argentinas, 1939.
Fabbri, Luce. *Camisas negras*. Buenos Aires: Ediciones Nervio, 1935.
Fabbri, Luigi. *La contro-rivoluzione preventiva (riflessioni sul fascismo)*. Bologna: Licinio Capellu, 1922.
Fanciulli, Giuseppe. *Canzoncine italiane*. Rome: Librería dello Stato, 1931.
———. *Letture di religione per le Scuole Elementare Italiane all'Estero*. Vol. 2. Verona: A. Mondadori, 1934.
Frola, Francesco. *Recuerdos de un anti-fascista, 1925–1938*. N.p.: Editorial Mexico Nuevo, 1939.
Gálvez, Manuel. *Este Pueblo Necesita . . . .* Buenos Aires: Librería de A. Garcia Santos, 1934.
Giuriati, Giovanni Battista, *La crociera italiana nell'America Latina*. Rome: Arti Grafiche Affini Roma, 1925.
Grandi, Dino. "Discorso alla Camera dei Deputati," March 31, 1927. In *La politica estera dell'Italia dal 1929 al 1932*, ed. Paolo Nello. Rome: Bonacci Editore, 1985.
Luisi, Luigi. *Manuale di cultura militare per le scuole italiane all'estero*. Rome: Ardita, 1935.
Maciel, Carlos Néstor. *La italianización de la Argentina: Tras huella de nuestros antepasados*. Buenos Aires: J. Menedez y Hijo, 1924.
Marchetti, Goffredo. *Risposte di buon senso alle principali obbiezioni che si fanno all'estero contro il fascismo*. La Plata: Mandolin and Bonaventura, 1940.
Micci, Alighiero. *L'emigrazione*. Rome: A. Mondadori, 1925.
Ministerio das Relações Exteriores. *Mensagem apresentado pelo Senhor Presidente da Republica ao Congresso Nacional em 3 de maio de 1925*.
Mussolini, Benito. *Opera omnia di Benito Mussolini*. Edited by E. Sumsel and D. Susmel. 44 vols. Florence: La Fenice, 1951–1963; Rome: Volpe, 1978–1980.
Opera Nazionale Dopolavoro. *Scopi ed organizzazione, bollettino ufficiale*. January 1, 1927.
Parini, Piero. *Gli Italiani nel mondo*. Rome: Fasci all'Estero, 1935.
———. *Italiani per il Mondo*. Milan: Mondadori, 1935.
———. "Italians in the World." In *Italy*. Chicago: Chicago Tribune, 1933.
———. *Norme di vita fascista all'estero*. Verona: A. Mondadori, 1937.
Pedrazzi, Orazio. *I nostri fratelli lontani*. Rome: Segreteria Generale dei Fasci all'Estero, 1929.
Raccolta ufficiale delle leggi e dei decreti del regno d'Italia. Rome: Regia Tipografia, 1889.
Scuole Italiane all'Estero. *Il libro della III classe elementare: Storia, geografia, aritmetica*. Verona: A. Mondadori, 1933.
———. *Sole d'Italia: Letture Classe V*. Rome: Librería dello Stato, 1934.
———. *Storia e geografia per la IV classe elementare*. Verona: A. Mondadori, 1938.
Volpe, Gioacchino. *I fatti degli Italiani e dell'Italia: Letture storiche*. Scuole italiane all'estero. Verona: A. Mondadori, 1932.
———. *Il Risorgimento dell'Italia*. Rome: Direzione Italiane all'Estero, 1934.

SECONDARY SOURCES

Albonico, Aldo. "Immagine e destino delle communità italiane in America Latina attraverso la stampa Fascista degli anni '30." *Studi Emigrazione* 65 (March 1982): 41–51.
———. *L'America Latina e l'Italia*. Rome: Bulzoni, 1984.
Aldrighi, Clara. *Antifascismo italiano en Montevideo: El dialogo politico entre Luigi Fabbri y Carlo Rosselli*. Montevideo: Universidad de la Republica, 1996.
———. "Luigi Fabbri en Uruguay, 1929–1935," *Estudios Migratorios Latinoamericanos* 12, no. 37 (1997): 389–422.
Anderson, Benedict. *Imagined Communities: Reflections on the Origin and Spread of Nationalism*. London: Verso, 1983.
Ascoli, Albert Russell, and Krystyna Von Henneberg, eds. *Making and Remaking Italy: The Cultivation of National Identity around the Risorgimento*. Oxford: Berg, 2001.
Atkinson, David, and Denis Cosgrove. "Urban Rhetoric and Embodied Identities: City, Nation, and Empire at the Vittoriano Emanuele II Monument in Rome, 1870–1945." *Annals of the Association of American Geographers* 88, no. 1 (1998): 28–49.
Baily, Samuel L. *Immigrants in the Lands of Promise: Italians in Buenos Aires and New York City, 1870 to 1914*. Ithaca, NY: Cornell University Press, 1999.
———. "The Italians and Organized Labor in the United States and Argentina: 1880–1910." *International Migration Review* 1, no. 3 (1967): 56–66.
Baily, Samuel L., and Eduardo José Míguez, eds. *Mass Migration to Modern Latin America*. Wilmington, DE: Scholarly Resources, 2003.
Baldassar, Loretta, and Donna R. Gabaccia, eds. *Intimacy and Italian Migration: Gender and Domestic Lives in a Mobile World*. New York: Fordham University Press, 2011.
Baldoli, Claudia. *Exporting Fascism: Italian Fascists and Britain's Italians in the 1930s*. Oxford: Berg, 2003.
———. "I Fasci italiani all'estero e l'educazione degli italiani in Gran Bretagna (1932–1934)." *Studi Emigrazione* 36, no. 134 (1999): 243–81.
Banti, Alberto Mario. *La nazione del risorgimento*. Turin: Einaudi, 2000.
Banti, Alberto Mario, and Roberto Bizzocchi, eds. *Immagini della nazione nell'Italia del Risorgimento*. Rome: Carocci, 2002.
Barbero, María Inés, and Susana Felder. "El rol de los italianos en el nacimento y desarrollo de las asociaciones empresarias en la Argentina." In Devoto and Rosoli, *L'Italia nella società Argentina*, 137–160.
Bartolini, Alfonso. *Storia della resistenza italiana all'estero*. Padova: Rebellato, 1965.
Ben-Ghiat, Ruth. *Fascist Modernities: Italy, 1922–1945*. Berkeley: University of California Press, 2001.
Bertagna, Federica. *La patria di riserva: L'emigrazione fascista in Argentina*. Rome: Donzelli, 2006.
———. *La stampa italiana in Argentina*. Rome: Donzelli Editore, 2009.
Bertonha, João Fábio. "Emigrazione e politica estera: La diplomazia sovversiva di Mussolini e la questione degli italiani all'estero, 1922–1945." *Altreitalie* 23 (2001): 39–61.
———. "Fascism and the Italian Communities in Brazil and America." *Italian Americana* 19, no. 2 (2001): 146–57.
———. *O fascismo e os imigrantes italianos no Brasil*. Porto Alegre: EDIPUCRS, 2001.
———. *Sob a sombra de Mussolini: os italianos de São Paulo e a luta contra o fascismo, 1919–1945*. São Paulo: FAPESP, Annablume, 1999.
Bezza, Bruno, ed. *Gli Italiani fuori d'Italia: Gli emigranti italiani nei movimenti operai dei paesi d'adozione, 1880–1940*. Milan: Franco Angelli Editori, 1983.
Bisso, Andrés. *El antifascismo argentino: Selección documental y estudio preliminar*. Buenos Aires: Editorial Buenos Libros, 2007.
Blengino, Vanni. "La marcia su Buenos Aires ('Il Mattino d'Italia')." In Scarzanella, *Fascisti in Sud America*, 205–34.
Bosworth, R. J. B. *The Italian Dictatorship*. London: Arnold, 1996.

Braun, Emily. "The Visual Arts: Modernism and Fascism." In Lyttelton, *Liberal and Fascist Italy*, 196–215.
Bristol, William B. "Hispanidad in South America, 1936–1948." PhD diss., University of Pennsylvania, 1947.
Burgwyn, James H. *The Legend of the Mutilated Victory: Italy, the Great War, and the Paris Peace Conference, 1915–1919*. Westport, CT: Greenword Press, 1992.
Calhoun, Craig, ed. *Habermas and the Public Sphere*. Cambridge, MA: MIT Press, 1992.
———. "Nationalism Matters." In Doyle and Pamplona, *Nationalism in the New World*, 16–40.
Cane, James. "'Unity for the Defense of Culture': The AIAPE and the Cultural Politics of Argentine Antifascism, 1935–1943." *Hispanic American Historical Review* 77, no. 3 (1997): 443–82.
Cannistraro, Philip V. *Blackshirts in Little Italy: Italian Americans and Fascism, 1921–1929*. West Lafayette, IN: Bordighera, 1999.
———. *La fabbrica del consenso: Fascismo e mass media*. Bari: Laterza, 1975.
———. "Mussolini's Cultural Revolution: Fascist or Nationalist?" *Journal of Contemporary History* 7, no. 3 (1972): 115–39.
Cannistraro, Philip V., and Gianfausto Rosoli. *Emigrazione, Chiesa e fascismo: Lo scioglimento dell'Opera Bonomelli, 1922–1928*. Rome: Studium, 1979.
Cannistraro, Philip V., and Brian R. Sullivan. *Il Duce's Other Woman: The Untold True Story of Margherita Sarfatti, Benito Mussolini's Jewish Mistress, and How She Helped Him Come to Power*. New York: William Morrow, 1993.
Capparelli, Filippo. *La "Dante Alighieri."* Rome: Bonacci, 1987.
Caprariis, Luca de. "'Fascism for Export?' The Rise and Eclipse of the Fasci Italiani all'Estero." *Journal of Contemporary History* 35, no. 2 (April 2000): 151–83.
Cárdenas, Eduardo J. *El primer nacionalismo argentino en Manuel Gálvez y Ricardo Rojas*. Buenos Aires: A. Peña Lillo, 1978.
Casali de Babot, Judith, and María Victoria Grillo. *Fascismo y antifascismo en Europa y Argentina en el siglo XX*. San Miguel de Tucumán: Instituto de Investigaciones Historicas, Universidad Nacional de Tucumán, 2002.
Cattarulla, Camilla. "Cosa direste a Mussolini se aveste occasione di parlargli? Un inchiesta de 'Il Mattino d'Italia.'" In Scarzanella, *Fascisti in Sud America*, 175–203.
Choate, Mark I. *Emigrant Nation: The Making of Italy Abroad*. Cambridge, MA: Harvard University Press, 2008.
Ciccarelli, Orazio A. "Fascism and Politics in Peru during the Benavides Regime, 1933–39: The Italian Perspective." *Hispanic American Historical Review* 70, no. 3 (August 1990): 405–32.
———. "Fascist Propaganda and the Italian Community in Peru during the Benavides Regime, 1933–39." *Journal of Latin American Studies* 20, no. 2 (November 1988): 361–88.
Colley, Linda. *Britons: Forging the Nation*. New Haven, CT: Yale University Press, 1993.
Corner, Paul. "Italian Fascism: Whatever Happened to Dictatorship?" *Journal of Modern History* 74 (2002): 325–51.
Croce, Benedetto. *A History of Italy, 1871–1915*. Translated by Cecelia M. Ady. Oxford: Clarendon Press, 1929.
De Felice, Renzo. *Fascism: An Informal Introduction to Its Theories and Practice*. New Brunswick, NJ: Transaction, 1976.
———. *Mussolini Il Duce: Gli anni del consenso, 1929–1936*. Turin: Giulio Einaudi Editore, 1974.
De Grand, Alexander. *The Italian Nationalist Association and the Rise of Fascism in Italy*. Lincoln: University of Nebraska Press, 1978.
De Grazia, Victoria. *The Culture of Consent: Mass Organization of Leisure in Fascist Italy*. New York: Cambridge University Press, 1981.
Delaney, Jean H. "Imagining *El Ser Argentino*: Cultural Nationalism and Romantic Concepts of Nationhood in Early Twentieth Century Argentina." *Journal of Latin American Studies* 34 (2002): 625–58.

Delzell, Charles. *Mussolini's Enemies: The Italian Anti-Fascist Resistance*. Princeton, NJ: Princeton University Press, 1961.
De Rosa, Luigi. "L'emigrazione italiana in Argentina: Un bilancio." In Devoto and Rosoli, *L'Italia nella società Argentina*, 73–89.
Deutsch, Sandra McGee. *Las Derechas: The Extreme Right in Argentina, Chile and Brazil, 1890–1939*. Stanford, CA: Stanford University Press, 1999.
Deutsch, Sandra McGee, and Ronald H. Dolkart, eds. *The Argentine Right: Its History and Intellectuals Origins, 1910 to the Present*. Wilmington, DE: SR Books, 1993.
Devoto, Fernando J. *Historia de los Italianos en la Argentina*. Buenos Aires: Editorial Biblios, 2007.
———. *Nacionalismo, fascismo y tradicionalismo en la Argentina moderna: Una historia*. Buenos Aires: Siglo Veintiuno de Argentina, 2002.
Devoto, Fernando J., and Gianfausto Rosoli, ed. *L'Italia nella società Argentina: Contributi sull'emigrazione italiana in Argentina*. Rome: Centro Studi Emigrazione, 1988.
Díaz, Claudio. *La ultraderecha argentina y su conexión internacional*. Buenos Aires: Editorial Contrapunto, 1987.
Doumanis, Nicholas. *Italy*. London: Arnold, 2001.
Doyle, Don H., and Marco Antonio Pamplona, eds. *Nationalism in the New World*. Athens: University of Georgia Press, 2006.
Eley, Geoff. "Nations, Publics, and Political Cultures: Placing Habermas in the Nineteenth Century." In Calhoun, *Habermas and the Public Sphere*, 289–339.
Escobar, Cristina. "Extraterritorial Political Rights and Dual Citizenship in Latin America." *Latin American Research Review* 42, no. 3 (2007): 43–75.
Fabiano, Domenico. "I fasci italiani all'estero." In Bezza, *Gli Italiani fuori d'Italia*, 221–36.
Fanesi, Pietro Rinaldo. "El anti-fascismo italiano en Argentina (1922–1945)." *Estudios Migratorios Latinoamericanos* 4, no. 12 (1989): 319–352.
Finchelstein, Federico. *Fascismo, liturgia e immaginario: El mito del General Uriburu y la Argentina nacionalista*. Buenos Aires: Fondo de Cultura Economica, 2002.
———. *Transatlantic Fascism: Ideology, Violence, and the Sacred in Argentina and Italy, 1919–1945*. Durham, NC: Duke University Press, 2010.
Floriani, Giorgio. *Scuole italiane all'estero: Cento anni di storia*. Rome: A. Armando Editore, 1974.
Fogu, Claudio. *The Historic Imaginary: Politics of History in Fascist Italy*. Toronto: University of Toronto Press, 2003.
Forgacs, David. "Cultural Consumption, 1940s to 1990s." In Forgacs and Lumley, *Italian Cultural Studies*, 273–90.
Forgacs, David, and Robert Lumley, eds. *Italian Cultural Studies: An Introduction*. New York: Oxford University Press, 1996.
Franzina, Emilio. *Gli italiani al Nuovo Mondo: l'emigrazione italiana in America, 1492–1942*. Milan: Mondadori, 1995.
Franzina, Emilio, and Matteo Sanfilippo, eds. *Il Fascismo e gli emigrati: La parabola dei Fasci italiani all'estero (1920–1943)*. Rome: Laterza, 2003.
Gabaccia, Donna R. *Italy's Many Diasporas*. Seattle: University of Washington Press, 2000.
Gabaccia, Donna R., and Fraser Ottanelli, eds. *Italian Workers of the World: Labor Migration and the Formation of Multiethnic States*. Urbana: University of Illinois Press, 2001.
Galli della Loggia, Ernesto. "La morte della patria." In Spadolini, *Nazione e nazionalità in Italia*, 125–61.
Gammage, Sarah. "Exporting People and Recruiting Remittances: A Developmental Strategy for El Salvador?" *Latin American Perspectives* 33, no. 6 (2006): 75–100.
Geisler, Michael E., ed. *National Symbols, Fractured Identities*. Middlebury, VT: Middlebury College Press, 2005.
Gentile, Emilio. "L'emigrazione italiana in Argentina nella politica di espansione del nazionalismo e del fascismo." *Storia Contemporanea* 17, no. 3 (1986): 355–96.
———. *La grande Italia*. Rome: Laterza, 2006.
———. "La politica estera del partito Fascista: Ideologia e organizzazione dei Fasci italiani all'estero (1920–1930)." *Storia Contemporanea* 26, no. 6 (1995): 897–956.

———. *The Sacralization of Politics in Fascist Italy*. Cambridge, MA: Harvard University Press, 1996.
Germani, Gino. *Autoritarismo, fascismo e classi sociali*. Bologna: Il Mulino, 1975.
Giudice, Gaspare. *Pirandello: A Biography*. London: Oxford University Press, 1975.
Giuliani-Balestrino, Maria Clotilde. *L'Argentina degli Italiani*. Rome: Istituto della Enciclopedia Italiana, 1989.
González de Oleaga, Marisa. *El doble juego de la Hispanidad: España y la Argentina durante la Segunda Guerra Mundial*. Madrid: Universidad Nacional de Educación a Distancia, 2001.
Griffin, Roger, ed. *Fascism*. Oxford: Oxford University Press, 1995.
Habermas, Jürgen. *On Society and Politics: A Reader*. Edited by Steven Seidman. Boston: Beacon Press, 1989.
Henessy, Alistar. "Fascism and Populism in Latin America." In *Fascism: A Reader's Guide*, ed. Walter Laquer, 255–94. Berkeley: University of California Press, 1976.
Hobsbawm, Eric. *Nations and Nationalism since 1780: Programme, Myth, and Reality*. Cambridge: Cambridge University Press, 1990.
Incisa di Camerana, Ludovico. *L'Argentina, gli Italiani, l'Italia: Un altro destino*. Milan: Servizi Promozioni Attività Internazionali, 1998.
Koon, Tracy H. *Believe, Obey, Fight: Political Socialization of Youth in Fascist Italy, 1922–1943*. Chapel Hill: University of North Carolina Press, 1985.
Lanús, Juan Archibaldo. *Aquel apogeo: Política internacional argentina, 1910–1939*. Buenos Aires: Emecé, 2001.
Leiva, M. L. "Il movimiento antifascista italiano in Argentina (1922–1945)." In Bezza, *Gli Italiani fuori d'Italia*, 553–82.
Lepre, Aurelio. *L'Italia addio? L'unità e disunità dal 1860 al Oggi*. Milan: Arnaldo Mondadori Editore, 1994.
Lyttelton, Adrian. "Creating a National Past: History, Myth, and Image in the Risorgimento." In Ascoli and Von Henneberg, *Making and Remaking Italy*, 27–74.
———, ed. *Liberal and Fascist Italy: 1900–1945*. Oxford: Oxford University Press, 2002.
Manfredonia, Gaetano. *La lutte humaine: Luigi Fabbri, le mouvement anarchiste italien et la lutte contre le fascisme*. Paris: Editions du Monde Libertaire, 1994.
Marella, Luigi. *I quaderni del Duce: Tra immagine e parola*. Manduria: Berbieri, 1995.
Mercadante, Luis. *La colectividad italiana en la Argentina*. Buenos Aires: Alzamor Editores, 1974.
Mosse, George L. *The Nationalization of the Masses: Political Symbolism and Mass Movements in Germany from the Napoleonic Wars through the Third Reich*. New York: Howard Fertig, 1975.
Mugnaini, Marco. "L'Italia e l'America Latina (1930–1936): Alcuni aspetti della politica estera fascista." *Storia delle Relazioni Internazionali* 2 , no. 2 (1986): 199–244.
Myers, Jorge. "Language, History, and Politics in Argentine Identity, 1840–1880." In Doyle and Pamplona, *Nationalism in the New World*, 117–42.
Newton, Ronald C. "*Ducini, Prominenti, Antifascisti*: Italian Fascism and the Italo-Argentine Collectivity, 1922–1945." *Americas* 51, no. 1 (1994): 41–66.
———. *The "Nazi Menace" in Argentina, 1931–1947*. Stanford, CA: Stanford University Press, 1992.
Oddone, Juan. "Serafino Mazzolini: Un misionario del Fascismo en Uruguay, 1933–1937." *Estudios Migratorios Latinoamericanos* 12, no. 37 (1997): 375–87.
Patriarca, Silvana. "Indolence and Regeneration: Tropes and Tensions of Risorgimento Patriotism." *American Historical Review* 110, no. 2 (2005): 1–26.
———. *Italian Vices: Nation and Character from the Risorgimento to the Republic*. Cambridge: Cambridge University Press, 2010.
———. *Numbers and Nationhood: Writing Statistics in Nineteenth-Century Italy*. Cambridge: Cambridge University Press, 1996.
Petriella, Dionisio, and Sara Sosa Miatello. *Diccionario Biográfico Italo-Argentino*. Buenos Aires: Asociación Dante Alighieri de Buenos Aires, 1976.

Pavone, Claudio. *Una guerra civile: Saggio storico sulla moralità nella resistenza.* Turin: Bollati Boringhieri, 1991.
Paxton, Robert O. *The Anatomy of Fascism.* New York: Vintage, 2004.
Payne, Stanley G. *A History of Fascism, 1914–1945.* Madison: University of Wisconsin Press, 1995.
Pisa, Beatrice. *Nazione e politica nella Società "Dante Alighieri."* Rome: Bonacci Editore, 1995.
Pluviano, Marco, and Irene Guerrini. "L'Opera Nazionale Dopolavoro in Sud America." *Studi Emigrazione* 32, no. 119 (1995): 518–37.
Pretelli, Matteo. *Il fascismo e gli italiani all'estero.* Bologna: Clueb, 2010.
Riall, Lucy. *Garibaldi: The Invention of a Hero.* New Haven, CT: Yale University Press, 2007.
Rock, David. *Argentina, 1516–1982.* Berkeley: University of California Press, 1985.
———. *Authoritarian Argentina: The Nationalist Movement, Its History and Its Impact.* Berkeley: University of California Press, 1993.
Rodriguez, Robyn Magalit. *Migrants for Export: How the Philippine State Brokers Labor to the World.* Minneapolis: University of Minnesota Press, 2010.
Romano, Sergio. *Finis Italiae: Declino e morte dell'ideologia risorgimentale.* Milan: All'Insegna del Pesce d'Oro, 1995.
Rosoli, Gianfausto, ed. *Identità degli italiani in Argentina,* Rome: Studium, 1993.
Ruberti, Alessandra. "Il fascismo e l'emigrazione italiana in Argentina nella stampa di Regime (1922–1930)." *Affari Sociali Internazionali* 20, no. 3 (1992): 107–16.
Ruiz Moreno, Isidoro. *La Neutralidad Argentina en la Segunda Guerra.* Buenos Aires: Emecé Editores, 1997.
Rusconi, Gian Enrico. *Se cessiamo di essere una nazione.* Bologna: Il Mulino, 1993.
Santinon, Renzo. *Fasci all'estero.* Rome: Edizioni Settimo Sigillo, 1995.
Santos, Viviane Teresinha dos. *Os seguidores do Duce: Os italianos fascistas no Estado de São Paulo.* São Paulo: Arquivo do Estado, Imprensa Oficial, 2001.
Savarino, Franco. "Bajo el signo del *Littorio*: La communidad italiana en México y el fascismo 1924–1941." *Revista Mexicana de Sociología* 64, no. 2 (January–March 2002): 113–39.
Scarzanella, Eugenia. "Cuando la patria llama: Italia en guerra y los inmigrantes italianos en Argentina." *Nuevo Mundo Mundos Nuevos,* March 12, 2007. http://nuevomundo.revues.org/3735.
———, ed. *Fascisti in Sud America.* Florence: Le Lettere, 2005.
———. *Sin fronteras encuentros de mujeres y hombres entre América Latina y Europa, siglos XIX–XX.* Madrid: Iberoamericana, Vervuert, 2008.
Schneider, Arnd. *Futures Lost: Nostalgia and Identity among Italian Immigrants in Argentina.* New York: Peter Lang, 2000.
Scobie, James. *Revolution on the Pampas: A Social History of Argentine Wheat, 1860–1910.* Austin: University of Texas Press, 1964.
Seitenfus, Ricardo Silva. "Ideology and Diplomacy: Italian Fascism and Brazil (1935–1938). *Hispanic American Historical Review* 64, no. 3 (August 1984): 503–34.
Sergi, Pantalcone. "Fascismo e antifascismo nella stampa italiana in Argentina: Cosí fu spenta 'la Patria degli Italiani.'" *Altreitalie* 42 (2007): 4–44.
Smith, Anthony. *National Identity.* Reno: University of Nevada Press, 1991.
Spadolini, Giovanni, ed. *Nazione e nazionalità in Italia: Dall'alba de secolo ai nostri giorni.* Bari: Laterza, 1994.
Sposito, Livio. *Mal d'avventura.* Milan: Sperling and Kupfer, 2002.
Sternhall, Zeev. *The Birth of Fascist Ideology.* Princeton, NJ: Princeton University Press, 1994.
Tasca, Angelo. *The Rise of Italian Fascism.* London: Methuen, 1938.
Tobia, Bruno. *L'altare della patria.* Bologna: Il Mulino, 1998.
———. "Il carteggio tra Filippo Turati e Torquato di Tella (1928–1931)." *Storia Contemporanea* 23, no. 4 (1992): 627–80.
Trento, Angelo. "Argentina e Brasile come paesi d'immigrazione nella pubblicistica italiana 1860–1920." In Devoto and Rosoli, *L'Italia nella società argentina,* 211–40.
———. *Os italianos no Brasil.* São Paulo: Premio, 2000.

Verdicchio, Pasquale. *Bound by Distance: Rethinking Nationalism through the Italian Diaspora*. Madison, NJ: Fairleigh Dickinson University Press, 1997.
Visser, Romke. "Fascist Doctrine and the Cult of Romanità." *Journal of Contemporary History* 27, no. 1 (1992): 5–22.
Weber, Eugen. *Peasants into Frenchmen: The Modernization of Rural France, 1870–1914*. Stanford, CA: Stanford University Press, 1976.
Zago, Manrique. *Argentina, la otra patria de los italianos*. Buenos Aires: M. Zago Ediciones, 1983.

Index

Alberdi, Juan Bautista, 16, 54, 155
Alighieri, Dante, 60, 139
Amigos de Italia, 170
Argentina: fascist Italian views of, 56–62; historical overview, 154–156
anarchists, 62, 120, 126–127, 131–132, 165
ancient Rome, 29, 94, 97, 107
Anderson, Benedict, 8, 154
antifascists: from the Italian community in Argentina, 133–144; Italian exiles in Argentina, 6, 64, 70, 126–133; native Argentine, 164–169
anti-Semitism, 43, 51n88, 158, 164, 175
Appelius, Mario, 66–68
Arias, Gino, 35, 73
Augustea, 60

Bagagli, Clementina, 90
Balabanoff, Angelica, 127
Balbo, Italo, 130
Balilla, 38–39, 71–73, 93, 103, 104, 169
La Bandera Argentina, 157, 159, 160–161
Bastianini, Giuseppe, 32–33
La Batalla, 165
Belgrano, Manuel, 54, 119, 125, 135, 144
Bolasco, Steno, 65–66
Bollettino dell'Emigrazione, 31
bolshevism, 33, 85, 89
Bontempelli, Massimo, 61, 73
Borsella, Giovanni, 56

Bosco, John, 75
Brazil, 20n6, 5, 14, 62, 72, 126, 128
Buenos Aires, 16, 154, 156, 159, 163, 167, 170, 173, 177; Italian community activities in, 117, 127–129, 131, 144; Italian fascist activities in, 54, 59, 62, 65, 66, 68, 73, 76–77, 103–104
Buenos Aires Herald, 172
Buffarini, Arsenio Guido, 117–119, 125, 179

Carulla, Juan E., 157, 159, 161
Castillo, Roberto M., 178
Catholicism, 75, 96–97, 157–158, 164
Ciano, Galeazzo, 45, 70
Ciarlantini, Franco, 60
Ciccotti, Francesco, 128
Cilla, Nicolas, 141–143
Circolo Venezia Giulia, 133
citizenship, 2, 30, 35–36, 170
Colombia, 190
Columbus, Christopher, 125, 135, 144
El Comité de Ayuda Antifascista, 169
Commissariato Generale dell'Emigrazione, 31
Communism, 126, 160, 161. *See also* bolshevism
Concentrazione Anti-fascista, 128
Congressional Investigation on Anti-Argentine Activities, 85, 101, 177–180
consensus, 5, 11, 12, 22n29, 22n31

Contra-Fascismo, 165
corporatism, 5, 156, 158, 161, 167
Corradini, Enrico, 27
Cozzolino, Hector, 142
Crisol, 157–159, 161
Crispi, Francesco, 34
Croce, Benedetto, 13, 129, 171
cultural consumption, 86

D'Annunzio, Gabriele, 56, 103
Damonte Taborda, Raúl, 174–175
Dante Alighieri, Società Nazionale, 5, 44–46, 58, 61; in Argentina, 73, 107, 117. *See also* Nuova Società Dante Alighieri; schools, in Rosario de Santa Fé
Daughters of Mary Help of Christians, 75
década infame, 153, 156
La Defensa Popular por las Victimas de la Reacción, 169
Del Croix, Carlo, 39
Delfino, Luigi, 134
Della Torre, Angelo, 90
Del Mineo, Rodolfo, 58
De Michelis, Giuseppe, 32
democracy, 4; in Argentina, 153–156, 159–160, 179–182; Italian community interpretation of, 121, 123–124, 126, 130, 136–137, 144
Department of Education, Argentina, 101, 103, 104, 176
De Rosas, Manuel, 157, 174
Dickmann, Adolfo, 128
Dickmann, Enrique, 174–176
Di Giovanni, Severino, 126
Di Marzio, Cornelio, 40–41
Dinale, Ottavio, 62
Direción General de Atención a las Comunidades en el Exterior, 190
Direzione degli Italiani All'Estero, 41–42, 43–44, 190
Di Tella, Torquato, 135
Dopolavoro, Opera Nazionale, 38, 73, 87, 104, 169
Il Duce. *See* Mussolini, Benito

Ecuador, 1
Edmondo de Amicis, 76
Einaudi, Luigi, 27

El Salvador, 190
emigrants, 13, 121–123, 140–141, 189–190; Fascist Italian views of, 27–36, 39–40; in school textbooks, 100–101
Enciclopedia Italiana, 158
Este pueblo necesita, 160
Ethiopia, 85, 102, 108, 124, 127, 141
European Union, 2

Fabbri, Luce, 131
Fabbri, Luigi, 131–132, 131
Fanciulli, Giuseppe, 90, 93, 96
Fasci Italiani all'Estero, 4, 32–33, 179; in Argentina, 63–64, 169
fascio (symbol), 93
fascism: Argentine interpretations of, 158–161, 165; Argentine. *See* nationalists, Argentine; historiography of, 11–12; Italian, 7, 117, 122, 123–124, 137, 139
fascist Grand Council, 32–33, 37, 60, 170
fascist Italy, 3, 6–7, 10–11, 27, 28, 47–48, 93, 103; Argentine views of, 158–159, 169; Italian community views of, 123–124, 129, 130, 136, 146
Fascist Party, Italy, 37, 60, 65–66, 73
Federazione Generale delle Società Italiane nell'Argentina, 117
Federazione Socialista Italiana nell'Argentina, 127
Federzoni, Luigi, 170–172
Felicioni, Felice, 45–46, 77
film, 70, 87. *See also* Luce films
France, 9, 60, 61, 64, 97, 127, 142
Franco, Francisco, 164
Freemasonry, 55, 62, 133, 161
Frente Único Popular Argentino Antifascista y Antiguerrero, 169
Frola, Francesco, 128–131, 135
La Fronda, 157–158, 161
fuorusciti. *See* antifascists, exiles in Argentina

Galileo, 60, 129, 139
Gálvez, Manuel, 17, 156, 157, 159–161
Garibaldi, Giuseppe, 9; Argentine depictions of, 168; fascist Italian depictions of, 54, 98; Italian community

depictions of, 126, 129, 135, 139, 141–142, 144
Gasperini, Domenico, 127
Germany, 10. *See also* Nazi Germany; Nazi Activity in Argentina
Giménez, Angel, 128
Il Giornale d'Italia, 120–123, 179
Giovinezza, 71, 102
Giuriati, Giovanni, 56–57
Graf Spee, 178
Grandi, Dino, 37, 39–40, 118
Great Britain, 4, 17, 54, 60, 97, 124, 142, 156, 159
The Great War. *See* World War I

Habermas, Jürgen, 12
hispanidad, 164
historical narrative, 8–9, 97–100, 105
Hitler, Adolf, 160
Hobsbawm, Eric, 14, 116
Hollywood, 70

imagery, national, 11, 91, 117, 125, 126, 129
immigrant assimilation: Argentine views on, 170–172; fascist Italian views on, 57, 61, 65, 89, 94–95
immigration, 14–15, 16–17, 35–36, 40, 54–55, 56, 146, 155, 161–162, 189–190; Italian community views on, 121–122, 143. *See also* emigrants; immigrant assimilation; Italian community in Argentina; International Conference on Emigration and Immigration
Imperatori, Ugo, 68
Intaglietta, Michele, 68–70
International Conference on Emigration and Immigration, 35–36
Isnaldi, Arturo, 105
L'Italia del Popolo, 6, 120, 138–141
Italia Libre, 141–143
Italian Community in Argentina, 54–56. *See also* antifascists, exiles
Italpress, 70
Italia Unita, 76

jus sanguinis, 35
jus soli, 35

Justo, Agustín P., 156

Labriola, Arturo, 126, 128
Il Legionario, 33, 37–38, 67, 72
Legión Civica Argentina, 66, 156
liberalism, 136, 143
liberal regime, Italy, 3, 27, 28–29, 34, 57, 75, 99, 133
liberty, 6, 11; Argentine depictions of, 155, 165, 168, 174, 181; fascist Italian depictions of, 62, 67; Italian community depictions of, 116, 123, 125–126, 129, 130–132, 136–137, 139–144
Libyan War, 60
Luce films, 73, 87
Lujones, Leopardo, 156

Macchiavelli, Nicolò, 9, 129, 139
Maciel, Carlos Néstor, 161–162
Malatesta, Errico, 131
Matteotti Crisis, 62, 128
Matteotti, Giacomo, 127, 129, 166
Il Mattino d'Italia, 5, 66–69, 179
Marchetti, Goffredo, 123–124
March on Rome, 25, 32, 100, 103
Martín Fierro, 120, 156
Mazzini, Giuseppe, 98, 126, 129, 132, 139, 141–142, 144
Mengiotti, Augusto, 59
MERCOSUR, 2
Mexico, 20n6, 62, 128
Michelangelo, 60, 129
Milani, Tommaso, 70
military service, 35, 56, 93–94
Ministry of Foreign Affairs, Italy, 32, 34, 37, 39–40, 45
Ministry of Popular Culture, 73, 87, 124, 158
Mitré, Bartolomé, 119, 155
monarchists, 62, 130, 116
Montevideo, 131, 178
Mosca, Vittorio, 138
Mussolini, Benito, 3, 123–124; on Dopolavoro, 38; on Emigration, 25, 27–28; on Fasci all'Estero, 37–38; on National Identity, 31; in school textbooks and curricula, 92, 105, 107; on the Scuole Italiane all'Estero, 101
myths, 8–10, 11, 28, 116, 117, 143, 155

La Nación, 118, 171
NAFTA, 2
nationalists, Argentine, 17, 69, 156–164; fascist Italian views of, 163
nationalists, Italian, 14, 26, 27, 40, 56
national identity, 1–7, 53, 85–87, 109, 145–146; Argentine, 16–17, 153–154, 180–182; discourses on, 9, 115–116, 187–189, 191; fascist conceptualization of, 46, 88–89; Italian, 8–12; New World, 4, 15–16, 131
Navello, Miguel B., 166
Nazi activity in Argentina, 173–174, 174–176
Nazi Germany, 63, 88, 153, 164
Nitti, Francesco Saverio, 117, 135
Nuova Società Dante Alighieri, 134–135

Ortiz, Roberto M., 156, 178
Oses, Enrique, 157, 159, 161

Palacios, Alfredo L., 167–168
El Pampero, 164
Parini, Piero, 3, 41–42, 48; and the Dante Alighieri Society, 45–46; and the Fasci Italiani All'Estero, 42; and the Scuole Italiani all'Estero, 43–44; *Norme di vita fascista all'estero*, 88–90; visit to Argentina, 65, 120
Pascoli, Giovanni, 27
La Patria degli Italiani, 6, 67–68, 135–138
patriotism, 5; Argentine, 160, 162, 177; Italian community views on, 115, 122–123, 129, 137, 141; Italian fascist views on, 29, 33, 56, 57, 62, 64, 67
Pedrazzi, Orazio, 95
Perón, Juan Domingo, 181
Peru, 20n6, 62
Philippines, 190
Pignatti, Bonifacio, 58, 66–68, 118
Pirandello, Luigi, 62
political religion, 10
Pro-Schola. *See* schools, Buenos Aires
La Protesta, 131–132, 165
public sphere, 3–4, 12, 109, 121
Puccini, Mario, 61

La Razón, 119
Renaissance, 121, 129, 168

Repetto, Nicolás, 167–168
Risorgimento, 8–9, 16, 54; Argentine antifascist depictions of, 168; fascist Italian depictions of, 98; Italian community depictions of, 125, 129, 132, 133, 139, 141–142, 144
Il Risorgimento (newspaper), 129–131
Il Risveglio, 63
Rivista Mensile della Federazione Italiana, 179
Rodríguez Araya, Agustín, 153
Rojas, Ricardo, 17, 155
Roma Press, 70

Saint Francis, 97
Salesian Society, 75, 97
Saló, Republic of, 63
Salvemini, Gaetano, 135
Sánchez-Sorondo, Matias, 157
San Sepolcro, 167
Sarfatti, Margherita, 130
Sarmiento, Domingo Faustino, 16, 141, 155
schools: antifascist, 76; Argentine investigation of, 90, 176–177, 180; in Bahia Blanca, 105; in Buenos Aires, 76–77, 103–104, 177; in Cordoba, 106; in La Plata, 104–105, 177; in Mendoza, 102, 177; in Rosario de Santa Fé, 107–108. *See also* Scuole Italiane All'Estero
Scuole Italiane all'Estero, 33–34; in Argentina, 74–77, 77; textbooks, 86–87, 90–101; religious instruction, 96–97
Sironi, Mario, 90
Smith, Anthony, 9, 13, 154
socialism, 127, 132, 158, 161. *See also* antifascists; Socialist Party, Argentina
Socialist Party, Argentina, 128, 164–169
socialists, 62, 126
Società Italiana di M.S. Belgrano, 133
Società Italia Unita, 133
Sonnino, Sidney, 27
Spanish Civil War, 70, 85, 108, 127, 157
Starace, Achille, 66
Stefani news wire, 70
Studi Sociali, 131
symbols, national, 10, 11, 116, 176

Swinburne, Algernon Charles, 139

teacher-agents, 43, 77
Testena, Folco (Comunardo Braccialarghe), 120–123
totalitarianism, 179–180
Trabalza, Ciro, 34
transnationalism, 3, 13–15
Tunisia, 95

United States of America, 35, 56, 124, 155, 178
Unknown Soldier, Italy, 98
Uriburu, José F., 128, 155–156, 157

Valdani, Vittorio, 63–64, 179
La Vanguardia, 127, 164, 165–168

Viaggio in Argentina, 60–61
Victor Emmanuel III, 91, 96, 130
Vittorio Veneto, 11, 29, 75
Volpe, Gioacchino, 90, 98–100

Washington, George, 124, 125
World War I, 29, 60, 65, 95, 98–99, 102, 117, 136
World War II, 153, 178–179

xenophobia, 161–162

Youth Organizations, 71–73. *See also* schools; Scuole Italiane all'Estero, Balilla
Yrigoyen, Hipólito, 155

About the Author

David Aliano is assistant professor of history and modern languages and literatures at the College of Mount Saint Vincent. He earned his PhD in 2008 and his MPhil degree in 2005 in European and Latin American History, both at the Graduate Center of the City University of New York, and his Bachelor of the Arts in Italian and History at Fordham University in 2000. His recent peer-reviewed publications include "Citizenship and Belonging: The Case of the Italian Vote Abroad," in *Ethnic Studies Review* (2010); "Revisiting Saint Domingue: Toussaint L'Ouverture and the Haitian Revolution in the French Colonial Debates of the Late Nineteenth Century, 1870–1900," in *French Colonial History* (2008); "Curing the Ills of Central America: The United Fruit Company Medical Department and Corporate America's Mission to Civilize," in *Estudios Interdisciplinarios de America Latina y el Caribe* (2006); and "Brazil through Italian Eyes: The Debate over Emigration to São Paulo during the 1920s," in *Altreitalie* (2005). He is also an associate editor of the *Ethnic Studies Review*, is on the Board of Directors of the National Association for Ethnic Studies (NAES), and is an associate member of the Columbia University Seminar in Modern Italian Studies.